The Final Mission of
Bottoms Up

THE AMERICAN MILITARY EXPERIENCE SERIES

John C. McManus, Series Editor

The books in this series portray and analyze the experience of Americans in military service during war and peacetime from the onset of the twentieth century to the present. The series emphasizes the profound impact wars have had on nearly every aspect of recent American history and considers the significant effects of modern conflict on combatants and noncombatants alike. Titles in the series include accounts of battles, campaigns, and wars; unit histories; biographical and autobiographical narratives; investigations of technology and warfare; studies of the social and economic consequences of war; and in general, the best recent scholarship on Americans in the modern armed forces. The books in the series are written and designed for a diverse audience that encompasses nonspecialists as well as expert readers.

UNIVERSITY OF MISSOURI PRESS

COLUMBIA AND LONDON

The Final Mission of
Bottoms Up

A WORLD WAR II PILOT'S STORY

Dennis R. Okerstrom

Copyright ©2011 by
The Curators of the University of Missouri
University of Missouri Press, Columbia, Missouri 65201
Printed and bound in the United States of America
All rights reserved
5 4 3 2   15 14 13 12

Cataloging-in-Publication data available from the Library of Congress.
ISBN 978-0-8262-1948-0

♾™ This paper meets the requirements of the
American National Standard for Permanence of Paper
for Printed Library Materials, Z39.48, 1984.

Design and composition: Jennifer Cropp
Printing and binding: Thomson-Shore, Inc.
Typefaces: Minion, Chicago Copperplate, and Brush Script

This book is dedicated to World War II

airmen, of all nationalities, who fought

their countries' battles in the sky.

Contents

Acknowledgments

This is the most terrifying part of publishing: acknowledging that the writer is not the lone ranger in the process, while fearing that someone who contributed will be left out.

Obviously, this could not have been written without the collaboration and cooperation of Lee Lamar. His collection of artifacts and his recollection of events is remarkable, and so was his enthusiasm for answering my hundreds of questions over the course of writing the manuscript. He was patient to a fault, and his insistence upon accuracy regarding each detail was a reminder of the task facing historians. Luka Bekic and the staff of the Hrvaska Conservation Institute literally unearthed the story while excavating another, older, story in the Istrian peninsula of Croatia. Without the curiosity and the perseverance of these men of science, a huge part of this tale would not be known; without their generosity and goodwill, it could not have been told.

Park University also needs to be in the spotlight. Without the generous monetary assistance in making the trip to Croatia, this story would not have been possible for me to write. A huge thank you to Olga Ganzen and Angie Markley-Peterson for their aid in setting up the trip and the class for Park Students. Park's former president, Beverly Byers-Pevitts, also was very supportive, and without her embrace of the project it could not have gone forward. Current Park president Mike Droge has been helpful in ensuring that I had time from my teaching to write this. I am deeply grateful to my colleagues Jane Wood, Virginia Brackett, and Steve Atkinson for their suggestions regarding several chapters of this work, and I appreciate the organizational skills of Cathy Boisen.

Several individuals and organizations were instrumental in bringing this book to completion. The Collings Foundation was very generous, inviting Lee and me to fly aboard the last remaining B-24J, from Colorado to Missouri, and allowing us to film inside the bomber while it was down for repairs in Kansas City. Members of the Commemorative Air Force, Heart of America Wing, were helpful in making available a number of volumes pertinent to this project. Lynn Gamma, at the Air Force Historical Research Agency at Maxwell Air Force Base, was gracious and prompt in sending me information from the archives of the 460th Bomb Group.

John Brenner, project editor at the University of Missouri Press, and John McManus, editor for the American Military Experience series, have been enthusiastic supporters, and both made very helpful suggestions for improving this account of Lee Lamar and his combat air crew. I very much appreciate their expertise, as well as the patience, professionalism, and unfailing good cheer of my copy editors, Sara Davis and Tim Fox.

Of course I need to thank the memory of my parents, Carl and Joan, for planting the seeds of passion about World War II. Dad was in the 8th Air Force stationed in England, where he met and married my mother before bringing her to the states. I miss their stories.

My wife, Jeanette, has been a supportive and helpful partner in this endeavor, always calmly coming to my aid each time a computer appeared to have swallowed whole my manuscript. I cannot thank her enough.

Despite my best efforts, surely mistakes have found their way into this book. I take full responsibility for those, while hoping they are few and minor.

The Final Mission of

Introduction

World War II was the age of death from above. Although in the earlier global war now called World War I stirring aerial combat among nimble fighters and the occasional bombing attack on cities were widely reported, the war of the 1940s was breathtaking in the employment of aircraft in the strategic decision to destroy the will and production facilities of opposing countries. That decision came with a high price, not only for those who were in the bullseye of bombing targets, but for the young men sent aloft in the service of their countries.

Deep within the entrails of the National Archives are roll after roll of microfiche files known as MACRs. These detailed Missing Air Crew Reports are crammed with fascinating minutiae regarding each of the 22,951 U.S. military aircraft that were lost on operational missions during World War II.

Anyone who is interested can order a copy of one of these reports, provided that the MACR number is already known. If not, a particular report might be obtained by knowing the name and organization of a missing airman. If that is unsuccessful, there are organizations and individual researchers available who might be able to shed light that leads to a single report.

But anyone setting out to learn more about a missing relative or friend should be forewarned: The reports are ripe with information that might be useful in identifying a crash site, but very lean on what an individual flier experienced. The prose is sparse; there is no room for description of the terror, or the courage, or the professionalism of those young men who climbed into the fighters and bombers and transports so many decades ago and faced the enemy and their own fears in skies over Europe and North Africa and the Pacific and Asia. The reports were typed by largely nameless soldiers doing an important job, but they were never meant to re-create the lives of those gone missing. How do you report that "a pair of neon blue eyes that would light up when switched on by a heart-breaking smile went missing today somewhere over northern Italy?"

One MACR, No. 9888, concerns one aircrew of ten such young men, flying a B-24J (AAF serial number 42–51926) out of Spinazzola, Italy, on 18 November 1944. The target, 9888 tells us, was Udine Air Drome, Italy; the mission, Bombing. The weather enroute was hazy, with cirrostratus clouds building from 23,000 feet; visibility was 10 to 15 miles.

The B-24J, nicknamed *Bottoms Up* according to the report, was part of the 460th Bomb Group (Heavy), 760th Bomb Squadron. It was equipped with three R-1830–65A radial engines, and one R-1830–43 engine; the serial numbers for each of the four are listed. Ten Browning M2 caliber .50 machines guns were aboard; the serial numbers of each of those weapons are duly noted.

Finally, nearly half-way down the page, is the chillingly impersonal query: Personnel listed below reported as (check one): Battle Casualty, Non-Battle Casualty. An X has been placed by the first choice for the following ten names:

Pilot: Darden, Randall B., 1st Lt;
Co-Pilot, Lamar, Edgar L., 2nd Lt.
Navigator, Craig, Wade M., Jr., 2nd Lt.
Bombardier, Reynolds, Donald, 2nd Lt.
Engineer, Webb, Hurston, S/Sgt.
Radio Operator, Norlund, Swante B., S/Sgt.
Assistant Engineer, Briganti, Mario A., S/Sgt.
Assistant Radio Operator, Nordback, John F., S/Sgt.
Air Gunner, Alder, Henry L., S/Sgt.
Air Gunner, Sturtz, Bernard C., S/Sgt.

The notation MIA (Missing In Action) denotes the "Current Status" of each man. Next of kin and address follow each name: Four Mothers, three Fathers, three Wives. The missing airmen hail from Texas, Missouri, Wisconsin, West Virginia, Minnesota, Connecticut, North Dakota, Pennsylvania, and two from Tennessee.

There follows page after page, about thirty in all, of follow-up reports. Four airmen in different aircraft who accompanied *Bottoms Up* and her crew to Udine give statements about seeing the Liberator hit hard by antiaircraft fire over the target, subsequently losing altitude and dropping behind the formation.

And to the credit of those nameless and unhonored keepers of the reports, additions to the file were made even after the war, as further information became available on the condition and whereabouts of various air crew.

Historians decades and centuries from now will doubtless find the MACRs to be valuable sources of information on the statistically horrifying war in the clouds, battles untraceable once the clear air swept away the smoke and the falling debris. Unlike ground battles of the Civil War or the thousands of other armed conflicts over the grim history of humankind, there are no old trenches or reconstructed forts or neatly marked trails to visit and reflect on the gallantry of young men or the misery of war or the inability of humans to arbitrate. The Missing Air Crew Reports are among thousands of documents available to historians as they formulate new theses, tabulate casualties, or critique campaigns.

What I have tried to do here is to introduce you to one man and some of his friends, a small fraction of the millions who served during World War II, and to tell the flesh-and-blood story of that war, of what happened to him and his friends, of the effects of that war upon him for the rest of his long life, and of the remarkable discovery by one persistent and curious archaeologist of the remains of his airplane, shot from the skies over Croatia more than sixty years before.

Lee Lamar is very much a product of mid-America, with roots in its fertile soil. He is a child of the Great Depression and a survivor of the war. A visitor to his home in Overland Park, Kansas, will wind through the tree-lined streets of his quiet subdivision and pull into the curving driveway of his brick ranch home. There, directly ahead through the windshield is a bumper sticker pasted to the window of his garage door. It is revealing. A waving American flag, upon which is superimposed an eagle with outstretched wings, and these words:

I believe in Life, Liberty,
and the Pursuit of those who don't.

Inside, sitting in his den, a visitor will also notice a wooden model of a tower, topped by a small shack, sitting beside his fireplace. That, Lee explains to your quizzical look, is a model of a German guard tower at a Stalag Luft, a prisoner-of-war camp for Allied fliers. It was made by another former POW, and Lee keeps it as a constant reminder that freedom comes with a high price.

There are other, less tangible, remnants of his experiences. More then six decades after being released from Stalag Luft I in May 1945, Lee is still unable to leave food on his plate. Long months of captivity with little to eat affected his stomach, but his mind still directs him to consume everything put before him. It may be a long time before the next good meal.

Researching and writing this book showed me some other aspects of Lee's character. As a result of his flying experiences and his education as an engineer, no detail is insignificant. Together Lee and I discussed various parts of his story, and I would dutifully take notes. Then I researched government documents, histories, memoirs, websites, and Air Force training manuals in order to tell his story as completely and accurately as I could. Lee would then carefully read my draft, and note that on a certain page I had the olive grove on the wrong side of the air base. Noted and corrected. We went through this waltz many times, until Lee was satisfied with every detail. As an engineer, he knew that every bolt in a bridge was crucial to its strength and integrity. As a pilot, he knew that what happened in training might be entirely different than what was done in combat, and the difference was important.

So, after many revisions, Lee's story is complete. No, not really. He is still going strong at ninety. He still drives veterans to their appointments at the Veteran's Administration hospital, is active in the Commemorative Air Force, POW organizations, Rotary Club, Quiet Birdmen, and other fraternal and community organizations. He still speaks to public gatherings and school classes about his war experiences, still relishes time with his family, including two grandchildren. His wife Bonnie will gently and lovingly chide him at times about his eating habits. Lee and Bonnie drive to church each Sunday. He attends talks by other veterans of that long-ago war on both sides of the globe. He reads prodigiously, and has strong opinions about government policies and politicians.

And if called upon, he would serve again. It has been a good life for Lee. I hope you enjoy his story.

Dennis Okerstrom
Independence, Missouri
January 2011

Chapter 1

Over Udine, Italy
1200 hours, 18 November 1944

The eight-day, wind-up clock crowning the instrument panel ticked to the top of the dial, the slender white reed of the second hand stark against the flat black of the face. The instrument, one of scores jammed into the flight deck of the heavy bomber, measured out the lives of the cockpit crew in quarter-hour dollops; nine hundred seconds on, nine hundred off. It was time for Lt. Lee Lamar to take over the wheel of the B-24J again, after his fifteen minutes of rest.[1]

For twenty bombing missions over targets in Germany, Italy, Yugoslavia, Austria, Hungary, Greece, and Rumania—all the places on the body of the earth where the cancer of Nazism had spread—Lamar and pilot Randall Darden had worked out a system overseen by the clock: a quarter of an hour flying, an equal amount resting while the other pilot flew. It doesn't sound strenuous today, in the age of fly-by-wire jets and light, single-pilot business planes.

But the Liberator was a huge airplane by the standards of the day: more than 67 feet long, with 110 feet of long, slender Davis wing upon which were hung four 1,200-horse Pratt & Whitney R-1830 14-cylinder engines. Up to 8,800 pounds of bombs could be tucked into its slab-sided middle section, to be dropped through two sets of bomb bay doors. The heavy bomber had a crew of ten young and fit men, and bristled with ten .50-caliber Browning machine guns.[2] Its official takeoff capacity was 65,000 pounds, but often it was loaded far beyond that as crews—and those who sent them out—began to view the numbers as cautionary, not absolutes. Had religion been their vocation, they might have viewed their guiding principles as the Ten Suggestions.

The B-24 was flown by the usual, contemporary arrangement of steel wires attached to the yoke pedestal and the rudder pedals, which ran through a series of pulleys before being hooked to ailerons, rudders, and elevators, the movable surfaces which controlled the pitch, roll, and yaw movements of the aircraft.

The sheer distance through the fuselage and the wings meant the force needed to change the angle of any of those control surfaces was considerable. A kink or twist in the wire, a slight wobble in the pulleys, a mote of stiffness in the pulley bearings magnified the resistance and increased exponentially the force required to herd the big bomber. An even bigger factor in the physical wrestling match of herding the big bomber was the size of the control surfaces themselves. Each aileron—one per wing—had a surface area of 41.5 square feet; the elevator was more than 60 square feet; the two rudders were 65 square feet. Each change of attitude meant putting one or more of these control surfaces into the teeth of a 200-plus miles-per-hour (mph) wind and holding it. That might be akin to standing in the back of a pickup truck going down the freeway at 70 mph and trying to hold a sheet of plywood vertical against the wind.

Lamar and Darden were big men; they could have played football for any number of college teams. Most crewmen and fighter pilots were small, averaging about 5 feet 9 inches and 154 pounds. But the Army Air Force selected big, muscular men to fly the heavy bombers: Lee was nearly 6 feet, and weighed 175; Randall, about the same. The AAF knew what it was doing: when the heavy bombers, with all their size and weight, were airborne and stacked up in a defensive box of dozens or even hundreds of aircraft, the turbulence from all those P&Ws was fierce. Despite their leviathan dimensions, the Liberators bucked, yawed, and pitched like fishing boats in a hurricane.

"Ready, Lee?" Darden pressed his throat microphone and looked over at Lamar in the right seat. Lamar looked back over the top of his rubber oxygen mask and placed a gloved hand on the control yoke.

"I've got it." Lamar, anticipating the hand-off, already had dialed back the rheostat on his electrically heated flight suit. The physical effort to control the big bomber made the suit far too hot while actually wrestling the yoke, a half-moon-shaped affair as big as the steering wheel of a commercial truck. The pilots turned down the heat while flying and increased it while getting their fifteen-minute rest as the below-zero chill at twenty thousand feet began to creep slowly into their bones.

The day was overcast, but even in the hazy air beneath the ceiling the white-draped Italian Alps were visible in the north, straight off the nose. *Bottoms Up*, their bomber that day, was one of twenty-eight Liberators from the 460th Bomb Group to target Udine Airdrome, a German-controlled fighter base in the north of Italy. It wasn't particularly a strategic target, but the mottled gray fighters that used its single runway were a nuisance on the long hauls from the 460th's home base in Spinazzola, near the heel of Italy, to targets in Germany. It was late in the war. The Luftwaffe had been steadily depleted, with many of the squadrons of Messerschmitts and Focke-Wulfs called back into the Fatherland to defend Hitler's thousand-year Reich, now being mauled by Allied bombers night and day. There were not enough fighters at Udine to attack the large formations of American bombers streaming over the Brenner Pass into Germany. Instead, they swarmed and buzzed at the edges of the flying task forces, picking out the wounded and attacking the crippled birds like wolves preying on the weak and young in a herd of caribou.[3]

They were nearly to the IP, the initial point, the beginning of the bomb run during which the bomber had to stay exactly on course and altitude. This enabled the bombardiers in each bomber to accurately unload the lethal cargo in the bays. Lt. Don Reynolds in the nose had the intervalometer in the Norden bombsight set to the mandated release sequence, but now he watched the lead bomber in his formation. When the olive drab explosives began to fall from the belly, he would release simultaneously. It was the time on the mission of the most extreme tension: they could not maneuver to evade flak or fighters now. That shouldn't be a problem today, however; the group intelligence officer had indicated that enemy fire would not be much of a factor on today's mission. The entire crew appreciated a "milk run."

With a start, Lamar leaned forward, staring hard as another line of bombers crossed in front of them at a distance of maybe five miles. It wasn't the bombers that had captured his attention; the sky was usually filled with them on every mission, wheeling and swarming like long trains of wasps. They were an everyday fact of life for a combat aircrew. Instead, he focused on the lethal puffs of black clouds that had suddenly appeared around the distant string of Liberators. The German flak gunners, despite the intelligence officer's prediction, were busy.

"Bomb bay doors coming open." Reynolds had pulled the lever that drew both sets of doors up and parallel to the fuselage. Lamar braced himself for the jolt as the doors disrupted the smooth flow of air down the fuselage and became drag, working against the thrust of the engines.

Lamar, flying from the right seat, tried to keep the Liberator straight and level. Despite his efforts, the aircraft rocked, rolled, and bucked, fighting both the turbulence of the planes ahead as well as the added violent blasts from the flak that had bracketed them now, and quite accurately. "Bombs away!" from Reynolds, and he felt the sudden rise of the heavy aircraft as three tons of bombs tumbled out of the racks. It was always as though a giant hand had lifted them forcefully toward the heavens.

"Bomb bay doors coming. . . ." Reynolds did not get to finish his sentence. Before he could say "closed," *Bottoms Up* was staggered by a tremendous explosion that blasted a hole in the left wing "big enough to drive a Buick through," according to crewmen in other Liberators. The bomber was knocked onto its side, the wings nearly vertical, and began to drop. The shell knocked out the hydraulic system, severed gasoline lines on the left side of the plane, and blew out the oxygen system. As the rest of the crew scrambled to snap on their parachutes and don their emergency walk-around bottles of oxygen, Darden joined Lamar in wrestling the bomber back into level flight. The plane was essentially falling out of the sky; no longer a flying machine, it was a 25-ton rock. It fell 15,000 feet in a matter of minutes.

Finally, at roughly 5,000 feet, *Bottoms Up* began to respond to the exertions of the two pilots as they pushed the nose forward and attempted to level the wings. It gradually, reluctantly, resumed a straight and level attitude. But now it seemed to Lamar that the bomber was precariously balanced on a tightrope, liable to fall off at any moment. No longer did the big bomber have the sense of stability and security that it had always afforded.

The '24 had achieved a reputation among some that it couldn't take a hit, that the Davis wing was fragile and would collapse at the slightest wound. Those stories were pushed to the back of Lamar's mind. Now, the immediate worry was the two port engines. Both power-plants on the left had begun to "run away," with the propellers speeding up beyond the safe range. They whined and screamed, and both pilots watched the tachometers wind up past 3000, past 4000, still climbing. It was possible, if they could not shut down the engines, that the propellers would spin off the shafts and come crashing through the aircraft squarely into the cockpit. The second worst scenario was being able to shut down the engines but not being able to feather the props; the blades would remain flat, creating huge amounts of drag on the left side, making control difficult and return to a friendly base unlikely. Lamar quickly pulled back the mixture control levers to kill the fuel supplies to engines one and two. Simultaneously, Darden reached to the bank of switches above the center windshield, lifted the safety bar, and punched the feathering buttons on the two left engines. Lamar continued to fight the yawing and bucking Liberator as the blades slowly wound down and turned into the wind.

That wasn't the end of their problems, only the solution to the most immediate. While Darden checked with the crew for injuries, Lamar began to trim *Bottoms Up* for straight and level flight. With both engines on one side now producing no thrust at all, it meant that the right engines, outboard of the centerline of the airplane, were pulling the right wing around faster than the left wing could go. This condition of asymmetrical thrust could be partly alleviated by increasing the power of the inboard engine, the one closest to the centerline of the plane, and slightly decreasing the outboard engine. The left wing had to be held slightly high and the right rudder pedal had to be depressed to counteract the tendency of the crippled bomber to continuously turn left.

The reports came in from the crew: miraculously, despite the dire condition of the machine, none of the human cargo had been injured. Or so they reported.

Now, however, they had to get *Bottoms Up* safely on the ground, along with its ten men and its totemic pigtailed blonde painted garishly across the nose. There was no assurance they could.

Darden and Lamar watched as the formation, now high above them, steadily pulled away. They couldn't hope for help there; no competent combat commander would endanger his formation by hanging back to assist a crippled bomber. Lamar, through the intercom, ordered the crew to lighten up the bird: throw out anything not essential to continued flight and a safe landing. Out went steel flak helmets and heavy flak suits, belts of .50-caliber ammunition, even the machine guns. In the minds of both pilots was the tiny island of Vis, a British fighter base with a single short runway in the middle of the Adriatic Sea. (Another B-24 pilot, a young Lt. George McGovern, would crash land his bomber at Vis, receive the Distinguished Flying Cross for his efforts, and go on to a long and distinguished government career.)[4]

"Mike, get us a course to Vis, the British base there." Mike Craig was the navigator, a twenty-year-old from Nashville and the youngest of the four officers in the ten-man crew. "Keep us just off the Yugoslavian coast, but close enough for us to glide in if we have to." The B-24 was notorious for breaking up in ditching attempts and sinking quickly. No one joined the Army Air Force to drown. There were plenty of ways to get dead flying in a bomber, but no one wanted a watery grave. They'd have joined the damn Navy if that was what they wanted.

Only a few minutes had passed since *Bottoms Up* was flak wounded. There was no panic; in the back of each crewman's mind had always been the thought that they would, if they flew enough missions, get hit hard on one of them. They trained for it, they prepared themselves mentally, they cross-trained for other jobs aboard the bomber. Just in case.

Other crews had been hit; many had been wounded, many more had died. In the 460th alone, at least one bomber had been shot down accidentally by gunners in another Liberator. There was nothing friendly about "friendly fire." Occasionally, a bomber would crash on takeoff, with full fuel and a load of bombs. Those deaths were quick.

One gunner had fallen from the catwalk over the bomb bays when he attempted to fix a problem that kept the doors open. He had not clipped on his parachute. There were crashes when crippled bombers tried to land, and midair collisions that wiped out two or more entire crews in the blink of an eye. Then, of course, there was the enemy, the actual human enemy, who fired machine guns and cannon at them from nimble gray-painted fighters, or who bombarded them in reverse with exploding anti-aircraft shells. In German it was called *Flugabwehrkanone*. Flak was easier to say, but it was just as deadly.[5]

The pilot's instrument panel in a B-24 is tall and the windshield small. Pilots could see ahead, but not down. Lamar likened it to flying a house while sitting in the basement and looking out through tiny, sunken windows. Now, barely ten minutes after being hit, Lamar and Darden stared out at the Adriatic, cognizant that they were a long way from their home base with only two working engines. Each silently calculated their chances of landing at the small emergency strip at Vis. The odds were not good, they both knew.

They had elected to fly down the western coast of Yugoslavia, avoiding the German gun emplacements that rimmed that sad country, then cross the Adriatic to Vis at the shortest over-water route. Both pilots knew the ditching qualities of the Liberator: the rather flimsy bomb bay doors would be ripped off on contact with the sea, tons of water would crash against the rear bulkhead, and the aircraft would break into pieces and sink rapidly. To avoid that, they would stay over land as long as possible, and once at Vis, if they decided a landing was not possible in the crippled bird, they could all parachute to safety over the base.

"Mike, I think that's Pola up ahead. Keep us out of the flak box around that place," Lamar radioed to his navigator. Pola was an ancient Roman city on the Istrian peninsula, jutting out into the Adriatic. It had a fine harbor that was dotted with small islands. In more peaceful circumstances, the crew probably could have picked out the second-century coliseum in the center of town, its circular walls a clearly visible icon.

But these were not peaceful times. As they approached the harbor, still out over the Adriatic, they suddenly were jolted out of any thoughts of making it to Vis. A Wehrmacht flak battery on one of the islands of Brijuni, northwest of the Pola harbor, had opened up, once more filling the sky around them with deadly black clouds, red in the centers. A dozen flak batteries ringed Pola, but there were also five batteries on the islands of Brijuni, and it was these that had bracketed the wounded bomber, now low, slow, and very large.[6] They needed to turn right, toward the sea, to get out of the deadly fire, but control now was extremely difficult. Both pilots had to stand on the rudder pedals with their backs braced against their seats. A left turn was easier, but each turn meant a loss of altitude they could not regain.

A bone-jarring explosion shook the bomber and Lamar's rudder pedals disappeared, shot away by exploding shells. Holes appeared throughout the plane, and soon it was apparent that flak fragments had also severed the cables to the elevators. *Bottoms Up* was mortally wounded, now staggering through the November sky with no control by its crew. It remained in a fairly level attitude, but the loss of the two left engines put it in a left turn that could not be countered. The bomber would continue the turn, which would gradually tighten into a spiral; with enough altitude, *Bottoms Up* would become a flying drill bit and auger a big, smoking hole in the earth.

The two pilots looked at each other. "I think this is where we're supposed to get off," Lamar said. Darden only nodded, and reached up to punch the bail-out button that would sound the alarm throughout the bomber. Lamar pressed his throat mic again. "Fellows, we're down to 3,500 feet and going down like a rock. Get out of here and get out fast." The two pilots stayed for a bit longer, holding the big control wheels all the way to the right in a vain attempt to regain some minimal control that would make it easier for everyone to jump. It was soon apparent that *Bottoms Up* was in the last minutes of her last flight.

Darden signaled for Lamar to exit the cockpit and bail out. "I'm right behind you, Partner." As captain of the ship, Darden would be the last out.

Lamar exited his seat, climbing awkwardly over the control console between the two pilot seats, and entered the radio and flight engineer compartment which was behind and a step down from the cockpit. There sat Hurston Webb, the flight engineer, calmly changing his bulky, sheepskin flying boots for his GI hightops. Lamar was incredulous.

"What the hell are you doing!? Get out of here, now!"

"But Lieutenant, the intel officer said for us to change into our walking boots if we ever had to bail out." The young sergeant was calm, as though jumping out of a crippled bomber were something he did weekly.

"You're not going to have to worry about walking anywhere if you don't get out of here right now. We're dropping like a rock!" The small engineer darted forward and slipped through the nose wheel door hatch. Lamar didn't follow him, instead turning aft to enter the dark pit of the bomb bay.

Originally, the pilot's escape route was designed as an overhead hatch in the cockpit. This emergency exit called for a flier to stand up, pull himself out, and crawl along the top of the fuselage before dropping over the side, much as a sailor might from a ship turning turtle. At least that was the theory. In practice, pilots tended to fall over the side immediately into the propellers of the inboard engines, or else they were hurled by the 150-to-200 mph relative wind into the tail. One was messier than the other, but in the end you were just as dead. The top hatch was now considered by veteran combat pilots solely an exit for crash landings and ditchings. An alternative bailout route was to crawl downward from the flight deck, shimmy through a narrow tunnel forward and exit through the nose wheel doors. This was the preferred emergency exit for the bombardier, navigator, and the nose gunner, who had already made it out, and the way chosen by Webb.

Lamar didn't think this was his best choice. The vagaries of government contracting during the war had produced a wide variety of items for warriors, and a decided lack of uniformity. For leather flight jackets, for example, the famous A-2, more than 20 companies stitched horsehide into the signature apparel of the flier. The results were hardly uniform: vast differences in color, in the shapes of pockets, the width of epaulets, the types of snaps holding down various-shaped collars. But none of this was a matter of life and death. Far more serious was the issue of parachute harnesses and the parachute pack that attached to it.

The chest 'chute pack attached to the harness by a system of hooks and rings; unfortunately, a lack of consistency and uniformity had resulted in potentially deadly mismatches. It was vital that a parachute pack with rings be mated to a harness with snaps, something assured if the maker of harness and parachute pack were the same. If not, there was a potential problem. It was possible to end up with two rings or two clip snaps, rendering the 'chute useless. This was only an issue on the chest-type pack, the type favored by most members of a bomber crew. A chest 'chute meant that they could leave the 'chute pack detached and stowed in a handy place while leaving them free to move about the plane relatively unencumbered. Seat-pack and backpack type parachutes were favored by fighter pilots, who could not move around their tiny cockpits and couldn't be restricted by a chest-type parachute. There was no potential mismatch problem with these, since they were a single unit.[7]

The pilots had heard of an incident before they arrived. A Liberator crew, so the story went, had made the decision to abandon their crippled ship. Unfortunately, each of them had been issued a parachute with clip-snaps—and a harness with the same hardware. They were unable to bail out, riding the bomber down to a crash landing. The story might have been apocryphal, but Lamar had brought the subject up with Darden and they had decided this would not happen to them. They had been issued backpack parachutes at their request. This was a bulky apparatus, much larger than a small chest pack, and included a back pad between the 'chute pack and their backs for comfort in the aircraft seat. However, it also increased the size of the apparatus.

The problem now was that both Darden and Lamar were large men, ideal for flying bombers but not so much for escaping from one. The backpack parachutes made going through the tunnel to the nose wheel door difficult, if not impossible. Additionally, Lamar reasoned that the exploding shell that blew away his rudder pedals had probably also damaged the entire tunnel area, leaving sharp, jagged edges that would snag and hold his flight suit or parachute. Despite Webb's apparently easy exit, Lamar decided on the bomb bays; Lib crews had been told that with a couple of good strong stomps one could force the doors open sufficiently to bail out. Might as well have been a cat, so weak were his kicks. He was exhausted from his wrestling match with the dying bomber; his legs trembled, and he was able to summon only a feeble tap against the doors. They didn't budge. He had to find another way out.

That left the rear section of the aircraft. Lamar would have to make his way aft over the six-inch wide catwalk between the two bomb racks then drop through the photo hatch behind the ball gun turret in the belly of the bomber. There were no windows in the bomb bays. It was dark in the belly of the beast, and the noise of the dying bomber joined with the thunder of exploding flak to create an unholy cacophony.

He took the first step. He couldn't take the second.

His unwieldy backpack parachute had become jammed between the narrow steel stanchions that held the catwalk in place. He was stuck, held fast by the very device that was supposed to save him. The irony of his predicament was not lost on Lamar. He pulled, twisted, jerked, but still he was held fast in the bowels of the airplane. He could hear the drone of the two remaining engines, the dull thuds of the now distant flak bursts, the wind roaring through a variety of holes throughout the plane, but above the din was the pounding of his own heart.

"I'm going to die. This is not a good day," the phlegmatic Lamar said to himself. It seemed an unlikely end for a farm boy from Missouri, to die in a smoking, ragged hole in the earth halfway around the world. He could not see out, but he knew the plane was getting very low now. It wouldn't be long before its final plunge, then blackness forever. In desperation, he summoned all of his strength and jerked once more against whatever restrained him in the Stygian darkness. He broke loose, nearly falling to his knees on the catwalk. He regained his footing and entered the rear bomb bay area. This time he turned to face the other side of the aircraft as if that might make the passage easier. Once more he found himself trapped in the small space. Again, he fought desperately to get through the narrow opening. Something slapped him in the groin. Lamar felt down, and the red-painted D-ring of his parachute ripcord was hanging loose, dangling free of its flexible metal sheath. It should have been at his chest, tucked into a small canvas pouch.

"Well, kid, you've really done it now. That parachute is out, all over the inside of this bomber, and you are never going to get out now."

Lamar slowly turned to look behind him, expecting to see a billowing sea of white silk that would serve as his funeral shroud. There was only blackness. Not knowing what else to do, he carefully pushed the wire with the D-ring back up into its tubing. Had it broken off inside the 'chute? Would it deploy his parachute canopy if he could make it out of the plane, or would he plummet to the earth holding the D-ring and a short bit of ripcord? There was no time to ponder the possibilities. He turned to enter the rear of the aircraft thinking he was the last still aboard. Suddenly, he was face to face with his gunners.

Henry Alder, Bernie Sturtz, and Mario Briganti were working to unbolt the ball turret from its overhead gimbal ring. Removing the six hexagonal nuts would allow the thousand-pound gun blister to drop from the belly. They had disconnected their radio headsets to work and had heard neither the bail-out bell nor Lamar's command over the intercom to jump. They were still trying to lighten the bomber in the hope of making it to Vis.

Three faces stared at Lamar, wide-eyed. It could not be good news that the co-pilot was back in their office. Despite their dedication to duty, Lamar blistered their ears and ordered them out without delay. Two quickly turned and dove through the photo hatch opening. But Alder, seeing the ground rushing by below, had second thoughts and backed away from the hatch. He approached again, and once more backed up. "Alder, if you don't jump right now, I will kick you through that hatch!" Alder looked at the face of his co-pilot and disappeared through the opening.

Lamar had no idea how close to the ground he was, but he knew it was too close for any sort of further delay. He thought he knew how a man in a burning building might feel, perched on a ledge and staring down hundreds of feet to a tiny net held by firefighters. He knew it was best to drop out the photo hatch from the rear to lessen the chance of the slip stream causing him to hit his head on the rear edge of the opening, but the time that would take seemed like eternity. The instructions for bailing out ran through his mind: Drop, tuck and do a full roll forward, then count to 10 before pulling the ripcord to ensure clearing the aircraft. Of course, that was with a parachute that you could count on to open, and with plenty of altitude.[8]

He was surprisingly calm. It was a revelation to him how little anxiety was felt by a man out of options.[9]

Lamar knew time was about up. He curled up his body and somersaulted into the maw of the abyss.

Chapter 2

Krvavici, Croatia
Fall 2005

The Istrian peninsula of what is now called Croatia juts into the northern head of the Adriatic Sea like a shark's tooth. At a crossroads of ancient trade routes, it has seen its share of violence and blood but today it is a natural gem, a bucolic land of charming old towns and villages, linked together by roads older than anyone's memory. From the altitude of an airplane, the roads can be seen to follow the natural contours of a rocky, rugged landscape, twisting and dodging around hillocks and karst pits and meandering gently from one village to another. The tiny fields edged with stone walls are a crazy quilt pattern laid out in a time when it was far more important to use every foot of arable earth than to make it easy on a surveyor.

The largest city in Istria is Pula. During World War 2 Istria was part of Italy, which curved up around the Adriatic like a collar, and the city was known as Pola. It lies east-southeast of Venice, on the eastern shore of the sea, and like that venerable, water-soaked city of palazzos, piazzas, and canals, Pula also was founded on trade. A wide, natural harbor, studded with achingly beautiful islands, has led merchant ships here since ancient Rome. One local tradition has it that the city was founded by Jason of the Golden Fleece. Be that as it may, the city and the surrounding countryside are friendly, intriguing, and full of archaeological wonders, evidence of a thriving humanity seeking to wrest a living here for thousands of years.

The Romans are the most visible of the occupiers, leaving behind grand and noble structures, many still in use. But the Romans were followed by the Eastern Goths, and then followed a couple of centuries of rule by Byzantium, and a succession of others. Franks followed the Byzantine rulers, and the Venetians extended their hand into the region. In 1379, the bright blue waters around Pula turned red when the Genoese destroyed the Venetian fleet and leveled much of Pula itself. In 1797 the area became part of the Austrian Empire, and in 1866 Pula became headquarters of the Austrian war fleet. World Wars 1 and 2 again brought death, misery, and destruction to the peninsula, but following the hostilities once more the people living here reclaimed the area and reconstructed their lives and the wonderful old stone buildings topped with the ubiquitous red tile roofs.

On a bright day in the fall of 2005, archaeologist Luka Bekic walked across a cleared track that defined the route of a natural gas pipeline to be constructed in the next couple of years. Bekic (pronounced BEK-ich) was three inches over six feet, and his long legs strode easily over the uneven, raw gash in the centuries-old fields. Although clear and cloudless, the day was cold, and Bekic wore a red parka, protection against the wind as much as the chilly temperature. Behind him on a ridgeline was a yellow marker that signified the main structure of the 1st century Roman villa that he and his colleagues were excavating, before pipeline construction would render useless any archaeological information to be gleaned from this site.

The country around the ancient village of Krvavici northeast of Pula was remote, rugged, and difficult to negotiate in anything other than a four-wheel-drive truck or by hard walking. Occasionally, a nearby farmer chugged through the area on an antique tractor, in search of an errant cow or to bring in firewood against the coming winter. The fields were still marked by centuries-old stone walls built of rocks plucked from the enclosures. The fields and walls were in the same locations as shown on a local map from 1800, in the hands of the same families for more than 200 years. Bekic, head of the division of archaeological heritage of the Hrvatski Restauratorski Zavod, the Croatian Conservation Institute, was searching for evidence of other outlying buildings on the grand Roman villa. For hundreds of years Romans had dominated the area around Pula, far up on the eastern coast of the Adriatic Sea, and it was not uncommon to find evidence of their tenure.

In Pula itself, which bills itself as 3,000 years old, a fine Roman amphitheater remains, still in use after two millennia and booked for gigs by such major talents as Norah Jones and Elton John. In the old town section of the city, temples and arches stand witnesses to a bustling past. The villa discovered near Krvavici was probably once the home of a wealthy merchant; the harbors at Pula and further north at Rovinj were notable for their ancient anchorages that helped establish the area as a trading center.

The entire peninsula of Istria is largely unspoiled, although the fuse is already lit for an explosion of tourism. Small towns and villages still play host to an agrarian economy; the silver-green leaves of olive trees shimmer in the slightest breeze, and grapes cluster richly on vines staked everywhere one looks. Fig trees offer up their jam-sweet fruit to anyone walking by. But the slow pace of life close to the land is rapidly changing. The towns along the Adriatic are becoming the playgrounds of Italians who come to enjoy the beaches and the many small coffee shops that line the narrow, cobbled streets of the old cities. The air is clear and bright, forming a dome over the sparkling blue-green waters of the sea. Inland, the land quickly rises, and the jagged peaks of Ucka Mountain are a constant blue backdrop.

The area around Krvavici is less populated than during World War II, as newer generations leave the task of working the rocky soil and gravitate to Pula or Zagreb or other cities. Now, many of the fields that used to grow hay or fence cattle are overgrown, with scrub oak trees sprouting like weeds. An aura of wildness belies proximity to small roads and tiny villages.

On this chilly day, Bekic walked through the rugged area, looking down as he always did. Not only was it necessary to keep from turning an ankle on the uneven and rocky ground, but years of training had taught him that artifacts often are essentially at your feet, if only you have the eyes for them. He had found many of the ancient baked bricks used for the outbuildings across the area that comprised the old Roman villa, and shards of pottery and terra cotta, as well.

Something gleamed dully a step ahead, and he kicked at it idly, thinking it a facet of a rock reflecting the Istrian sun. It didn't move, and he bent to examine it, discovering that it was a scrap of aluminum, doubtless an old tractor part left from a field repair sometime in the not-so-distant past. He tugged at it, and pulled a jagged and twisted piece of sheet aluminum from the half-inch of soil that covered most of it. In size, it was about eight inches by a foot or so, and Bekic looked at it with little interest. Obviously not part of the Roman villa and doubtless belonging to a more quotidian and recent past, it was not an item for his professional interest. He started to toss it Frisby-style toward a stone wall nearby, but he stopped his arm in mid-throw and pulled it back for a closer look at the opposite side. Stenciled in red paint was an advisory in English:

"If this airplane is equipped with a G-6 starter . . ."[1]

Bekic, fluent in English, stared at the twisted scrap of metal for several moments, trying to make sense of this serendipitous find. Scuffing around with his boots, within minutes he uncovered several more bits and pieces of jagged metal. He called for his assistants, Mladen Mustacek and Tihomir Percan, and the three searched with metal detectors for another hour or so. In that time, they found dozens of machine-gun bullets and several hundred bits and pieces of aluminum, some painted with a greenish zinc oxide primer, and many with English words painted or imprinted on them. All were ripped and twisted, silent evidence of a violent end to an American or British aircraft.

Luka Bekic was a veteran of the 1991–95 war in which Yugoslavia broke up into Serbia, Bosnia, Montenegro, Slovenia, and Croatia. It was a deadly, ghastly conflict, one in which he saw many of his fellow infantrymen die painfully from horrible wounds. They had fought using cast-off weapons from other conflicts, wearing cobbled-together uniforms from a score of nations, and with medical supplies virtually nonexistent. Croatia was largely unprepared for the war, but Bekic and his comrades fought for two years, taking and retaking small villages, killing and being killed.[2]

The fledgling Croatian Air Force had flown a handful of outdated Soviet-built MIG fighters. For bombers, they had relied on the ancient, bi-winged Soviet Antonov AN-2 Colt, a single-engine, propeller-driven anachronism. Ground crews had fashioned bombs from water heaters, which were filled with explosives and old hardware, and dropped on enemy positions. Bekic understood wars, and he understood what happens to young men destined to fight in those wars.

After the war, he determined that he would not be a professional soldier, wishing instead to add to human knowledge through understanding the past. He entered a graduate program in archeology at the University of Zagreb, and over several years had participated in or led excavations in the areas of Istria, Primorje, Dalmatia, Lika, and other places. Recently, while excavating the Bronze Age fortress of Munkodonja atop a hill overlooking the Adriatic, he had discovered evidence of a massacre. The skeletons of a score of men, women, and children had been dumped unceremoniously into a crypt by the main gate, an area that would have been used as a scrapheap for garbage. The right arms of each of the men had been hacked off, evidence to Bekic that they had been newcomers from outlying areas and had raised their arms in defiance of the forces in control of the fortress. Wars had raged across the region for millennia, untold numbers of humans had died violently.

Now, holding the original scrap of aluminum from a more recent conflict, he looked up at the sky and imagined an airplane spinning downward, perhaps on fire, out of control. He thought of the young man or men in that machine, and a sense of the brotherhood of arms permeated him. What had happened here, and when? What happened to the young soldiers in the aircraft? Were remains buried here? Did aviators die violently in a long-ago conflict? What were their stories? Were any still alive, and what had happened to them?

Driving into the village, he asked to speak to the oldest resident. He was directed to an ancient at the far end of the tiny village. Did he recall an aircraft crashing in the area? Yes, the old man replied. It was an American bomber, very big, and the Germans had shot it down late in World War II. There were parachutes in the sky, but people remembered finding charred boots and a glove with a hand in it.[3] Germans had been in the area for several days, and they had dragged the largest pieces of the plane to one of the deep pits, numerous in the karst region, and villagers had cleaned up much of the remainder.

Word spread of the archaeologist's interest in the plane crash, and various residents came to show him pieces of the bomber that had been pressed into daily service. One farmer had sawed an oxygen tank in half, added a bail, and used it to feed his cows. Another had a large piece of aluminum with a piano hinge running its length: he used it to cover his wood pile. It would prove to be pivotal in identifying the aircraft as local researchers identified it as a B-24 bomb bay door.

But which B-24? Who had crashed here more than sixty years before, and what had happened to them?

For Bekic, this was a mystery that had to be solved. But where to begin?

Chapter 3

The 1930s

Faucett, Missouri

William Urvie Lamar parked his Model T Ford outside the Bank of Faucett, a small, nondescript brick building on a dirt street that was the only thoroughfare in the small, northwest Missouri town. Faucett in the early 1930s was nearly indistinguishable from thousands of small communities across the country, clusters of commerce that sprang up to serve the needs of nearby residents, but never incorporated as a city or even a village. False-front buildings lined both sides of the packed-earth street—feed stores, sundries, hardware, a café or two—without pretension or dreams of conglomeration or growth. The town was said by locals to be "a mile long and a block wide." That wasn't strictly true, however. In a couple of places, it was two blocks deep.

Unpretentious was a word that, if anyone were asked and thought about it for a bit, might have been used to describe Urvie Lamar, who owned and worked a small farm a couple of miles south of town. The Lamars were not the local gentry, but had been in the area for a couple of generations and were respected for their hard work and piety. This day, Urvie needed to settle up a minor debt to the owner of the feed store, but he wanted exact change. Finding spare dollars to make change had become a bit of a problem for some lately, and Urvie didn't want to embarrass anyone.

He walked up to the teller's window and smiled at the cashier, a smallish, balding man in a gray suit jacket and a wide gray tie.

"Morning." Lamar's greeting was laconic, typical of the sparseness of everyday life in the gently rolling farm country between St. Joseph and Kansas City. The cashier nodded, and Lamar pushed a rumpled $5 bill across the counter. "Change, please." The clerk took the bill and opened a drawer nearby. Urvie thought he looked a bit flustered, and became concerned when he turned to go into a back office. Lamar waited. Another customer had entered the bank, and stood patiently a few feet behind him. Several minutes went by, and Lamar grew more uneasy. Had he been passed a counterfeit bill? Of course not, he considered. Even now in the throes of the Depression, no one bothered to print a fake five spot.

At last the harried cashier emerged from the tiny back office, and somewhat officiously counted out four dollar bills, three quarters, two dimes and a nickel. "There you go, sir." The clerk smiled thinly. "Thanks for coming in." Lamar nodded, thanked the clerk, and went to settle up the two dollars he owed for feed. His own funds were in a bank in nearby Wallace, where he attended the Methodist church. But his oldest son, Charlie, had an account in Faucett.

"Better get your money out of the bank," he told his son when he returned home. "It won't be open much longer." Three weeks later, like hundreds of banks across the country, the struggling bank of Faucett closed its doors forever. The Great Depression had claimed another victim.

The incident defined much of the early life of Lee Lamar and perhaps others of the crew of *Bottoms Up*. Rich, perhaps, in personal relationships and full of those incidents often called "character building," today Lamar's early life would be called economically deprived. He is more direct. "We were poor."[1]

For the youngest Lamar, growing up on a hardscrabble farm in rural northwestern Missouri, south of St. Joseph and north of the impossibly large city of Kansas City, the days were neither idyllic nor grinding. But the details of daily life then have the capacity to make that time seem much longer ago, the changes difficult to imagine occurring in a single lifetime.

The responsibility for raising Lee—like his father, he was known by his middle name—fell largely on the shoulders of his older sisters, Mildred and Thelma, and Lee might have been spoiled in such a setting if the family had not lived on a self-sufficient farm, where hard work was not just expected, it was absolutely necessary.

So Lee grew up and attended one-room school houses (where, because one teacher taught all eight grades, he skipped sixth grade, did eighth grade work in the seventh, and seventh grade work in the eighth. The day after the poor, harried teacher died of cancer, the entire eighth grade class failed to be promoted and repeated the grade). His first school bus was a wooden box with canvas sides mounted on the running gear of a farm wagon, and drawn by four horses, with a bench seat running down each side of a narrow aisle. More like a Conestoga wagon than a contemporary school bus. Students entered from the rear. During the winter, the driver stayed warm by keeping a small stove burning beside him. Lee and the other children of farm couples waited patiently at the end of their drives, in good weather and bad, for the wagon-bus to pick them up and haul them over unpaved roads to the consolidated school. Holes in the ruts during wet weather were a major problem, and children often had to disembark and walk while the horses strained to pull the wagon through the soggy tracks.

As the depression dragged on, life for the Lamars, never extravagant, became more precarious. One day Lee was approached by his father, a man of few words but proud and self-sufficient. The elder Lamar needed to borrow from Lee's piggy bank. Without hesitation, or asking why, Lee removed all of the change from the bank and handed it to his father. It came to one dollar. Lamar took the dollar and went into town, where he purchased an ax. He needed it to cut firewood to keep the family warm that winter.

Despite the complexities and obstacles of the arcane world of education, Lee was able to enter high school at Faucett, and he rode a pony to school his first year. By his sophomore year, a motorized school bus was in operation.

The family was quietly religious, faithfully attending the Methodist church in nearby Wallace until it closed its doors during the depths of the depression. When Lee was in his mid-teens, while lying on the bank of the small creek that meandered through the farm, he looked up at the clouds. The immensity of space suddenly weighed mightily on him. A few years later, the great French writer and aviator Antoine de Saint-Exupery lay on his back in the North African desert and felt something similar, a feeling he described as vertigo and a sense that he would fall off the earth into the sky.[2] But Lee was far too grounded to experience that, and his logical mind next followed the line of inquiry to the opposite extreme. How small were the basic building blocks of all life, of all matter, and how did they get here? It was a deep and largely unanswerable query. But for whatever reason, his mind next turned to a small, colored postcard he had been given in Sunday school years before. It was a picture of Jesus, along with several Bible verses, and as the first color picture that he could recall, it had made a deep impression on him.

Quietly, with no public display, no trembling acquiescence, Lee made the decision that he would try to live in a way that Jesus would approve. He didn't talk to anyone about his decision, just made up his mind that this man from Nazareth was a symbol of all that was good and right in the world. Lee determined to pattern his life after him. This deep conviction of the right way to live would prove vital in just a few years as his quiet faith carried him through trials of deprivation, destruction, and widespread death.

To help the family's financial situation, young Lee worked a variety of jobs during the summer and after school, including delivering water to harvest crews, raising heifers, and stoking the school furnace early each morning for the sum of $5 for the winter.

High school proved no problem for the serious-minded young man. He did well in mathematics and science. He was strong and lean but not particularly gifted as an athlete. However, his gangly frame was nearly six feet tall and he was told by the principal his freshman year that he WOULD play basketball. Lee played for four years, never as a starter, but always ready to go in when needed. A photo from the time shows a handsome young man, blond hair smartly combed, dressed in a suit coat, a collar pin behind the knotted tie adding a dapper signature. His head is dropped ever so slightly, his eyes raised in order to look straight ahead. It would become a trademark look, and gives a viewer the impression that Lee is looking skyward.

By the time he graduated high school in the spring of 1939, there were few realistic opportunities for Lamar to do anything other than farm or to find other low-paying jobs. Growing up in Faucett, Lee had seen barnstorming pilots land and take passengers up for the chance to see their farms from the air. But the elder Lamar was dead set against airplanes, muttering as so many others did that if God had intended for men to fly he would have given them wings. Or more money.

But the sight of the planes ignited in Lee a fierce secret desire to be closer, to get into one, to fly above the countryside. Once while still in grade school he had gone to St. Joseph to visit one of his sisters, now married, and she and her husband took the young boy out to the airport. He walked through a couple of hangars and touched the airplanes inside, admiring the tightly-stretched fabric, the clean lines of the fuselage. He couldn't get inside one, certainly didn't get to fly that day, but that opportunity came along in the summer of 1939 shortly after graduating from high school.

A cousin, Lloyd Ussary, invited Lee to go with him and his family on a visit to Kansas City for a picnic with relatives. Then Lloyd had borrowed the family car, and Lee and his cousin ended up at Kansas City Municipal Airport (now Wheeler Downtown Airport). There, a large crowd had gathered near a biplane whose pilot was taking people for sight-seeing flights. Although he didn't have much money, and what he did have had come dearly, Lee could not resist. He shelled out the few dollars and climbed into the front cockpit alone—Lloyd opted not to go—and took off to the south over downtown Kansas City with the barnstormer in the rear cockpit. He never mentioned the flight, or the extravagant waste of hard-earned cash, to his father.

He was hooked. The feeling of freedom, the wind in his face, and the view from the heavens, were enough to capture the imagination of any young man. But the country was still in the grip of the Depression, and such heady dreams of flight were quickly dashed.

With high school graduation behind him, Lee was in a bit of a quandary. What now? Few jobs were available, and college was out of the question. Rarely did farm boys go to college. No one in his high school class of twenty seemed to have considered it. Only rich kids went to college, and the Lamars were anything but well-to-do. Farming seemed a likely route, but there too were obstacles: it took land and capital to get started, and Lamar's father was already deeply in debt and trying to work off the aborted farming plans of Lee's brother. He spent the summer of 1939 working hard on area farms for a dollar a day, and by the end of the harvest season had the princely sum of $85. And still no real prospects for the future.

Lee's brother-in-law, Norman Crouch, had worked his way through St. Joseph Junior College, then had managed to complete a teaching degree at the University of Missouri by working a couple and sometimes three jobs during school. In mid-August of 1939 his sister and Norman came to visit the Lamars. As it worked out, Lee and Norman were alone outside the house when Norman turned to him and, seemingly casually, remarked that he had talked to the dean of the junior college, Miss Nellie Bloom, about Lee.

No jobs for students were available, having gone to those who applied in the Spring. But if Lee could register and make it through the first 30 days of class without a scholarship or work-study job, the dean thought Lee might be able to snag one of the National Youth Administration jobs funded by the federal government. Students in those jobs had to work a minimum number of hours to stay in the program, and Miss Bloom was fairly certain that at least one would fail to keep up his end of the bargain. An additional financial hurdle was eliminated by the understanding Miss Bloom. Since Lamar lived outside of the St. Joseph School District boundaries, he should have been required to pay out-of-district tuition. Norman Crouch had told her that Lee would be living in St. Joseph with him and going home to Faucett on weekends. The dean chose to overlook this detail. Still, it would take all of his hard-earned cash to enter the junior college, and there was no guarantee that when his money ran out he would be able to continue. It sounded like a poor investment to a financially strapped boy from Faucett. He was noncommittal to Norman, and he was not particularly enthusiastic about his college prospects. A few days later, all that changed.

Lee picked up the *St. Joseph News Press* and saw a two-paragraph article that re-ignited the smoldering desire to fly.

The U.S. government was aware that a war might be possible in Europe at any time (this was just weeks before the Nazi blitzkrieg rolled over Poland, prompting England and France to declare war on Germany). Someone in the administration had looked ahead and determined that more pilots might be needed quickly. To do this in the least expensive way possible, without increasing the size of the armed forces, the Civilian Pilot Training Program had been instituted, the article said. The CPTP was to be conducted at flight schools around the country, with the costs subsidized by the federal government. One of the schools would be at St. Joseph Junior College, with flight training at the city airport, Rosecrans Field. For $10, students who were eligible—a physical examination and written test had to be passed—could obtain a private pilot's license.

Lee could scarcely believe his eyes. Carefully, he reread the short article. There it was. Ten dollars and he would be trained as a pilot. It seemed an impossible dream that a farm boy from tiny Faucett, Missouri, with no college and few prospects, could become a pilot and obtain a college education.

That's what his mother thought also. "Lee, there is no way you can go to college."

For the hard-working mother of four, poor all her life, the glamour of a college degree was beyond anything she could envision. It was past any possibility. But Lee was determined, and he enrolled at the St. Joseph Junior College with no clear idea of a course of study other than he wanted to fly. At the college he learned that a pre-engineering program would transfer to the University of Missouri, and there he could complete a bachelor's degree in engineering. It was as good as anything, he decided. But he was disappointed to learn he was too late to enroll in the CPTP for that year. He could enroll in the ground school, however, with the promise of the flight program the following year.

Miss Bloom was true to her word. She found a job for Lee, a janitorial position that required forty hours of work a month for the princely salary of $5. But he was not dunned for out-of-district tuition, and Lee would be able to pursue his dream of flight.

The CPTP was one of those government programs that seemed to surpass its original goals and to provide a healthy return on the dollars invested. The Army Air Forces in 1939 had only 4,502 pilots, according to the National Museum of the Air Force. The CPTP was one of several efforts to significantly ramp up the numbers, and paralleled similar programs in other countries, notably Germany and England throughout the 1930s. In 1942, the CPTP was renamed War Training Service. From its start in 1938 until discontinued in the summer of 1944, the program trained 435,165 pilots. Many of these went on to become military combat pilots; others became liaison, service, or glider pilots, or served as civilian fliers in the Air Transport Command operating around the globe. The program was operated through 1,132 colleges and universities, in partnership with 1,460 flight schools. Those enrolled in the CPTP continued to be enrolled in colleges, and it was assumed many would enter military service when called.[3]

Despite not being able to fly his first year at St. Joseph Junior College, Lee was fascinated by what he was learning in ground school. The theory of flight, emergency procedures, weather, and flight regulations all seemed like practical and valuable information that would be applied when he was in a cockpit, and he enjoyed the stories of those in ground school who were also in the flight portion of the program. The summer following his first year of college Lee delivered ice to farmhouses around the region. Ice was a necessity for those rural dwellers, many of whom did not have electricity for refrigerators. The ice box, which needed to be refreshed with new ice periodically, was vital to keep food from spoiling, and Lee was glad to be free of the uncertainties of farming to ensure his return to school in the fall.

That summer of 1940 he got his second airplane ride, one that influenced his later decision to become a bomber pilot. An air show at the St. Joseph airport featured Ben Gregory, a pilot from Kansas City, who thrilled the crowd with his two Ford Tri-motors, flat-sided, thick-winged flying machines sheathed in corrugated aluminum with a radial engine hanging from each wing and one on the nose. One of the Tri-motors was for taking up passengers; the other was rigged for an aerial, smoke-trailing display of flying. The engines were rigged to inject oil onto the exhaust pipes when triggered by the pilot, which of course generated a trail of smoke. Gregory's trick was to fly above the airfield, perform a few standard maneuvers, then do a low pass over the crowd. He would release the oil, and while the smoke billowed he would also flick on large lights mounted on the wings which appeared to the crowd to be flames. He climbed slightly, then dove behind a line of trees at the edge of the Missouri River where he released a smoke bomb. The stunned audience believed they had just witnessed a tragic crash. Gregory kept the plane low, out of sight of the crowd, and circled around to the other side of the field to make his landing.

After landing his specially equipped plane, Gregory then began hawking tickets for his flight-seeing Tri-motor. Apparently, the crowd bore no ill will for the trick, nor did it discourage them from flight, for usually the sixteen seats were full. Lee was one of the paying passengers that summer of 1940, and Gregory invited him to sit in the co-pilot's seat for the flight. He was fascinated to watch the pilot's use of the throttle levers to taxi the ungainly airplane.

Gregory kept the palm of his right hand on the center lever, effortlessly rotating his hand to advance the right lever, increasing power to the right engine while simultaneously retarding the left engine by pulling back the left lever. This use of differential power was used to turn the airplane in either direction, and the young would-be pilot was mightily impressed with this casual display of piloting finesse. He vowed that if possible, he would fly multi-engine aircraft some day.

That fall, Lamar finally realized his dream of flying. But it was nearly over before it started.

Lamar and the other young men starting the flying regimen were sent to a local doctor for a flight physical. Lee was unable to read the required line on the eye chart. It was a crushing disappointment.

"You're a student at the Junior College, aren't you?" the physician asked him. Lamar affirmed that he was. "I suspect that you have been studying a great deal. Go home, rest your eyes, and come back in the morning." A despondent Lamar trudged back to his room, wondering what he would do now that his dream of a flying career was apparently shattered. He didn't read, his usual occupation in the evening, and went to bed early, sick at heart. The next morning, back at the doctor's office, he passed the visual acuity test and all the other eye functions, including color and depth perception. He was allowed to proceed to the flight line.

A few days later, prior to his first entry into a Piper J-3 Cub, the instructor, Tommy Ogle, showed Lamar how to properly put on a parachute, which was a requirement for all flight training under the CPTP rules. Cinching tight the thick, white cotton webbing of the harness, Lamar soberly contemplated the significance of donning the equipment. He knew that if a pilot flew long enough, he would probably jump out of his airplane someday. Newspapers in the 1920s and '30s routinely carried stories of airmail pilots forced to jump when their ships ran out of fuel above a thick layer of clouds.

"Someday, you may need to use this," he thought. "If that day comes, you are going to use this parachute as quickly as possible. There will be no ifs, ands, or buts. You will just use it."

The Piper J-3 was a basic airplane that in many ways was only marginally advanced from the Wright Flyer. It was powered by a 65-horsepower engine, whose cylinder heads jutted out of the side of the narrow nose for air cooling. A six-foot wooden propeller had to be swung by hand to start the engine. The wings and fuselage were covered in doped cotton, and a pilot and a single passenger—the student—sat in tandem, the student normally in back. Because of its small size and weight and the center of gravity, it was always flown solo from the rear seat. A spartan instrument panel housed an airspeed indicator, an altimeter, a compass, tachometer, and oil pressure gauge. Sticks rising up between the legs of both pilot and passenger controlled the ailerons and elevator, and conventional peddles acted upon the rudder. The throttle was on the left side of the cockpit wall, along with the trim tab that resembled a window handle on a Buick. The fuel tank was behind the engine, in front of the pilot, and the fuel gauge was a wire attached to a cork that floated atop the gasoline just outside the center of the windscreen. Fuel amount was determined by how much wire projected through the top. There was no radio, no flaps, no electrical system, no lights, no generator, and no starter. On warm days, the tiny plane could be flown with the single door on the right side open, making the experience somewhat akin to flying a motorcycle.[4]

In August, 1940, Lamar took his first flight as a student pilot. His logbook was later stolen, but he recalled the regimen: straight and level flight, climbs, turns, and descents, the time-honored "four fundamentals" of flying. These basic maneuvers of flight were drilled and practiced and reviewed. All aerial maneuvers stem from some combination of those four fundamentals, he learned. Recovery from aerodynamic stalls was emphasized, as was spin recovery. After a few hours of higher aerial work, Ogle and Lamar spent several days in the traffic pattern learning the basics of landing. The Cub landed slowly, about 40 mph, and was light enough to float just above the runway on warm days when hot air rose in waves from the earth. Landing a tail-wheel equipped airplane was a matter of slowing the plane to a speed just above a stall, cutting all power, then as it slowed still further and began to settle to earth, pulling back on the stick to touch down on all three wheels at the same time that it stalled.

Stalling an airplane is not the same as stalling a car. It has nothing to do with the engine, and—as many Navy dive bomber pilots learned—could happen in any attitude at any speed. It means that the wing exceeds an angle (relative to the direction of flight) wherein the air that is supposed to flow smoothly over the top of the wing can no longer do so, and begins to burble and swirl, thus killing the lift that is necessary for continued flight. In the event of landing, that is what is intended. Otherwise, stalls are normally not a desired condition for flying. They have killed many pilots when they occur at low altitude.

The old Rosecrans Field had been close to the river bluffs that were considered a hazard, so a new one, well away from these obstacles, had been constructed a couple of years earlier. The new field boasted two concrete runways and two grass strips. To save tire rubber, student pilots would use the grass strips and not the runways.

In October, after about eight hours of dual instruction from Ogle, the instructor climbed out of the Cub.

"You're ready. Take 'er around three times, three landings to a full stop." He winked at Lamar. "I'll be watching from here. If I need to talk to you about something, I'll walk out to the plane so keep an eye out for me." He punched Lee's shoulder, and walked to the edge of the mowed grass strip.

Lee wasn't sure he was ready. But the instructor judged him so, and student pilots are not encouraged to argue with their instructors. With a pounding heart, he lined up the Cub in the center of the runway, applied full power with his left hand, and kept the stick forward. Gradually the speed increased and his eyes flickered to the airspeed indicator every few seconds. He could not see over the nose of the small plane, so he had to watch the edge of the grass strip at the side of the cowling. When the ASI showed about 30 mph, the tail began to rise and he eased the stick back to neutral. At 50, he pulled back the stick and the Cub rose in the air, for the first time with young Lee as the only occupant. He was exhilarated, but busy, carefully keeping the airspeed at a constant 60, watching the altimeter climb through a few hundred feet. He turned left to crosswind, then left again to downwind parallel to the runway. He reduced the throttle to about two thousand revolutions per minute (rpm) as he leveled at eight hundred feet and lowered the nose slightly.

The loss of weight of Ogle in the front seat had caused the Cub to fairly leap from the grass runway, it seemed to Lee, and now in level flight he realized that it also had shifted the center of gravity, causing the nose to want to rise. He carefully twisted the trim control until the plane flew level with no pressure from Lee on the stick. Looking down, he could see the tiny figure of Ogle beside the runway at the midway point. Passing the end of the strip, Lee reduced the power to 1,700 rpm. He turned left to base leg, and once more to final approach, where he pulled the throttle all the way back and watched the near end of the runway to ensure that he was not too high, or worse, too low. He sailed over the end of the grass strip, held the Cub level as the speed gradually bled off, and as it began to settle he pulled the stick back. The bright yellow Piper settled onto the grass, bounced once slightly, then rolled on all three tires down the runway.

Lee saw Ogle salute him, then wave his arm to indicate he should do another circuit. A huge grin split the young man's face as he taxied the aircraft back for another takeoff. He had done it. He had flown an airplane, taken it off, landed it, all on his own. He could feel like a pilot at last.

So, through the fall of 1940 Lamar and other young men enrolled in the CPTP pulled on their white mechanic's overalls, embroidered on the back with the name of the flight school and a large winged propeller, and showed up at the airport after their classes. One day late in the fall, and early in the morning, Lee and Ogle departed on Lee's first dual cross-country flight designed to teach navigation skills. They flew for an hour and ten minutes into a strong headwind trying to reach Topeka, Kansas. Ogle finally signaled that it was fruitless to keep going, so they turned around and in ten minutes had landed again at St. Joseph. A few days later, on the third leg of a triangular course that took them from Fairfax airport in Kansas City, Kansas, to St. Joe, Lamar was able at last to see his family home and all the familiar landmarks of his youth. Ogle, noting his careful attention to the scene below, assumed Lamar was lost and began asking him the names of small towns easily seen from 5,000 feet. Lamar did not consult his map, able to rattle off the names easily. Ogle was impressed, and he signed his logbook qualifying Lamar for a solo cross-country flight over the same route.

Late in the semester several inches of heavy snow were dumped on the St. Joseph area, threatening the flight operations of the school and thereby possibly delaying the training of the current crop of student pilots. Snow removal was a fledgling art, and the entire flight curriculum was in danger of running out of time if a solution could not be found. Someone suggested skis, and the fleet of Cubs was soon fitted out with smooth, curved-tip skis. Students and instructors alike had to learn how to handle the plane on the ground, since now it had no brakes. It was interesting and challenging, but Lee never flew on skis after that winter.

By the middle of Lamar's second year at St. Joseph Junior College, he had completed the course prescribed by the Civil Aeronautics Administration, forerunner of the Federal Aviation Agency, and received his private pilot's license. He had learned how to fly a small plane, and along the way he had made many friends with the same desire. He graduated from St. Joseph Junior College with an Associate Degree, and he warmly shook the hand of Nellie Bloom, the college dean who called out the names of the two hundred graduates without ever referring to a written list.

He was to learn that flying was fun, challenging, and sometimes unforgiving of mistakes. After the war started, he was to lose an average of one friend a month in training accidents. He lost track of the number later, when he was posted overseas to a combat unit.

But for now, Lamar's next step was to transfer to the University of Missouri to begin work on a Bachelor's degree in engineering. He knew the chances of finishing that degree before being called on by Uncle Sam were remote.

Chapter 4

1941–42

You're in the Army Now

Lee worked at delivering ice the summer of 1941, and that fall, with a bit of money for school but none left over for flying now that he had completed the CPTP, he entered the University of Missouri. He found a room in a large house in Columbia, across the street from the engineering school, where he roomed with another transfer student from St. Joseph. A widow operated the rooming house, where seven students were grateful for a place with a bed and she was glad to have the income.

Classes in structural analysis, fluid mechanics, and differential equations kept Lamar busy, but his practical mind was fascinated at the process of understanding and applying principles of physics in practical ways. He was not interested in philosophy, and literature held little appeal. But he reveled in new-found knowledge that made it possible to look at a bridge or a building and consider the use of materials and stress points in a particular design. It was, in some ways, an extension of the physics of flight; an understanding of the principles of lift, gravity, thrust, and drag were as essential to being a good pilot as an understanding of material strengths was to a civil engineer. Disregarding physics in either profession would mean disaster at some point.

The war continued to rage in Europe. France had fallen the previous summer, and now the British were alone, slugging it out against Erwin Rommel in North Africa after rescuing most of their expeditionary force at Dunkirk. The teenage pilots of the Royal Air Force had beaten back the onslaught of the Luftwaffe, and would forever be known as The Few. Control of the air was necessary for Hitler's plan to invade England, and the RAF had thwarted that scheme. The daily news stories of the fall of 1940 had been inspirational to young men like Lamar. The air war was dangerous but glamorous, and it seemed to verify that now, wars would be fought in the clouds.

These were serious times, but for Lamar and other struggling and overwhelmed college students, their concerns were closer to home. He was vaguely aware that the war in Europe was going badly for Britain, but he also needed to get through his classes.

December 7, 1941, was another Sunday of studying in the widow's rooming house. Life changed in an instant, however, that afternoon. A medical student who roomed there shattered the friendly silence, shouting that the Japanese had attacked Pearl Harbor. The United States was at war. While most eyes had been watching Europe, Japan had struck in the Pacific.

The next day, one of Lamar's professors brought a radio to his classroom, and the somber engineering students sat quietly while President Roosevelt asked Congress for a declaration of war on Japan. Three days later, Germany sealed its own fate by declaring war on the U.S., which then reciprocated. It was to be a two-front war for the Americans.

It wasn't long before recruiters began showing up on college campuses, and Lee opted for the Air Corps Enlisted Reserve. He would be allowed to stay in school until the Air Corps needed him and had the training facilities built to accommodate him and hundreds of thousands of other young fliers. But first he had to pass a battery of mental and physical exams.

He sailed through the mental tests, and the physical examination was not difficult for a young, fit farm boy, albeit a bit out of shape while at college for the past couple of years. But once more, his eyes posed a challenge: he could only read the 20/40 line on the eye chart. As earlier in St. Joseph, he was devastated. This surely was the end of the road on his journey to becoming a pilot. Lamar and several others in the same predicament were asked to come back the following day for a vision re-test. If they failed that, they could not be admitted to the aviation program.

That evening, a despondent Lamar was wandering the streets of Columbia. As he trudged down Conley Avenue, his mind was ticking off his alternatives. He could muster enthusiasm for none of them. Flying was the only thing he wanted to do.

"Hey, Lamar!"

He looked up to see several young men that he recognized, all of whom had failed their initial visual acuity test. They waved for him to cross the street and join them.

"Lamar, you're going to love this." One of the young men leaned toward him while a couple of other conspirators looked around anxiously. "We got back into the eye exam area and copied down the last line. It's easy to memorize." He recited a quick mnemonic ditty that arranged the letters in such a way that it was impossible for Lee to shake them from his mind. Like the lyrics to a song that you cannot banish from your brain, it followed Lamar through a series of upcoming eye exams and later created some anxious soul-searching for the earnest young man.

The next day, Lamar passed his eye exam, though he could not honestly tell if he passed on the strength of his eyes or his memory. But through a series of misunderstandings, minor accidents, and impatience by recruiting officers, he was not sworn in immediately. Later he received a letter from his local draft board advising him to report, and another from the Air Corps Enlisted Reserve advising him that he had completed all the requirements for that program but still needed to be sworn in. Lamar borrowed his brother's car, drove to St. Louis, and was sworn in, a procedure that took about thirty seconds. He was then able to write his draft board that he was already obligated to the military through the Enlisted Reserve.

Time was passing, and in the spring of 1943 Lamar finally received orders to report to the federal courthouse in Kansas City for induction. His parents drove him there, and after some awkward and teary-eyed goodbyes, they left their youngest child on the sidewalk staring after them as they headed back to the farm. Late that afternoon, he was on the train bound for Jefferson Barracks, near St. Louis, dispirited and weak from a recent bout of measles.

Lamar had hoped to report directly to the Aviation Cadet Center in San Antonio, but the facility was simply overloaded. Additionally, the sheer numbers of young men needed to fight this world war was astonishing, and the Air Corps, which changed its name in 1942 to the Army Air Forces, had to change its requirements for cadets. For acceptance into pilot training (and commissioning as an officer in the service of the United States), the requirement had long been a minimum of two years college. However, very few young people of the 1930s and '40s went to college, far fewer than today, so as the war went on the pool of potential aviators was rapidly depleted. The requirement was lowered to a year, and by the last years of the war high school graduates were going directly into the aviation cadet program. To bring cadets up to a higher educational level, however, college training detachments were established, and young men in khaki or olive drab uniforms began to sit in classrooms with civilian counterparts at colleges around the country. In this way, they were given a rudimentary start on higher education.

After a few cold and miserable weeks at Jefferson Barracks, Lamar and two hundred other young men were shipped north to Eau Claire, Wisconsin, where they enrolled in a variety of classes at the state teacher's college. Once there, he learned that his group of forty cadets would be the first to be assigned to San Antonio based on the results of the tests conducted at Jefferson Barracks. In the meantime, he enrolled in a European history class and conversational Spanish, but before he could complete the classes, he was ordered to San Antonio. At last he was on his way to a pair of silver wings.

The San Antonio Aviation Cadet Center turned out to be the exact epicenter of every possible physical, emotional, and mental examination ever devised by humans, Lamar and all other aspiring cadets were to discover. For days on end, they were probed, prodded, squeezed, injected, monitored, measured, and quizzed; they underwent humiliating physical examinations of every nook and cranny of their young bodies, including their private parts; they marched, ran, ate, slept, and did calisthenics in unison; they sweated through a series of tests that made no sense to them; they were asked to read maps, interpret aerial photographs, complete math problems. Lamar's engineering classes prepared him well for these tests, and he excelled. To check eye-hand coordination, presumably, other tests were devised: holding a metal disc against a point on a rotating wheel, or holding a long metal rod through a hole in a metal plate without touching the sides. Breathe in, breathe out; hold your breath, exhale. Turn your head and cough. Listen to the heart. Run in place, listen to the heart again.

And still ahead, after days of this, was the dreaded eye examination. Color differentiation, fine. Depth of field, fine. Peripheral vision, fine. Acuity—hold your breath, Lamar. It turned out to be a different bottom line from his memorized old friend. It made no difference. He was able to read the bottom line. He breathed a huge sigh of relief as he left the examining room, and his discomfort over how he might have passed previous acuity tests simply dissolved.

All of the results of all of the tests were somehow tabulated into a score, called a Stanine Rating, which was supposed to indicate how well a cadet might perform as a pilot, bombardier, or navigator, on a scale of one to nine. Each cadet was asked to rank his first, second, and third choices, a decision which would be made primarily on the needs of the government but which would consider, at least, the desire of the cadet. All flight positions were voluntary, and the government realized the unsatisfactory situation of forcing someone into pilot training who desperately wanted to be a navigator, for instance. Lamar listed pilot, then navigator where he could utilize some of the math and other courses he had excelled in. He had no interest in the bombardier's position, and did not list a third choice.

There was one more test before he would learn the Army's decision on his future: a chat with a psychiatrist.

Each day since arriving at the SAACC, young men simply vanished. At any point, for failing any of the dozens of tests and assessments, they would be given fifteen minutes to pack their gear and report for reassignment to another military duty such as infantry. For some, the reason for their rejection was obvious to the other cadets. The departing former cadet had failed at some physical test, in a very public, very visible way, or they had scored poorly on a test of mental agility. But for some, there was no simple explanation. Rumors swirled around the psychiatric exam. Suspected latent or open homosexuality was said to be one sure ticket out. Lamar finally was called in for his interview by the shrink. The questions seemed innocuous, the conversation innocent enough. Lamar relaxed.

"So, how about the girls around here, Lamar? Anything catching your eye?" The psychiatrist, a major with a deeply tanned face, smiled disarmingly. By now, Lamar had grown into a handsome young man, tall, lanky, blond, with neon blue eyes that were startling in their intensity.

"I have absolutely no idea, Major." Lamar looked forlorn. "We've been confined to the base since we got here." He leaned forward slightly, and grinned. "Tell you what, though. How about you arrange a weekend pass for me, I'll go into town, and when I get back we can talk some more." The major laughed heartily, and told Lee he was free to go—but there would be no weekend pass!

The young men who had survived the weeks of testing were now set to become aviation cadets, a distinction that meant they now packed up their meager belongings—nearly all government issue—and those who had been selected for pilot training moved across the base to Pre-Flight, on the other side of a set of railroad tracks which bisected the sprawling development that was as large as many cities. Navigator and bombardier trainees would head elsewhere. Earlier they had been notified of their selection for one of the three officer flying ratings, and Lee was jubilant to learn he was headed for pilot training. Later, he learned that his Stanine Rating had been a nine, the highest possible, and he also had scored a nine for navigator and bombardier training.

As full-fledged Aviation Cadets, Lamar and his classmates now received $75 monthly, a sum that seemed impossibly large to the young man who just a few years earlier had worked bucking hay bales for a dollar a day. In addition, he received food, clothing, and housing. Army life was not bad, he decided.

Army pilot training was divided into four nine-week courses: Pre-Flight, and Primary, Basic and Advanced Flight Training. At each step of the way, candidates would be eliminated from training in an impersonal, calculated culling of the inept, the slow, and the unsuited. There were many more applicants than the military needed, and the instructors at each phase were generally merciless in their decisions. Their reasoning could not be faulted: lives would depend on a pilot being fully qualified.

One day the cadets queued up and marched to a nondescript building, a place they had all heard about. Inside was the hyperbaric chamber, a large, sealed, steel tank with an airtight door. Air could be withdrawn from the chamber to simulate flying at high altitudes, and the purpose of the lesson was to impress upon the fledgling pilots the effects of loss of oxygen on their performance. As a sober and hard-working young man, Lamar had never experienced inebriation, not even a mild alcoholic buzz. The earliest stages of hypoxia—lack of oxygen—replicate the effects of alcohol, but it was not a connection he could make.

Twenty cadets entered the chamber and sat on benches built along the sides. They were instructed to don their oxygen masks, and slowly the oxygen was drawn out of the sealed hyperbolic chamber until they were at a simulated altitude of 30,000 feet, a height at which many combat missions were flown.

"Lamar, take this writing tablet and pencil, and remove your mask." The instructor handed him the pad and pencil, and Lamar dutifully removed his oxygen mask while the other cadets watched closely. "Now, I want you to start writing backward from one hundred by threes."

By 97, the numbers were shaky, 94 was illegible, and the young cadet, try as he might, was not able to determine the next number before passing out. It was a lesson he never forgot, and presumably neither did any of those watching wide-eyed as the instructor quickly replaced Lamar's oxygen supply.[1]

At the end of July 1943, after sailing through most of his classes—and scraping by in Morse code—Lamar and 160 other cadets left San Antonio and reported for Primary Flight Training at Hicks Field in Fort Worth. Here, at last, they would get to fly—and here the most severe elimination process would begin. The group forever would be known as the Class of 44B—indicating that they were scheduled for graduation as fully-qualified pilots in February 1944. When that date arrived, however, the number would be much smaller than the 161 who started the rigorous process.

On his first day at Hicks, he encountered stark evidence of the seriousness of this flying business. Walking after lunch in an area north of the administrative offices, he stopped short. There, in front of him, was the wreckage of a PT-19, the very primary trainer that he and the class of 44B would soon be flying. He walked closer, hesitating to get too close for fear of being challenged. The two-place airplane was crumpled and twisted, the engine pushed far back into the fuselage, one wing ripped from the airplane and lying next to it as one might stack old furniture at the curb after cleaning out the attic. It was obvious that no one could have survived the horrific crash.

It didn't take long to learn the story on this one. An area near the field had been established for flying practice by students who had soloed. Most of this area was over timbered, uninhabited land, but there were occasional houses in the clearings. One of these had a swimming pool, and on summer days it was frequently a popular area for young women in bathing suits. Of course, it also became popular for young, male, flying students. The novice flier of this now-wrecked PT-19 had been flying low and slow over the pool and failed to notice his airspeed had dropped. He stalled, was unable to recover, and killed himself when the trainer slammed nose-first into the hard Texas earth. It was a difficult lesson, one that Lamar never forgot. When in a cockpit, keep your mind on flying.

Lamar, despite his enforced hiatus from flying, found that his private pilot license and training in the Civilian Pilot Training Program made primary training in the military a fairly easy transition. The Fairchild PT-19 was about as simple as a Piper Cub, and nearly as easy to fly in his opinion.[2]

Lee soloed the PT-19 in about eight hours with little difficulty. Not all cadets were so fortunate. After a solo flight to a nearby practice field, he entered the traffic pattern at Hicks and saw another trainer preparing to land. It rode down the final approach path, then the pilot applied full throttle to go around. Lamar landed, and watched as the student repeated the attempt to land again and again. Nothing went right. He either stalled it too high above the runway and dropped it in, causing it to bounce back in the air, or didn't stall it at all and slammed onto the strip, also causing a giant bounce. In both cases, a go-around was necessary, and this had been going on for a long time before Lamar arrived. It undoubtedly was the longest solo of any student pilot in 44B. The student eventually got the airplane down to stay, but was washed out of the program. By then, he probably didn't care.

But for most aviation cadets, "washing out" was the stuff of nightmares. It meant the end of a dream, and the threat of not making it was constantly with each of them. For Lamar, flying was his ticket out of a life of hard physical labor and low pay. He worked incessantly, determined to do well on every test, to excel at each requirement. In a letter to his parents written while he was at Hicks Field, he noted that he was one of only a few cadets who were not going into town that Friday night:

"Most of the boys are going in to town tonight, but I am going to stay in and review for a test in 'weather.' I just found out I made the best grade in our class in a test on 'engines.' 97% that helps my average a lot too. . . . They sure are a lot of fellows being 'washed out.' Several in our class have already left and several more are waiting to leave. Can't tell I might be next. I sure hope not."[3]

And to his sister, Lamar expressed similar fears:

"We flew Saturday since we are behind on our time. I will probably leave here in two weeks provided I get all my time in and don't 'wash out.'"[4]

Death continued to be a silent partner in pilot training, but never so dramatically as one day when Lamar and the other cadets were lined up in formation in front of their barracks. A low rumble overhead turned into a roar, and the entire formation looked up to see two B-24 heavy bombers slam head-on into each other and fall in a shower of twisted, flaming debris. Both had been piloted by newly commissioned pilots training on the large bombers at nearby Tarrant Field. All aboard both bombers were killed.[5]

On September 29, 1943, Lamar graduated from Primary Flight School at Hicks Field. He had completed 29 hours, 18 minutes of dual instruction, 31 hours, 20 minutes of solo flight time. He had recorded 142 landings, and logged 5 hours of instrument training on the Link trainer.

Twenty-five of the original 161 cadets had washed out, and several others had been held back for a following class. But their luck had held; none had been killed in training.

Perrin Field at Sherman, Texas, was the next stop, where cadets from several primary training fields became the Perrin class 44B as they started Basic Flight School. The designation did not change, but the membership did. Here they would fly the BT-13. In addition to being an enclosed all-metal ship, it had a 450-hp radial engine, a two-speed propeller, and a radio, along with an intercom.[6]

The '13 proved to be a reasonably easy airplane to fly, despite its imposing appearance to new pilots. Lamar and most others in 44B soloed after a few hours of dual instruction, then it was on to more complicated flight maneuvers than they had previously mastered: stalls and spins, of course, and chandelles and Immelmanns, flight routines that had been developed during combat in World War I. Additionally, students in Basic would learn formation flying, instrument flying, and night flying.

Training was tough, washouts and accidents greeted many, and a future of combat flying did not look rosy. While Lamar and other cadets were focused on the basics of navigation, essential flight maneuvers, and the idiosyncrasies of radio communications, the war was taking a heavy toll on fliers overseas. According to historian Donald L. Miller, the early returns on casualties indicated a disaster in the making. Seventy-three per cent of the combat fliers arriving in England in the first year of America's entry into the war failed to complete their tour of duty; fifty-seven per cent were killed or missing in action, the remaining sixteen per cent seriously wounded, killed in accidents, or permanently grounded for severe mental or physical disability (frostbite was a recurring problem at high altitude).[7] The completion of 25 missions by Robert Morgan and his crew of the B-17 *Memphis Belle* was cause for celebration and a much-ballyhooed documentary film.

But for Lamar and the other thousands of air cadets, those facts didn't dull the gleam of the silver wings that awaited their graduation. For this phase of his training, there remained but a final check ride with an Army Air Force major, and Lamar would be shuttled along to Advanced training, where most completed the training on high-performance aircraft. By that time, a majority of the inept had been culled, and the military had a great deal of money and time invested in the young pilot trainees. They did not want them to fail at this stage. After Perrin's graduation ceremony, he was on his way to Ellington Field, near Houston, for twin-engine training.

Ellington Field was close to the Gulf, and low-lying. Thus it was prone to fast-forming fog, a thick blanket that rolled in quickly when warm breezes swept inland and met the cooler land. The cadets soon learned that when there was an indication of fog they needed to land promptly, either at Ellington or one of several auxiliary fields in the area.[8]

One evening during night training in the twin-engine Beech AT-10, the fog crept in unseen by some. The call went out for all aircraft to land immediately, but as Lamar and the others on the ground listened, they could hear one of their planes droning overhead, unable to see the field. Eventually the sound of the plane moved away, and the small waiting crowd dispersed. They learned the next morning that a cadet and instructor had been killed.[9]

The young men were nearing the end of their training, and they began to get a bit cocky. They told themselves that low-level flying—"hedgehopping"—would be necessary to their survival in combat, and without clear authorization but with few recriminations they made life miserable for many of the farmers around Houston. When safely clear of the base area, they commonly dropped to just a few feet above the earth, ripping along in the snub-nosed AT-10 at 190 mph, lifting up to skim over cottonwood trees and fences, and leaving terrified cows and angry farmers in their wake. One of Lamar's close friends was with an instructor at the close of a session of formation flying, and the instructor announced that each in the formation would head for Ellington at low level. They dove for the ground, leveled off about the height of a Ford coupe, and firewalled the twin-engine Beech. The cadet popped over a line of trees into a clearing with a farmhouse on the far side. It was evening, and a farmer was surveying his holdings, leaning on a pillar on the front porch, no doubt thinking back over a day's hard work when the AT-10 burst into his reverie. The cadet held it steady, just off the deck, and aimed straight for the farmer—who swung himself around his porch pillar and into his home, slamming the door just as the light twin roared a couple of feet over the roof.[10] It must have been a common occurrence across the country as hundreds of thousands of boys, some still in their teens, others in their early twenties, were given control of some of the fastest, loudest, and most dangerous machinery ever made.

Transitioning to twin-engine aircraft was relatively easy for Lamar, and he went through the course with little difficulty. The end was in sight, and for all the fledgling aviators, the excitement was palpable. A couple of weeks before the end of their training, the cadets were issued a clothing allowance and told to get measured for their new officer's uniforms. It was a proud young Missouri lad who walked into one of the men's clothing stores in downtown Houston that evening with several friends. They were treated very much like gentlemen as they were measured for jackets, pants, and shirts. It was the first time in his life that Lamar had had his clothing tailored, and the $200 he paid for two complete outfits seemed like an astronomical figure.

On February 8, 1944, Lamar and the class of 44B, resplendent in new "pinks and greens," received their silver wings and gold bars. They were officially rated as pilots in the Army Air Forces, and were commissioned as Second Lieutenants. They now were allowed to eat in the Officers' Mess Hall, and they rated salutes from enlisted soldiers. The enlisted men were savvy, and many were waiting outside the auditorium where the new "butter bars" had been sworn in. Tradition had it that the new second looies had to pay a dollar to the first enlisted man to render a salute. Some corporals and sergeants made a nice pile of greenbacks when each new class of officers turned out.

Second Lieutenant Lamar was asked where he wanted to go next for further training, and he quickly opted for B-24 transition training. A B-24 base was in Liberal, Kansas, somewhat closer to home than his bases in Texas, and he was duly assigned there. It would be only months now before he was in combat, he knew.

But hopes and plans often have detours.

The huge influx of men and equipment severely strained the available resources of the sleepy Midwestern town, as it had to many others across the country. There were virtually no rooms to let for married servicemen, and the quarters on the base were cramped and crowded for single men. Lamar reported to his assigned quarters, and was certain a mistake had been made. Even in basic training things had not been this stuffed with men, bunks, and gear. At Liberal, he found, new second lieutenants were stacked in bunks three high, with only enough room between the tiers of bunks to walk sideways. In every corner and in any available space, boxes and B-4 bags were stacked precariously.

The training bases were at last at peak production, turning out thousands of new pilots and other fliers each month, but transition-to-combat training bases had not kept up. Additionally, at Liberal bad weather was endemic, it seemed, and as a result several students from the class ahead were still trying to complete their flying hours. There were, it seemed, not enough B-24s or rooms to accommodate the flood of new pilots, so Lamar and his friends waited. And waited.

But not for long, it turned out. The Army had decided that the base at Liberal was not prepared for the tsunami of new fliers and that at least half of the would-be bomber boys would be sent to basic flying training centers as instructor pilots. Since Lamar had been unable to get in any B-24 time, he was sent to Independence, Kansas, to teach basic flying students. Disappointed, he packed his government-issued belongings once more and left the crowded base.

His arrival at the Army Air Forces base in Independence was less than confidence-inspiring. As he and five other new instructors from Liberal entered the gates, they saw the U.S. flag was flying at half-mast. Why? he queried. Two instructors had just recently been killed in a flying accident, they were informed.[11]

The next day, they met Capt. James E. Small, commander of the squadron of instructors to which he had been assigned at Independence. Lamar and Marquis Lillick, who had been in each training school with Lamar since Pre-Flight at San Antonio, were wearing their new "pinks and greens" (the wool trousers had a slight tinge caused by microscopic red fibers; the four-pocket dress jacket was a dark olive green) and a crusher-style hat. They saluted smartly. The "crusher" was one of those items of equipment that had become a symbol of the exalted status of fliers. To facilitate the wearing of a headset while flying, aviators were allowed to remove the metal ring that stiffened and gave shape to the crown. Soon, companies were selling soft-billed versions to the style-conscious fliers, with names like "Flighter," "Air Flow," and "Fly-Weighter." The cap, along with the famous A-2 leather flight jacket, became prized possessions of those who achieved flight status. Ideally, the sides of the cap would be folded over to effect a fairly shapeless form, which became known as the "50-mission crush," and it would be worn at a jaunty angle. It was the mark of a veteran flier, whether achieved overnight by twisting and kneading it in a stateside barracks or sweating through flak-filled skies over Germany.[12]

"Let me see your cap, Lieutenant." Captain Small held out his hand to Lamar, who turned the headgear over to his commander. The captain looked inside, where the large gold eagle emblem of an officer was attached, held in place by a screw through a grommet in the front of the cap and secured by a brass nut.

"I just had an instructor badly injured by this, Lieutenant." He pointed to the threaded screw which projected about a half-inch beyond the brass nut. "Cut it off, right down to the nut. You get slammed into the canopy or forward into the panel and hit your head, that screw is going to go right through your skull and into your brain."

The two young officers quickly snipped the offending piece of the badge.[13]

He did enjoy his status with the young ladies, however, most of whom were taken with the dashing young pilots in their custom-tailored uniforms. A period photograph shows a handsome, smiling young man wearing his summer khaki dress uniform, silver wings above his left pocket, gold bars on shoulder epaulets. He has assumed a relaxed pose, right elbow resting on a covered backdrop, hands loosely clasped. His close-cropped blond hair is just visible below his crusher hat, and he is looking at something just beyond the camera. He is a handsome man by any standard.

On March 25, the weight of what they were doing was made known to them. Flying was fun and games, exhilarating and exciting, and although accidents might occur they always, always happened to the other guy. But on this day, a sober-faced major spoke to a quiet room full of pilots, and advised them on how to fill out their Last Will and Testament. The document, a single page with spaces for names, addresses, and the like, was emotionless in the way legal papers always reduce death to an event to be recorded and assets disbursed, a neat bundle of necessary acts to which the possibly horrendous death of the party of the first part is merely incidental. Lamar dutifully named his father as the beneficiary of his estate, cognizant of the fact that it consisted of a few uniforms and a government life insurance policy. War, Herodotus wrote, is the time when fathers bury their sons.

But still the war seemed no closer. Lamar was in the middle of the country, training cadets to fly the BT-14, keenly aware that many he trained would soon be headed overseas to a combat zone. He was disappointed and frustrated not to be sitting in the cockpit of a bomber, flying over the enemy.

That changed quite soon in a way completely unexpected by Lamar. He was in the office of Captain Small in late April, when Small remarked that he was preparing a list of eight instructors who would ship out to become B-24 co-pilots.

"Captain, why don't you put my name on that list." Lamar unconsciously leaned forward as he said it.

The young commander of instructors looked closely at Lamar's intense face and narrowed blue eyes. He was preparing a list he surely did not want to make. Without any doubt, some of the boys on the list would be going to their deaths. A few seconds ticked by.

"Are you sure you really mean it?" Unspoken was the knowledge that while occasionally there were deaths in training, combat flying was certain to be far more dangerous. It was a plum job to be an instructor pilot, with great benefits, good pay, nice uniforms. Why give it up?

But Lamar did not enjoy instructing, and he felt cheated at not having gotten into heavy bombers. He was at peace with the possibility of his own death. Yes, he told the captain. I am sure. Put me on the list.[14]

On May 10, Lamar received orders transferring him to Lincoln Army Air Field in Lincoln, Nebraska, along with seven other instructors. He was able to stop by his home in Faucett for a couple of days, where he left his Ford coupe with instructions to his brother to sell it. Then, with the knowledge he was at last back on the trail to war, Lamar headed for Lincoln.

He waited two weeks, each day checking the board for the list of names assigned to Combat Crew Training. Finally, his name was posted as an alternate to Pueblo, Colorado. He would go if someone else were unable. That would be fine with Lamar, since he had an aunt who lived in Pueblo. As it turned out, someone was unable to go then—he never learned why—and Lamar, with packed bag and lifted spirits, boarded a train for Colorado.

On the long ride across Nebraska, others in the crew to which he would be assigned learned he was aboard and looked him up. He enjoyed meeting them, and knew he would fit in. But there seemed to be a problem, a festering sore that Lamar was certain was going to become a major issue in the very near future.

The pilot, he learned, was also on the train. He was drunk, deep into a crap game, and already had borrowed money to continue his gambling. Worse, he had tried to borrow money from the enlisted men of his crew, whose pay and benefits were less than half of his own pay. Lamar listened to the tales, certain that he would end up nose to nose with this pilot. It was a clash of lifestyles, beliefs, and temperaments that was certain to cause friction to the point of explosion, he was sure of that. At last, as dusk pulled its darkening curtain across the vast stage of western Nebraska, Lamar fell asleep to the comforting rhythm of wheels on tracks.

Chapter 5

The Crew
Hometown, USA

It was a monumental task, this training of young men for the business of war. Armed conflicts had been occurring since the Paleolithic era, when bands of early humans clashed violently over territorial rights and hunting privileges. But progressively, the weapons of war had become more lethal, more complicated, as the bow replaced the spear, the muzzle-loading musket rendered obsolete the bow, and the machine gun made a single soldier more deadly than a platoon in armies of the past. This particular war was going to be vastly different than other conflicts, with the advent of the flying machine. The First World War had had its aerial battles—so-called knights of the air dueling at two miles high, and the attacks on London by German Gotha bombers. But in truth, those desperate and deadly struggles were mere sideshows to the main event, the ghastly ground warfare fought savagely in a tangle of barbed wire, muddy trenches, and a hellish fog of mustard gas.

The second global conflict began in the air, when Luftwaffe First Lieutenant Bruno Diller and his wingmen launched their Stuka dive bombers against a pair of railroad bridges in Poland on 1 September, 1939. Their early morning strike preceded the ground Blitzkreig that stunned the Poles and left the rest of the world agog.[1] But tit for tat, the Royal Air Force and the young pilots of its Fighter Command stymied the German plans for a cross-channel invasion in an epic Battle of Britain; the course of the fierce conflict was marked in contrails in the high summer sky of 1940.[2] For Americans, the war came home with the attack by Japanese carrier-based torpedo bombers on the Pacific fleet at Pearl Harbor at the close of 1941. The daring raid on Tokyo in April 1942 by Jimmy Doolittle and his boys, taking B-25 medium bombers off the deck of the USS *Hornet*, was the first good news of the war.[3] The Battle of Midway, two months later, resulted in the sinking of four Japanese carriers by hundreds of American Navy fliers, and was possibly the turning point in the Pacific campaign.[4] In Europe, raids by hundreds of heavy bombers on German industrial centers brought the horrors of global war to the Third Reich's homeland, but at a terrible cost: more than 49,000 dead or missing, presumed dead, in the 8th and 9th Army Air Forces alone.[5] And the end blow in the war would be administered to two Japanese cities by single bombers carrying but one bomb each. The mushroom cloud would be a symbol of war from above for succeeding generations.

For the United States, still struggling to emerge from a worldwide economic depression, the war was something they had hoped to avoid. Nazi Germany was certainly no one's national ideal, but it was largely Europe's problem. Still, as the fighting raged and Europe fell before the German war machine country by country, until only England was left, most Americans began to suspect that President Franklin D. Roosevelt might find a way to bring them into the fray. There was Lend Lease, for example, the program that allowed the scrappy Brits to take possession of American-built ships and planes without the U.S. actually violating the technicalities of neutrality laws. Hundreds of young men had gone to Canada to enlist in the Royal Canadian Air Force while Uncle Sam looked the other way. American navy ships were battling U-boats in the North Atlantic in a fierce unofficial war.

And the build-up of the armed services, and programs such as the Civilian Pilot Training Program, convinced many Americans that we would enter the war against Hitler at some point.

Of course, few were looking West, and the attack on Pearl Harbor shattered any illusions of peace or of a one-front war.

The decision was made very early that the U.S. would commit more technology and less blood to the winning of this war. There was no doubt that the nation geared up its industrial might and cranked out ships, airplanes, bombs, tanks, and guns at a stunning, mind-boggling rate. Whether this decision by the military and industry resulted in less American blood being shed is open to debate. Whether it ultimately won the war, though, is not.

Once committed, the entire nation turned its attention to winning the war. In small towns and large cities across the country, drives were held to collect scrap metal, sell bonds, and encourage victory gardens. Women went to work in factories to replace the men who had been called to arms. Rationing was instituted for fuel, tires, food, clothing. Young men began to disappear from neighborhoods and reappear, for brief periods, in khaki or green or dark blue.

For the military branches involved with flying, the problems were manifold. They needed men, lots of them, and airplanes by the thousands. They needed facilities to cope with housing and training these youngsters, many of them just out of high school or with a year or two of college. They needed landing fields, and the equipment and systems to smoothly transform civilian kids into military fliers. And of course, they needed to do all of these things very, very quickly.

Given unlimited time and the luxury of peace, no doubt all of these things could have been accomplished nearly painlessly, without the subsequent horrendous number of training accidents and snafus and sometimes poor selections. But they didn't have the time, and it was war.

So it was that Lamar ended up in Pueblo, Colorado, at the Combat Crew Training Center. Here, men from across the country, small towns and farms and big cities, college graduates to high school drop-outs, the wealthy and the poor, the bright and the cunning, were to combine all of the various duties for which they had been trained for many months and learn to fly and fight as a unit, a small team among many in a big war. War novels and battle movies have made a cliché of the combat crew as cross-section of America. But hackneyed or not, it was the truth, and it cannot be portrayed differently for the sake of originality.

Here, in the hot, parched high country of Colorado, farm boy and college student Lee Lamar met the nine men who would train with him for combat, nine men who each had to be trusted completely to do their own job as well as being cross-trained to perform another crewmember's tasks in case . . . well, just in case.

He shook hands with 2nd Lt. Randall Darden, the pilot and aircraft commander. His crew would always be known as the Darden crew, although later decisions in the airplane might not be made solely by him. He was 22, a bit younger than Lamar, and was from Mart, Texas. He and Lamar were both from class 44B, graduating as pilots and second lieutenants in February, but Darden had been to B-24 transition training while Lamar was instructing on BT-14s in Kansas. He was tall, able to look Lamar squarely in the eye, and looked like he might have played some ball. Darden was married, and he had been a truck driver before the war. Lamar, having heard stories about Darden that he didn't like, looked closely at the smiling face of the pilot and saw only a self-assured and confident young man. He decided to withhold judgment.

Next was 2nd Lt. Don Reynolds, 21, from Wisconsin, the bombardier. Quiet and serious, he too was married, and emanated a sense of dedication and competence. In the coming months, he would become Lamar's closest friend on the crew.

Corporal O. R. Bozarth was the flight engineer and top turret gunner, but as things were to work out he would not make the flight to a combat zone with the rest of the crew. Corporal Swante B. Norlund, a youngster who also was married, was from Floodwood, Minnesota. He would be the radio operator, and would fire one of the .50-caliber machine guns from an open side window of the B-24. Corporal Joseph R. Betine from Chicago was the assistant flight engineer and the other waist gunner, but he would not be involved in the final mission of this crew. Corporal Henry L. Alder, a 19-year-old from Sneedville, Tennessee, was the ball turret gunner. His job was to curl inside a Sperry gun turret that hung below the belly of the bomber and defend her from attacks by fighters. For hours, he would sit in a tiny bubble with two .50-caliber machine guns, his knees around his ears, connected to the rest of the crew only by his headset. It was for most bomber crewmen the least enviable position on the crew.

The front and rear gun turrets, each sprouting two .50-caliber guns, were manned by two privates first class, John Nordback in the nose and Bernie Sturtz in the tail. Nordback, 21, from Fargo, North Dakota, had been a farmer before the war; Sturtz, 19, hailed from Chambersburg, Pennsylvania, and had been a machinist. Neither was married. The navigator position had not been filled yet, but within a few weeks, 2nd Lt. Wade Craig, always known as Mike, arrived straight out of navigation school in Ellington, Texas, where Lamar had completed his advanced pilot training. Craig, 20 years old, was from Nashville, Tennessee, and had joined up to fight when just 18.

So here they were, four officers in their early 20s, six enlisted men in their late teens and early 20s. All had been civilians a year or so ago, youngsters interested in sports, in girls, in cars, worried about their studies or their paychecks perhaps, and keeping an eye on the progress of the war. Now they were part of it, and they knew that in just a couple of months they would be seeing it firsthand.

What none of them knew, it is all but certain, was that they were there partly as the result of some bad miscalculations by what have been called the Bomber Mafia by later historians. In truth, the miscalculating precedes the American advocates of air power—Billy Mitchell, Hap Arnold, Tooey Spaatz, and Ira Eaker—and in one of those ironies that so often are found in war, were in large measure the concepts of an Italian air commander, Gen. Giulio Douhet. In the early 1920s, Douhet published his vision of future wars in *The Command of the Air*. Here, he forecast huge fleets of aerial bombers, heavily defended ships of the air that would focus their fury on civilian population centers. By reducing cities to rubble, instead of concentrating on the traditional military route of smashing armies, Douhet insisted that the ability of a nation to produce war material would be reduced or eliminated, and the will of the people to continue fighting would be sapped. Strategic bombing—aimed at cities and production centers—would become the prevailing Allied doctrine of the war.[6] The big mistake by Douhet and others in the "Bomber Mafia" was in believing that bombers alone could accomplishment all this, without need of fighters. And thousands of airmen paid for this unwarranted optimism with their lives as their bomber formations were ripped to shreds by German fighters.

It was ironic, of course, that Lamar and his crew of bomber boys would end up in Douhet's own native country as they flew those strategic bombing missions.

But the Darden crew, including Lamar, didn't know about all that. They weren't necessarily even able to see that they were part of a long pipeline connecting American training to war zones around the world. They were in the Army now, and they did what they were ordered to do. While cognizant that things happened in a sequence—primary, basic, advanced flight training, combat crew training, combat—they didn't have the historical view that what they were doing was revising the ancient precepts of war, throwing out the von Clausowitz dictum that wars were won by pulverizing the enemy's armed forces. They did know that they were trying to weld themselves into a fighting unit, that to do that they would have to know the vagaries of the B-24 and each of her systems, would have to be able to deliver bombs to a target and unload them accurately, that they would be asked to navigate precisely and fly with skill and shoot moving targets like marksmen. It meant rising before six, or flying half the night, it meant daylight bomb practice and low-level tactical flying and shutting down one or two engines at inconvenient times. In short, it was going to be no picnic.

For Lamar in particular, combat crew training was going to be a crash course that combined elements of what to expect in combat as well as how to actually fly the four-engine B-24 Liberator. He should already have been qualified on the Lib, and had been assigned to B-24 transition school. Of course, an unlucky series of events resulted in his being reassigned as an instructor pilot before being able to even sit in one of the leviathans. It was going to be on-the-job training for Lamar, but he eagerly anticipated the challenge.

The B-24 would be a challenge for anyone. More than 18,600 were produced during the war, more than any other aircraft ever built in the USA. And for many who flew her, the Liberator was temperamental and fragile, something like the rugged-looking boxer who turns out to have a glass jaw. For others, she was the awkward sister to the belle of the ball, the Boeing B-17, a wasp-waist beauty of a bomber that looked almost delicate parked on a ramp. The thick-bodied Liberator's beauty, however, was in her performance, her admirers said: she could carry more bombs further and higher than the Flying Fortress. Couldn't take a hit? Tell that to the dozens of crews who made it back to their bases in England or Italy or Espiritu Santo in the Pacific with huge holes in their wings or half a rudder shot away, they said.

It was big, it was complicated, and it was a very effective bombing machine. The sheer size of the B-24 would dwarf anything that Lamar had previously flown. In fact, for many of the flight crew except for Darden, this would be the first time they had been in a ship of this size. The wings spread across 110 feet tip to tip, and were 14 feet from leading edge to trailing edge at the fuse-lage. The square, boxy fuselage itself was 67 feet, 2 inches long, and 10 feet, 5 inches high. Parked, the top of the twin rudders stood one inch shy of 18 feet, about the height of a 2-story house, and were 26 feet apart, outside edge to outside edge.

But no one would ever mistake this ungainly craft for a civil passenger plane. The interior was devoid of anything like creature comforts. The metal of the skin was naked, sprayed with a putrid green, anti-corrosion paint; bright yellow oxygen tanks were strapped at locations around the aircraft. Browning .50-caliber M2 machine guns sprouted from turrets in the nose, the top, the belly, the tail, and the waist windows, and their long belts of shells snaked out from plywood boxes throughout the bird. There were ports for oxygen hoses at each crew station, as well as outlets for electrically-heated flight suits and radio leads. For the waist and ball-turret gunners, there was no place to sit, save against a bulkhead on takeoff, and for all except the pilots their seats were little larger than those on a bicycle.

The Lib came into existence nearly by accident. The B-17 had been accepted by the Army Air Corps, and in October 1938 Consolidated Aircraft Corporation was asked to begin building the Boeing aircraft to supplement the facilities of that company. General Arnold, the head of the Army Air Force, had stated that what we needed was a bomber that would fly farther, faster, higher, and carry more bombs than the B-17 and be easily mass produced. The chief engineer at Consolidated, Isaac Laddon, said they could build a much better bomber than the Fortress. They submitted a design using the long, slender wing advocated by David Davis, a heavy-lifter that promised both greater payload and greater distance. Approval was granted for a prototype, and the first Liberator flew in December 1939 after the first clashes of World War II in Europe.[7]

Soon the '24 was in production on a scale never before seen. The Consolidated factory in San Diego was enlarged to triple its original size, and new plants were set up outside Fort Worth and near Dallas. But it was the incredible new Ford plant at Willow Run, outside Detroit, that showcased America's production ability. The plant, at the time the largest production plant of any kind in the world, was built on a farm owned by Henry Ford. It covered eighty acres, and was billed as the world's largest single room. The line was more than a mile long, and included a turntable which rotated the bombers on the line 90 degrees. Workers believed it was constructed to avoid crossing into the neighboring county where taxes were higher. The plant employed forty thousand workers, and by 1944 they were building a brand-new B-24 every fifty-six minutes.[8]

So the Combat Crew Training phase would have as its goal the melding not only of ten diverse young men into a single, smoothly operating team, but also a team that would know every nut and bolt, every electrical and hydraulic line, every switch and gauge and control in a large and complex piece of flying machinery. The idea was that in the end they would know their jobs thoroughly, and could stand in for another crewman in an emergency. They would know each other and trust each crewman completely, as well as know and trust the bomber that was to take them into harm's way on each mission they flew. And they would do that in about two months.

As he suspected on the train across Nebraska, Lamar would have a run-in with Darden. It didn't take very long.

Darden had graduated from Army pilot training as part of the class 44B, the same class as Lamar although at a different air base. Like Lamar, he had requested heavy bomber transition training, and had graduated from that course while Lamar had been reassigned as a flight instructor. Thus it was that Lamar was assigned as a co-pilot, instead of perhaps getting a crew of his own.

From their first training flight as a crew, Lamar knew it was only a matter of time before his quiet and serious outlook on life, war, and flying would clash with Darden's more outgoing, devil-may-care demeanor. He had already learned to carry his cash in his trousers and not in his billfold. On those frequent occasions when Darden tried to borrow money for his gambling, Lamar would pull out his wallet and dolefully exhibit its empty currency pocket.

But it wasn't Darden's exuberant lifestyle that eventually caused the blow-up. Lamar disapproved of Darden's ways, but he was willing to accept differences. He had met many men during his college and cadet days who differed greatly from him in temperament, values, and outlooks. Those he could accept. It was flying itself, and his duties as co-pilot, that brought the simmering clash to a boil.

Darden knew that Lamar had never flown a B-24, and despite—or perhaps because of—this fact he allowed Lamar to perform only the smallest of tasks in the cramped cockpit. Surrounded by dozens of black-faced round gauges, banks of switches, rows of circuit breakers, a complex array of levers for propeller angle, fuel mixture, throttle, as well as landing gear and flap controls, switches for automatic pilot, radios, intercoolers, de-icing equipment, lights, booster pumps, engine starter, primer, and a host of other equipment monitors and regulators, Lamar sat mutely in the right seat while Darden did all of the flying of the Liberator. His only duties were to raise or lower the landing gear and flaps as Darden directed. Lamar found himself a highly trained passenger, one rated as a pilot but without any real flying duties. He was angry at what he felt was demeaning treatment.

On the third flight of the Darden crew, a check pilot rode with them, standing behind the two pilots on the flight deck. Pueblo is more than 4,600 feet above sea level, and in the warm air of that May morning the B-24 started sluggishly down the runway. Even without a load of bombs, the thin air was having an effect on the performance of the engines as well as the lift of the wings, and when Darden pulled back the control wheel to lift the nose, the Liberator struggled to leave the earth. Just as the wheels lifted grudgingly off the pavement, the check pilot reached forward and pulled back the throttles on the two right engines. The bomber swayed and dipped like a boxer who has been staggered by a lightning quick jab to the jaw.

Lamar watched as Darden fought to keep the Liberator in the air, standing on the left rudder pedal while straining to turn the control wheel to the left. It was not clear that he was going to succeed in keeping the bomber flying, but Lamar made no move to assist. He could see the ground rushing by in a blur through the low wind screen. It looked very close.

"Dammit, Lamar, give me a hand here!" Red-faced, Darden shouted for Lamar to apply left rudder and left aileron. The combined strengths of the two big men gradually brought the Liberator to straight and level flight. Airspeed crept up, and they were able to establish a climb of a few feet per minute. Satisfied at their performance, the check pilot leaned forward and pushed the two starboard throttles forward, and the bomber resumed a normal climb under full power.

They went through a series of maneuvers as directed by the check pilot, and they finally returned to the air field. As the crew gathered their gear and climbed down through the open bomb bay, Darden and Lamar went through the shut-down checklist. They chatted for a few minutes with the check pilot at the nose of the big bomber while he debriefed them on his assessment of their performance. When he left, Lamar turned to Darden and quietly unleashed the seething anger of the past week on the lanky Texan.

"Listen, Darden. I don't ever want to have happen again what happened up there on the takeoff." Darden cocked his head slightly to the side and narrowed his eyes, but did not say anything as Lamar continued.

"I didn't get on the rudder pedals because you haven't been doing your job in letting me learn how to fly this aircraft. You've been hogging all the time. My job is to learn to fly this aircraft just as well as you do and I am not going to be able to do it unless you let me have some time to do it." That the usually stoic Lamar was furious was obvious, and Darden did not try to interrupt or stop him.

"We'll be going into combat soon, and it isn't fair to me and it isn't fair to the rest of the crew for me not to have the time to fly the aircraft. Now make up your mind: are you going to do your job, or do I have to go into the office and request a transfer to another crew?" Lamar stared at Darden, his hands on his hips, chest heaving slightly. He was quite prepared to jump ship if something were not changed immediately.

To Lamar's surprise, Darden did not defend his actions nor argue any point of Lamar's unhappiness.

"You're right, Partner. How's this—from now on we split the flying time, fifty-fifty. When we get through this, you'll be able to fly this bomber as well as anyone." Darden's word on this point proved to be good.[9]

The rest of the crew were honing their own skills as well as cross-training. The Army Air Force's Manual 50–12, *B-24: Pilot's Training Manual for the Liberator,* is instructive in gaining an appreciation for how seriously cross-training was emphasized. It isn't hard to read between the lines for the reason: flying a large, slow airplane over an enemy who is shooting at you will obviously result in casualties. Examples given in the handbook are that the pilot will also be a navigation specialist; the co-pilot will also be a navigation specialist, in addition to being the gunfire control officer; the navigator will be a qualified nose turret gunner and an assistant bombardier; the engineer will be a top turret gunner, and also be qualified for co-pilot duties; gunners would be expected to be assistant engineers or turret specialists or assistants to an armament or parachute officer.

The regime for combat crew training was unrelenting. The B-24 *Pilot's Training Manual* urges the aircraft commander to keep each crew member busy throughout each training flight:

"Get position reports from the navigator; send them out through the radio operator. Put the engineer to work in the cruise control and maximum range charts. Require the co-pilot to keep a record of engine performance. Give them a workout. Encourage them to use their skill. Let them sleep in their own bunks—not in a B-24. A team is an active outfit. Make the most of every practice mission."[10]

For Lamar, learning to fly the complex, highly demanding Liberator was a challenge, but one he relished. He was building time in his logbook, but more importantly was seen by his crew as having the ability to get them home safely if Darden were wounded or killed. He spent hours pouring over the charts in the flight manual, learning load factors on the wings at various airspeeds and angles of bank (a 60 degree angle of bank created a factor of 2.0, or twice the load on the wings as straight and level flight). The maximum diving speed at 56,000 pounds was 275; for take-off at sea level, the Liberator needed 2,410 feet of ground roll when loaded to 50,000 pounds, 2,850 feet if at 6,000 elevation. He learned how the supercharger on each engine worked (it was exhaust driven). He studied the hydraulic, electrical, oil, and fuel systems. He learned emergency procedures for hydraulic or electrical failure. For hours when the plane sat on the ramp, Lamar sat in the cockpit, memorizing the position of each gauge, switch, indicator, and control, until he could close his eyes and place a finger on each of the hundreds of important cues to the performance and health of the airplane.

When not concerned with the actual flying of the airplane, Lamar was busy learning the operation of both the Sperry and Norden bombsights. In a large hangar on the Pueblo air base, a special trainer had been built. A tall platform on wheels had been constructed with electric power that moved it over a painted map on the hangar floor. Bombardiers and secondary-duty officers operated the "bomber" using mockups of the two types of sophisticated bombsights, dialing in factors such as airspeed, altitude, and wind speed and direction, while steering the moving platform to a specified "target" painted on the floor. The novice bombardiers would then "release a bomb" and the place where the bomb hit would be marked. Hitting a stationary target was a challenge; sometimes the target would be moving, simulating a ship at sea, and the difficulty was increased exponentially.

The bombing range at Pueblo provided more authentic practice for bombardiers, and Don Reynolds was kept busy in the nose of the Liberator when they flew practice bomb runs. One-hundred pound practice bombs, painted blue and with no explosive, were used for these flights. While not explosive, they were filled with a white powder that would scatter on impact and form a small cloud that could be seen from the airplane. In the middle of the range was a small wooden structure that was known as the "shack," and for most of the bombardiers it became the bullseye of their target. To actually drop a bomb into the structure was known as "getting a shack."

The bombsights were extremely complex instruments, and the Norden in particular was a closely guarded classified secret. It was linked to the aircraft's autopilot, and on the bomb run, the lead bombardier actually took over the control of the bomber to fly it to the target. In addition to airspeed, altitude, and drift, the weight of the bombs and the interval between the release of each bomb was factored into the bombsight.

The Norden, in addition to being linked to the autopilot, operated a small instrument called the Pilot Directional Instrument, or PDI, located in front of the pilot. It had a needle that swung right or left to tell the pilot where the bombardier wanted him to fly. The pilot was supposed to keep the vertical needle centered at the top or at the 0 point to satisfy the bombardier's needs. The crew practiced both kinds of bomb runs, auto-piloted by the bombardier, and PDI-directed.[11]

One day they were flying a practice bombing mission and made several passes over the target. Reynolds was doing quite well, although he had not scored a "shack." On the final run, Lamar—the back-up bombardier—climbed into the tight confines of the nose for a crack at it. He released the practice bomb, and it arched gracefully from the belly of the bomber and struck the center of the wooden shack.

Surprised as anyone, Lamar turned to the incredulous Reynolds. "Easy, Don. Nothing to it. Secret's in the wrist." He later admitted it was entirely luck, that he knew nothing about the intervelometer or how to enter any of the myriad other factors into the bombsight.

So members of the Darden crew spent the summer of 1944 honing their skills and learning to function as a single unit, a cohesive team that could count on each other to do both a primary task and a secondary or tertiary one if need be. The intensity of their training was leavened by the sheer thrill of being young and flying in a warplane at speeds and altitudes that more mature and sober adults, aware of their own mortality, might have found frightening. Several areas east of Pueblo were largely arid, vacant spaces where they could, with near impunity, roar at top speed only a few feet above the baked landscape, hopping over ridges and rock formations and then swooping back down to leave a billowing roostertail of dust rising and swirling behind them. Factories and other buildings in the area became "targets" for their high-level bombing runs, which were generally conducted in a large formation of B-24's and sometimes at night. Surely the workers inside must have silently prayed that the boys in the bombers did not miscalculate.

On one occasion, a gunnery practice flight, Darden and Lamar had flown the Liberator at low level while the gunners, using live .50-caliber ammunition, fired at lines of targets on both sides of the plane. The racket from 10 machine guns firing simultaneously from inside a metal fuselage drowned out even the roar of the four unmuffled radial engines; the vibration of the recoil could be felt in the control columns by the two pilots. It was undoubtedly exhilarating to have that much firepower at your fingertips, while flying fast and low above the high plains of Colorado. On this day, after completing several passes over the alley between gunnery targets, Lamar was surprised by a tap on his shoulder. He turned to see Hank Alder smiling at him.

"Your turn, Lieutenant." Alder jerked his head to indicate his position in the ball turret. Now Alder, like most ball-turret gunners, was a smallish young man, far shorter and lighter than Lamar. Not wanting to appear a bad sport, Lamar grinned and heaved himself out of the right seat in the cockpit. Making his way over the catwalk in the bomb bay to the rear compartment of the Liberator, he squeezed himself into the fish bowl of the belly gun turret and radioed that he was set and in position. It was a strange new perspective for Lamar. Instead of the comforting presence of a cockpit full of gauges that had become like old friends, he was hanging suspended below the whale-like body of the bomber. It was disorienting, it was cramped, and it offered absolutely no way for him to escape should the Liberator slide into the earth.

Darden had been climbing from the last gunnery run, and now Lamar watched the scene below him rotate as the pilot banked through a turn and descent that would bring them once more on a high speed run through the targets. The earth rose, and Lamar was acutely aware of his discomfort as the landscape seemed inexorable in its upward march toward him. They were closing on the target area now, and still the Liberator descended. He was certain now that he could open the back escape hatch in the turret and touch the ground that rushed by in a blur just below his hunched body. Ignoring the proximity of Mother Earth, he squeezed off a few bursts at targets that were flashing by, with no hint or even interest in whether he had hit anything or not.

The bomber sank just a bit further, and now Lamar was certain that they were much, much lower than they usually flew the gunnery mission. It was terrifying, and he was keenly aware of the fragility of his own body as he pictured the ball turret being scraped off on the cement-hard crust of the earth when Darden miscalculated or they encountered a sudden brief down current. When he emerged from the turret after the run, he knew from the grins on the faces of the crew that he had been set up. He grinned back, and knew he had passed their test. But he never, ever got into a ball turret again.[12]

The nine-week combat crew training course was nearing an end, and the routine of flying simulated combat missions was becoming almost second nature. The crew would pile into a bomber, fly high or hedgehop, fire their guns or drop their practice bombs, monitor the radios and record the engine performance and calculate their position. Both Darden and Lamar could handle the big bomber with aplomb, respond quickly and correctly to a variety of simulated emergencies, and communicate crisply and clearly with each crewman.

For some reason, bridges have fascinated pilots since the dawn of aviation, and they experience a nearly irresistible urge to fly under them in spite of the hazards. One day close to the end of their training, they were flying with all their crew aboard. They had completed their simulated bombing run; Darden turned to Lamar and said he wanted to fly under the Royal Gorge Bridge over the Arkansas River near Canon City. Darden grinned broadly as he mentioned it. Now Lee had recently been to the site of that bridge, walked across it and gone down the incline to the bottom and even walked across the Arkansas River on a small swinging bridge to look up between the narrow, winding canyon walls. "You might fly under that bridge, but you're never going to do it while I'm in here." Lamar stared hard at Darden. The Texan dropped it. He had seen an angry Lamar before.[13]

As the days neared the end of combat crew training, the men got to see each other in circumstances other than simulated bombing missions. Sometimes that glimpse beyond the khaki uniform was heartwarming. Sometimes not.

For Lamar, Pueblo meant that he was able to see his Aunt Myrtle, his mother's sister, who lived nearby. On several weekend trips, she took her nephew to Royal Gorge and Colorado Springs, where they took in all the tourist sights. Once, she served as tour guide for all four officers, plus the wives of Reynolds and Darden, on a trip to San Isabel Lake. Here, they relaxed, had a picnic, and rowed boats around the small mountain lake.

It was fun and relaxing, but Lamar also was aware of a knife edge of tension, one that went beyond the unstated fact: the men would very soon be sent to a combat zone. The biggest unspoken tension was the fact that Reynolds's wife was obviously pregnant, and Reynolds had quietly passed on to Lamar his certainty that the child could not be his. Such human lapses were doubtless common throughout the war, but for Lamar, this intrusion into his idealistic world was more than uncomfortable, and he felt a deep sympathy for his good friend. He also witnessed crass behavior on the other side.

Darden's wife, Virginia, had come up from Texas to spend a weekend with her husband. Darden borrowed $200 from Lamar to take his wife to dinner and show her around. Lamar went out for the evening, and when he returned to his quarters there was Darden with his crap-shooting buddies. The pilot was drunk and broke, and never did go into town to see his wife. Lamar was furious.[14]

He did see the other side of love, however. Bernie Sturtz, the tail-gunner, shyly approached Lamar one day. His girlfriend, Betty, was coming to Pueblo with her mother for a weekend. Enlisted men were paid much less than officers, and generally were sending an allotment home to their families. Sturtz asked if he could borrow $20 to get through the weekend. Lamar didn't hesitate, and pressed him whether that would be enough. Later, he saw Sturtz with Betty and her mother strolling around Pueblo, but the gunner apparently did not see Lamar. Afterward, the pilot gave him a bad time.

"Man, Sturtz. Now I know what kind of a guy you are. I finance your weekend with a good-looking girl, and you don't even introduce me." Sturtz, embarrassed and pleased at the same time, always insisted he had not seen the lieutenant in town.

Lamar's mother came out to visit her son and her sister, the first time she had been to Colorado. Lamar was able to get a weekend off, and the three of them took in all the local sights. Myrtle knew, of course, that combat crew training was the last stateside assignment for the boys, and must have told her sister. But it was never mentioned, to Lamar's relief.

Then, on August 10, 1944, the Darden crew completed their combat training and officially transferred to Topeka Army Air Base. It was almost anticlimactic, after all the weeks honing their skills, learning to work together and cross-train for several positions aboard a heavy bomber. Their orders were to proceed to Topeka AAB to pick up a new B-24 for transport to a combat zone. With all of their razor-sharp skills and elite status as a flight crew, they were on their way at last. Lamar was keenly aware of the irony. They were going by train.

Chapter 6

Overseas at Last
Summer 1944

The war had been raging for nearly five years, but clearly it was not over. Many millions would yet die, cities would be laid waste, lives would be ruined and ways of life altered forever. But there was a sense, finally, that the endgame was now being played. The Nazi war machine had been ground down, and German invincibility had long been proven chimerical.

Allied planners had been slow, it seemed to many (Joe Stalin chief among them), to finally start a second front. The Soviets had long clamored for an invasion by Americans and Brits to relieve the pressure on the Red Army; Russian men and women had exacted a brutal toll on the Teutonic invaders, while paying an enormously high price in blood themselves. Finally, in June of this summer, the largest invasion force in human history had been launched from England; thousands of vessels offloaded tens of thousands of combat infantrymen onto the beaches of Normandy, and Allied armies were racing across France to drive Hitler's war machine back into Germany.

Another invasion—Operation Torch—had occurred much earlier, however, in North Africa. In November 1942, American and British troops had landed in Morocco and Tunisia and drove across the sands and rock of the African continent to launch a strike into Italy. It had been revealing: American troops, while fresh and full of esprit de corps, had come up against grizzled veterans of the Afrika Korps and had suffered some sobering defeats, particularly at Kasserine Pass. It was obvious to Eisenhower and his staff that America's industrial might would eventually turn the tide, but it was not going to be an easy war.[1]

By clearing North Africa of the Wehrmacht and Luftwaffe, it would be possible to drive into Germany and German-occupied countries on yet another front. Strategically, it would mean Hitler's armed forces would be fighting the

Russians on the east, and would face allied armies sweeping across France and pouring up through Italy. Additionally, Italy would provide the opportunity for heavy bomber bases, making more accessible strikes against such premium targets as the Ploesti oil fields and the Schweinfurt ball bearing factories. Although the Italians had signed a secret armistice with the Allies in September 1943, the Germans had continued to fight fiercely as they slowly withdrew to the north.

Giggling. It was definitely giggling coming from the interior of the B-24J parked on the flight-line at Topeka. Unmistakably, female laughter and the urgent whisperings of young men emanated from the heavy bomber in what was supposed to be a highly secure area, entrance to which was restricted solely to the flight crew.

Lamar could not believe his ears. The crew of the bomber, which had trained together for many weeks at Pueblo, Colorado, now awaited departure for a war zone, destination yet unknown and to be learned only after takeoff the following morning. Thursday, August 15, 1944, they were restricted to base— quarantined, they called it—and the four officers on the crew were assigned to overnight quarters adjacent to the flight-line. The six enlisted crew were billeted overnight on the aircraft itself, assigned to guard it against any unauthorized approach by anyone not on the crew.

But as is always the case in such troop movements, the young women who worked at the Army Air Forces base always knew before the crew itself what was coming next. They knew, for example, that the personal gear of the crew would be loaded aboard that evening, that the aircraft would be moved to a secure area of the ramp, and that the officers and enlisted flight crew would be quartered near or in the big, slab-sided bomber. It is the way of things always. The women knew, the crew could only guess.

Now, late at night, Lamar stood outside the aircraft he was soon to co-pilot to a war zone, and pondered what to do. He was an officer in wartime, charged with ensuring the safety of his crew and aircraft. He had taken an oath, and each phase of his training reiterated that his was a position of incredible responsibility. Everywhere around him for the past two-and-a-half years, discretion, secrecy, and silence had been the nation's watchwords. Posters everywhere warned: "Loose Lips Sink Ships." Now, on the eve of their deployment, here was a violation of orders, a serious security breach. The weather in mid-August was warm, and the bomb bay doors stood open to allow some circulation of the humid air through the body of the ungainly aircraft. He remained in the darker shadows of the enormous wings, and once more heard the tittering of young women. There was no doubt, none whatsoever. The enlisted crew had arranged for women to board the aircraft on their last night.

If he sounded the alarm, there would be delays and recriminations. Some of his men would be punished, and they would all be delayed in getting to a combat zone. But to turn a blind eye to this egregious and flagrant breach would be a dereliction of duty. How was he to discern between a minor disregarding of the rules by young men who might be going to their deaths, and a more serious violation that could lead to the deaths of many others?

He looked at his watch, the hands glowing softly in the darkness. Abruptly, he swung on his heel and walked quickly back to his temporary quarters, forgetting why he had gone out to the aircraft in the first place. He never said a word about the extra visitors.[2]

Early the next morning, about two hours before sunrise and with no sign that women had ever graced the harsh, stark interior of the war machine, Lamar and the nine men known as the Darden Crew lifted off from Topeka for Grenier Field, near Manchester, New Hampshire. It would be the first stop on their way to war.

They were headed out with some misgivings and foreboding. For nine weeks the ten men comprising a heavy bomber crew had trained together, gotten to know each other's strengths as well as foibles. One of the purposes of Combat Crew Training in Pueblo had been to bond, to grow to trust each other and have complete confidence that each would perform his tasks correctly, with dedication and precision. But now, as they lifted off from Topeka, they were missing a key member: the flight engineer.

It was silly, really, an accident that never should have happened. A few days before, each crewman had been issued a shoulder holster—easier to carry on an airplane and perform their duties—and a .45-caliber Colt pistol. Darden had found a sergeant who was willing to provide some ammunition and a ride to the firing range in a 6X6 truck for the entire crew. It was unauthorized, of course, and no range safety officer was present. For several minutes, they stood in a line and awkwardly loaded their magazines with the stumpy, round-nosed bullets, each the diameter of a man's finger. Carefully, adopting the stance taught them earlier, they squeezed off a few rounds at targets they had set up fifty feet down range.

The .45 auto pistol had been adopted before World War I, in response to the poor performance of .38-caliber revolvers in the Philippines against insurgents following the Spanish-American War. It was a heavy, slab-sided pistol with little grace but with tremendous stopping power: it was said that hitting a man anywhere with a .45 would knock him off his feet as though he had been kicked by a mule. In any case, it had tremendous recoil, the barrel rising sharply with each shot.

After a few minutes of carefully controlled firing, a certain bravado had set in. They were, after all, trained killers now, and a few of the men began an improvised game of Old West quick-draw from their shoulder holsters, snapping off a shot at the target. This required that the bottom part of the leather holster be held in the left hand to facilitate smoothly extracting the pistol, or the entire rig tended to ride up with the handgun. Lamar, who had been raised around guns, often using a .22-caliber rifle to bolster the family larder, grew concerned with the lack of shooting discipline and respect for what a gun can do. He quietly moved back to a small shack behind the firing line.

And of course something bad happened. Not lethal, but bad enough. Corporal O. R. Bozarth was holding the lower part of his shoulder holster while quickly drawing his Colt. Unfortunately, the pistol was cocked, the safety catch off. The handgun fired and a slug nearly half an inch in diameter removed the tips of two of his fingers.[3]

They rushed Bozarth to the base hospital, where doctors decided very quickly that the flight engineer could not be sent overseas anytime soon. The risk of infection was far too great, they determined.

The next day, Hurston Webb of Marnet, West Virginia, was assigned to the Darden crew for the long flight to a combat zone, in the important role of flight engineer. He was to prove very skilled at his job, but for now the crew was wary, if not despondent, about what appeared to be a very bad start. If their story were a Shakespearean play, this would be seen as foreshadowing.

They lifted off from Topeka well before dawn, the first of several shiny new bombers to be dispatched from the heartland to a combat theater that day. They were off, finally, to test themselves and to win a war. The mood aboard the B-24 was artificially light, a bit like a high school locker room before a championship football game. The routine for takeoff was the same as for every other flight in the heavy bomber, and yet as they slowly gained speed rumbling down the runway Lamar too felt a sense of relief that finally they were on their way.

It seemed like light years since he had first enrolled at St. Joseph Junior College and the Civilian Pilot Training Program. Fifteen or twenty of his friends or fellow cadets had been killed along the way, many more had been dropped from the exacting regimen of flight training. Now, with several hundred hours in his logbook, Lamar believed himself prepared for any emergency he and the crew might face. He was sorry to not have a last leave home to say goodbye. On their first test flight a week earlier, he had swung the big bird toward Faucett, a short flying time to the east. His intention—he was 23 years old, on his way to war, and he had a great big bomber to play with, after all—was to give the homeplace a royal buzz job, roaring in low and fast with all four engines at full throttle. Let them know that Lee Lamar had made it, had achieved his dream of wings, and that he was here now, right above them, saying goodbye 'til later.

They had arrived over the Lamar place, and the young pilot looked down and spotted his father cultivating a cornfield behind a team of horses. Urvie looked small and fragile from this altitude, and Lamar knew that the horses would spook if he were to swoop down over their heads. Instead of a spectacular low buzzing, Lamar circled overhead once, calling out to his crew over the intercom. "Fellas, wave goodbye to my Dad. That's him down there on the cultivator." The tiny figure did not look up.

Coming into Grenier Field in New Hampshire, Lamar was certain they had made a navigation error. They were turning to final approach, and still there were only small fields, an apple orchard, and a small village below them. Darden turned the bomber to final, and lined up on the approach to what appeared to be a small municipal airport. He grinned at Lamar. Only then did the copilot see that the large military base had been disguised so as to be virtually invisible from overhead. War production plants and military bases on both coasts had adopted similar camouflage in the event they were attacked, and Darden, briefed on what to expect, had not shared this classified information with Lamar. It was a good joke, and Lamar grinned back.

That evening, with nothing to do but wait for morning and a set of additional orders, Lamar and others were sitting around a clubhouse on the base when a pilot sitting not far from him suddenly went into epileptic seizure. There was a flurry of activity, as someone lowered him to the floor, someone else loosened his tie, and the unfortunate young pilot thrashed about. Lamar thought it strange that someone who had undergone so many rigorous physical exams should now manifest such an incapacitating condition. But it was a strange war. He learned later that the pilot and his crew continued their flight into combat as though nothing had happened.

Early the next morning, the Darden crew were up to eat breakfast, pre-flight the airplane, and await their orders. They came soon enough: verbal instructions to proceed to Gander Lake, Newfoundland, and a sealed brown envelope that was not to be opened until they had flown one hour beyond the U.S. border. They laid the envelope behind the control console in the flight deck and took off for Newfoundland. They began speculating on their destination after they leveled off and trimmed up the bomber for the hop to Gander Lake. Smart money was on England, where the entire second air division was comprised of Liberators. It made sense that they would join up there as replacement for a crew that had completed its tour. Or been shot down.

Finally, an hour after leaving the coast of Maine, Darden reached behind the control console and held up the envelope, waving it slightly in a theatrical gesture of suspense. He tore it open using a gloved finger as a knife, and Lamar watched his face closely as he read the typed form. Darden's face revealed nothing, and after reading the form, his lips occasionally forming silent words, he handed the communiqué to Lamar. Smart money lost. They were to proceed by way of the North Atlantic on leg routes to be supplied by Air Transport

Command to Naples, Italy, for further assignment in the 15th Air Force. Specific additional orders would be forthcoming at stops en route.

They reached Gander Lake without incident. At the time, the base was the last jumping-off point for aircraft headed across the Atlantic, and it was packed with U.S., Canadian, and British aircraft and fliers. After checking in and finding their quarters, once more the Darden crew found itself with little to do but wait. They were not overly concerned, however, because they would be leaving for the Azores in the morning.

The wait turned into two weeks.

The airfield in the Azores was small, able to accommodate only a few aircraft at a time. Bad weather at Gander or across the Atlantic grounded all flying for several days and backed up the line of planes destined for the Azores. When it did clear off, a number of priority aircraft were the first off, including B-24s that had been converted to tanker aircraft to fly fuel over the Himalayas—the "Hump"—to waiting B-29s at forward bases in China. Then the weather closed in again, and more priority aircraft waited impatiently ahead of the Darden crew. More bad weather, more priority aircraft. The cycle seemed without end to the impatient fliers.

Darden found ways to pass the time, of course, since there was always a crap game going somewhere on the base. Soon that became a problem for Lamar, Craig, and Reynolds, as the aircraft commander went through his own funds and began to borrow money from the others. They all had been told to take some extra funds along, since it might be a while after reaching their combat base before the accounting system would catch up with them. Now, those extra funds were dwindling rapidly, and Darden was down to borrowing enough to eat on.

The time dragged on. The entire crew, officers and enlisted, went bowling at the alley on base, where the pinsetters—operated by foot—proved to be a comical sideshow. They also went canoeing on the large glacial pond on the airfield, and the tippy craft proved another source of hilarity as some of the men soon swamped theirs. Lamar's concern soon turned to laughter when the men in the water discovered that the pond was no more than four feet deep.

The long wait finally ended, and the Darden crew and their bare aluminum Liberator lifted off for the long leg across the North Atlantic, glad finally to be flying again. Once more the atmosphere was light, as crewmen wisecracked and jibed over the intercom. Lamar, himself as happy as anyone to be back on the trail, somewhat reluctantly advised the crew to observe radio discipline. The men settled into a long flight, one that eventually became boring despite the unspoken danger of the cold water below them and the Liberator's notorious inability to ditch without breaking into sections and quickly sinking. The four Pratt and Whitney engines were in sync, and the hypnotic droning finally began to work on the crew. After several hours, Mike Craig came up from his lonely position in the nose and Lamar offered him his seat on the flight deck. Lamar, who had not slept well during the nights at Gander Lake, moved to the radio room behind the cockpit and sat down on the long bench there. Webb, the new flight engineer, and Norlund, the radio operator, were in the radio room quietly talking, and Lamar was aware that the nose gunner and Reynolds, the bombardier, were in the waist with the other gunners.

Lamar drifted off, unable to fight off the siren call of sleep. Sometime later, he awoke suddenly, looking around to orient himself. He could see Webb strapped in the top turret, asleep, and Norlund was also dozing, his head cradled on his arms atop the small desktop in the radio room. Up front, Darden was sound asleep, nearly falling out of the left seat, and Lamar could see Craig reaching for the knob on the autopilot to make a course adjustment. That was the extent of his knowledge of flying, so Lamar decided to shake himself alert and get back to the flight deck.

The weather stayed clear for the trip across the big pond, and they landed at the field in the Azores without difficulty.

Around the world, in Europe, the Mediterranean, the Pacific, military engineers grappled with the new demands of an aerial war. From soggy England to sandy islands, soft ground threatened to curtail the use of heavy bombers as they leaped ahead of the capability to construct hard-surfaced runways that would support their enormous bomb-and-fuel cargoes. The solution was acres of interlocking, slotted steel mats, known as Marston mats, that were laid down in sand bogs and mud pits on hundreds of airstrips. They were quick to construct, ideal for bearing weight, easy to ship. And they were very, very noisy when an airplane weighing several tons plunked down on a steel runway and clattered along during the landing run and taxi.

The runway at the Azores was constructed of Marston mats, but the two pilots did not inform the crew, which had done all of its training on relatively quiet macadam runways. When the Darden Liberator touched down in the Portuguese-owned islands, the noise was terrific and must have sounded like the bomber was falling apart. Great fun for Darden and Lamar, less so for the rest of the crew.

That evening, the crew wandered around the small base and looked over a steep cliff onto the crashing surf below. A few fliers were swimming, but Lamar wasn't tempted. Later, they took in a forgettable USO show, while searchlights cast pillars of light across the black sky. The sweeping lights reminded Lamar that he was indeed approaching a war zone. After a mostly sleepless night in an unheated plywood shack, Lamar and the other officers ate and headed for the flight line.

There, they found the crew recovering from a night of riotous drinking, begun when enterprising Portuguese entrepreneurs had wandered by with sacks full of sherry and other spirits. One man was propped against a tire, passed out cold. Lamar watched in fascination as large green flies ventured in and out of his open mouth. The inebriated crewman was oblivious. Others were not quite so impaired, and in short order they had the plane ready for takeoff to Marrakech, Morocco. The crew lifted the unconscious man into the space forward of the bomb bay and placed the end of an oxygen line in his mouth. Fliers had long recognized the sobering effects of pure oxygen on an alcohol-addled brain. Sometime after taking off, the crewman regained consciousness and retreated to the waist of the Liberator.[4]

The Darden crew was about to enter the Mediterranean Theater of Operations. They were about to enter the war zone.

Why would anyone volunteer for duty that was considered so hazardous that flight allowance amounted to 50 per cent of their basic pay? In England, the Royal Air Force Bomber Command was losing half their flight crews to accidents, German fighters, and ground fire. It was slightly better for the American Army Air Forces, but losses continued to be horrendous.

There was patriotism, of course. America had been attacked, so the war was seen as a necessary duty. And flying was the most glamorous of professions. The entire generation of young men during World War II had grown up with tales of Lucky Lindy, Amelia Earhart, Wiley Post, Wrong Way Corrigan, and Jimmy Doolittle. Magazines like *Eagles of the Air* and *Air Trails,* selling for a quarter or less, fed the appetites of adolescent males for stirring adventures. The elitism that surrounded the selection and weeding out of potential airmen didn't hurt its appeal any, and the awarding of wing badges was a virtual guarantee of dates with young women who a year before would not have given them a second glance.

So they volunteered, despite the rigorous selection process and the loss of face for those who washed out. They volunteered, choosing to ignore the hundreds of casualties that were bound to result when training young men to fly high-powered aircraft, young men who often could not even drive a car. They volunteered, thinking that while combat losses were high, it would always happen to the other guys, not to them. They volunteered because they didn't want to walk, or hated camping out, or because they heard the food was better for aircrews, or because of the flashy uniforms, or the promise of coming home after completing twenty-five or fify or seventy missions—the numbers went up as the war progressed—and getting on with their lives. They volunteered for a thousand reasons, and later had trouble putting into words why. When asked fifty or sixty years later why, in the face of such dangers they had volunteered, most of them would only stare blankly at their interlocutor, unable to comprehend the question. Why? Why the hell not?

Chapter 7

Spinazzola, Italy

The flight to Marrakech was through dismal weather, cloudy with bouts of rain that lashed the fuselage and pelted the small windscreen. The Liberator yawed and pitched through the turbulence while the two pilots held onto the yoke and the rest of the crew grabbed onto anything handy. They were all feeling miserable as they neared the coast of northwestern Africa, and uncertain as to when they might actually make landfall on the African continent. Then a small break in the clouds allowed them to glimpse waves slamming against the shore near Casablanca, so they were able to mark the time of their arrival over land. Marrakech is in central Morocco, founded by Arabs as a regional capital a thousand years ago, and often described as exotic by visitors.

But finding the ancient city was not going to be easy. The weather was no better inland, and they had to be concerned with flying too far. The Atlas Mountains were just east of Marrakech; some of their peaks rose to thirteen thousand feet. Darden and Lamar were flying blind, using instruments that depended on a less-than-precise system of radio signals that tended to ebb and distort as the storm wrapped itself over the earth. Finally, Lamar was able to locate a signal and "fly the beam" to the air base. They broke through the clouds as they descended to the Red City. Minarets and the ancient clay-brick Kasbah were visible to the crew as they came over the old city, along with the bewildering walled Medina with its maze of narrow alleys and overhanging balconies. The vast open square of the Djemma al Fna and the minaret of the Koutoubia mosque were clearly visible, although their names were unknown to the crew. They touched down, emerging into the heat of late summer in North Africa. The smells from the souqs were faintly evident even over the pervasive odor of aviation fuel.

Lamar watched a small crowd of men in jallabas, wearing their inevitable yellow Ali Baba babouches with the curled toes, sitting near the runway. They were intently breaking rocks roughly the size of basketballs into fist-sized stones, filling two metal cans which periodically were emptied into low areas of the hastily-extended runway. The image stayed with him, these Berbers working so diligently. With their long robes and headgear, they were as distant from rural Missouri as anything Lee could imagine. Had they been pressed into service, or had they volunteered, grateful for the opportunity for work? He never learned, but it was evidence that the war touched lives far beyond the khaki-clad swarms of soldiers that were so ubiquitous in the States.

They spent the night in Marrakech, the officers housed in a former French Foreign Legion building. That evening, they pondered the mysteries of the bathroom facilities. After much discussion, the lieutenants decided that the strange device was a bidet, something one of them had heard would be found in the ultra-chic, expensive hotels of New York City.

Now that Over There was Over Here, the crew created their Short Snorters. This was one of those traditions that seems hard to understand from a distance of sixty or seventy years: each crewman took out a dollar bill, and each signed everyone's currency. Thereafter, in any bar anywhere as long as they were in the service, anyone could demand to see their "Short Snorter." Failure to produce it meant that they had to buy drinks for the entire party. For Lee, who drank almost no alcohol, this was not a probability, but he went along with the custom as a form of future protection.

The next morning they departed for Tunis, flying over the now-visible peaks of the Atlas, and landing at a former German air base. For once, all the buildings were permanent, with no sign of the sea of tents so evident at the previous airdromes at which they had landed. To one side, a pile of wrecked German and Italian aircraft marked the passage of ownership from the Axis to the Allies.

All transient crews were supposed to be restricted to base, a fact that rankled Lee when he saw men of the permanent party routinely walking through the front gate to savor the night life of Tunis. Lee, never before one to rebel or to flaunt authority, now encouraged the others to join him in sauntering out the main gate.

"We'll just keep walking until someone stops us," he urged. They did, but the other three officers uncharacteristically got cold feet. They turned around and spent a boring night on the air base, and were chagrinned to learn that other transit crews had simply walked into town without any hassle.[1]

The next morning, the crew headed out over the Mediterranean Sea, the morning sun sparkling like diamonds off the waves below them. It was a brilliant, pellucid day, the sky overhead like a luminescent blue dome, with visibility nearly to forever, it seemed to the cockpit crew. Darden and Lamar were in good spirits. This was to be the last leg of the long flight to the war zone.

Then, off the right wing, a P-47 appeared, a single-engine American fighter, the young pilot obviously enjoying the day as well. He began a series of rolls and loops, showing off his agile and lethal plane, silently boasting in his private air show. Lamar looked at Darden and grinned, and they quickly shut down one of their four engines. The big bomber proceeded on course while holding altitude. Try that, Single Engine! The fighter pilot quickly left.

The B-24J flew over Sicily and entered the pattern for the sprawling air base at Gioia del Colle, Italy, a supply depot where the crew would report to the 15th Air Force. The 15th was the strategic air arm of the ground forces in Italy, while the 12th, flying mainly twin-engine medium bombers such as the B-25 and B-26, was the tactical force.[2] They were cleared to land at Gioia, and the lumbering '24 touched down on clanging steel Marston mats.

They were directed to a spot on the north end of the field, on the left side of the runway, and there they shut down the engines and performed the multitude of after-landing checks. Finally, Darden and Lamar climbed down from the cockpit, exiting through the bomb bay doors, and joined the rest of the crew who were stretching and walking out the kinks engendered by the long flight. And then, before they had flown their first mission or even been assigned to a group and a squadron, the war came to them.

Another B-24 was landing, directed to the large facility at Gioia after a hard mission. It was shot up and the landing gear, as it turned out, was damaged. As the lumbering bird touched down its left gear collapsed, and the two propellers on that side began to chew up the metal runway. Trailing a rooster-tail of sparks and emitting a fearsome, grinding howl it hurled toward the Darden crew, now transfixed in fascinated horror. At the last moment, the asymmetrical fusion of drag and damage caused the '24 to spin around and stop just short of the wide-eyed neophyte crew. They watched as fire equipment and ambulances surrounded the battle-damaged bomber, and men swarmed aboard to drag the crew out safely.

The thunderous report of a Browning machine gun froze the Darden crew, and they stared in amazement in front of their feet at the hole in the ground from which powdery dirt drifted away on the slight breeze. One of the .50 caliber machine guns in the crippled bomber had cooked off a round. They knew not to get in the line of fire of any of the guns on any fighting machine; the weapons had a bad habit of firing at unexpected times even when no one was around. There was little they could do in this instance, however.

Someone in Darden's crew said "Welcome to the war, boys." No one bothered to answer. Each man was lost in his own private thoughts.[3]

They spent four days at the replacement center and supply depot of Gioia del Colle, once more with little to do. They wandered into the small town of Gioia after dinner, finding a refreshment establishment that was apparently operated by Americans. There, with little else to do, the officers were pulled into a game of blackjack. Lamar, never a drinker, had few choices and finally opted on gin and juice, heavy on the pineapple juice. Throughout the evening, he sipped sparingly from his glass that seemed to never diminish. Darden disappeared to find a crap game.

Late that night, as they left to head back to their pyramid tent, it was obvious that nearly all of the young men were drunk, their movements and judgment seriously impaired. This might not have been a problem had they been on a familiar base, but they had only been to their tent once to leave their gear before heading out to dinner and the bar. Now, a dozen or more disoriented flying officers sought to find their digs among the sea of tents that rose up in the dark. Lamar alone was sure he knew the way to the Darden crew tent; the others were bunked nearby.

"Hold hands, fellas. I can find the tent." So hand in hand, the jolly group snaked through the tent village, occasionally tripping over tent ropes or stakes, swearing and laughing. Lamar halted the train in front of the proper tent, and from there the others found their own quarters. Reynolds was impressed.

"I can't believe this," the young bombardier announced. "All night I tried to get Lamar drunk." He grinned at his co-pilot. "Every time you turned your head I filled your glass. You must have had a quart of that gin, and you were still the only one who could find the tent in the dark." He just shook his head. They crawled into their GI cots and quickly fell asleep.

Some time in the early hours, Lamar was aware of a hulking figure looming above him fumbling with his blanket. Thinking he was about to be robbed, he lashed out and the figure stumbled over to Craig's cot. Lamar saw the navigator jump up and stumble over to Darden's empty bunk. The pilot had come in, drunk and cold, and was trying to crawl in with one of the crew to warm up.

The next morning, bleary eyed and with pounding heads, the men slowly struggled to rise. Reynolds went outside to get his shoes.

"Dammit to hell!" The young bombardier threw his GI shoes to the ground and stood flipping his hands. "Darden, you jerk! You pissed in my boots!" When they left Gioia the sodden shoes were still outside the tent, unclaimed.

On September 11, 1944, the boys of the Darden bomber crew were assigned to the 460th Bomb Group, comprising the 760th, 761st, 762nd, and 763rd bomb squadrons. The group had begun life in May 1943 in Clovis, New Mexico, as little more than a signature on General Order No. 78. Col. Robert Crowder, a Military Academy graduate, qualified to fly gliders as well as four-engine bombers, was the first commanding officer, and Lt. Col. Bertram C. Harrison, another Academy man, was deputy group commander. Both were experienced military flyers, each with more than 2,000 flight hours in their log books. By August, the group was shipped to the new Army Air Forces School of Applied Tactics (AAFSAT) at Orlando, Florida. Delays en route meant they arrived at the school a week late, and they missed many of the lectures on battle flying from experienced officers returning from the combat theaters.[4]

Original members of the group remembered the ten-thousand-foot runways for AAFSAT near Pinecastle, about ten miles from Orlando. The base had been created by draining a swamp, and it stank after each rain. Swarms of mosquitoes in the dank air meant sleepless nights, despite the netting supplied for each bunk, and in the finest tradition of armies throughout history, the men complained about the cooking. A unit history written many years after the war noted that long hours in miserable and primitive conditions meant that the men got to know each other well in situations that would prepare them for what was ahead. The flight crews flew simulated bombing raids on surrounding cities as a run-up to their combat tour.[5]

From Orlando, the group was transferred in mid-September to Camp Kearns, twelve miles southwest of Salt Lake City, where they continued to train amidst a lack of facilities. The most notable accomplishment of this brief posting was a contest, judged by Col. Crowder, for the best drawing of a black panther, which had been selected as the symbol of the 460th. Soon group members were sporting on their flight jackets white leather patches with a snarling, green-eyed panther, its threatening, raised paw displaying extended claws. The symbol also would become a standard painting on the nose of each group bomber (to supplement, not replace, the iconic nose art inspired by Vargas and other artists of the female form).[6]

But of course they stayed in the dry and crisp environs of Salt Lake for barely a month before being ordered to Chatham Field, near Savannah, Georgia, a facility that would allow them more flying and combat training. The group officers were advised to expect overseas deployment about the first of January, 1944. At Chatham, the young flyers often flew simulated missions against eastern seaboard cities, frequently mixing it up with young Marine fighter pilots training at Parris Island. The mock combats taught them quickly about the speed and surprise inherent in being "bounced" by enemy fighters; it was far more effective than the hours of lectures they had sat through on the subject. Training closed up for the 460th Bomb Group in the week sandwiched between Christmas and New Year's, and the young fliers prepared to move out to a combat zone. New supplies, from uniforms to Thompson submachine guns, were issued all around, and sixty-two B-24H bombers were assembled to transport the unit overseas. In the mysterious ways of assembling armies, the men and machines were ordered to Mitchell Field, near New York, for processing, and then back south to Morrison Field, West Palm Beach, there to be under the aegis of Air Transport Command. There followed a month of careful checking by ATC to ensure that each aircraft and crew could make the trans-Atlantic flight safely. Finally, the first crews and bombers of the 460th lifted off into the dawn air for a long flight to Natal, Brazil, then on across the South Atlantic to Dakar, Senegal. It was a series of boringly long legs, followed by quick naps, refueling, maintenance of the airplanes, and more flying, often over or around bad weather, or sitting on the ground waiting for it to clear.[7]

When the group finally arrived in Italy in February 1944, they stepped into biting cold, deep snows, howling winds and deep, ubiquitous mud. The mud was nightmarish, a sticky, thick paste that, depending on the temperature, became either a frozen, rutted moonscape or ankle-deep muck that tugged and sucked at their boots as they walked. The veterans of that campaign would remember the bone-aching, debilitating cold and the constant fear of losing their boots in the mire.

Combined with a complete lack of facilities, the weather sapped the spirits of the crews, flight and ground, of the 460th. Originally designated to form up part of the 49th Bomb Wing, headquartered at Torretta, the group instead was assigned to the 55th Wing and stationed at Spinazzola.

The town of Spinazzola is in southern Italy, above the so-called "heel" if the country is seen as a boot, on a line drawn between Bari on the Adriatic coast and Salerno on the Tyrhennian coast. The town was on a railroad line, abandoned since the start of the war, with a central plaza called Piazza Plebiscito. Caribineri, the police with Napoleon-style hats (Hemingway's characters in *A Farewell to Arms* call them "airplanes") and white bandoliers, strode through the town in pairs, while occasional shoppers strolled the Corso Vittorio Emanuele heedless of the slow-paced horse-drawn carts that were the principle means of hauling goods and produce. The only motorized traffic was the military vehicles that occasionally sped through the town.

South southeast of the old town was the raw and cluttered Army Air Forces base, which sprang up on a thousand-acre former wheat farm owned by Giacinto Lorusso. All of the houses and outbuildings of the prosperous farm had been commandeered for the Allied war effort: the pink two-story villa became headquarters for the 460th group, with offices for several functions of the 460th on the first floor and administrative officers living on the second floor. Elsewhere, a machine shed became a carpenter shop, a granary became a briefing room, a barn was converted to a movie theater. Since an army—even a flying one—travels on its stomach, construction of mess halls for enlisted men and officers had a high priority. That left living quarters still to be reckoned with.

Improvement was badly needed. The young air officers were living miserably in muddy tents. The leading officers gave out strong encouragement to make better provision for their living comfort. Soon various forms of improvement began to take place. Captain Keith Mason, Operations Officer of the 760th Squadron, discovered his office was a tent, which he found to be completely unsatisfactory. He located a quarry nearby, where tufa blocks—a kind of soft stone, of seashell origin—could be cut and delivered by locals for very little cash. Local Italians were excellent masons who would work for what seemed to the Americans to be peanuts (for $200, the Yank airmen could have a sound, comfortable cottage with a red tile roof, fireplace, and tile floor), and soon a small village of stone huts sprouted about a half-mile southeast of the flight line. Wooden timbers stout enough to support the heavy roof tiles were rare and in high demand, and in the spirit of armies before them, the soldiers acquired what they needed by "midnight requisitioning."[8]

Tufa Town, as the camp was quickly designated, became a fantastic array of imaginative designs. Some of the huts contained fireplaces, wash basins, running water, and a quixotic array of windows and other materials scrounged, borrowed, or pilfered from the large number of wrecked aircraft that cluttered the wartime airbase. Many even had electricity, although the put-put that supplied power throughout the base only operated from dark until around 10:00 P.M.[9]

At Gioia, the Darden crew had received a shock. Brand new, shiny bombers were delivered to the war zone by brand new, shiny crews—but they didn't get to keep them. New crews and new aircraft were assigned to bomb groups as needed. If an aircraft was shot down and both the crew and the aircraft were lost, both were replaced. If an aircraft was wrecked and the crew was still functional, only the aircraft was replaced. If a crew completed their missions and went home, only the crew was replaced.

A 460th bomb group B-24 had been sent to pick up the Darden crew. They left their gleaming B-24 sitting on the ramp at Gioia, to be flown by a lead crew somewhere in one of the bomb groups. Newbies flew the older, battle-worn aircraft, still serviceable, but more subject to malfunctions. It simply didn't make sense for the lead crew, or the deputy lead, to fly a battle-worn bird which might malfunction while a new factory fresh aircraft was being flown farther back in the formation by a crew flying their first mission.

They learned something else. New crews were assigned to live in a tent, not one of the many tufa stone houses they saw in the area. If they wanted to live in a house, they had to build and pay for it themselves.

They strolled through the haphazard lanes of Tufa Town, noting the variety of styles. Some of the houses were little more than four walls and a roof. Others were imaginative creations with names like "Characters Cottage," "Casino," "Stagger Inn," and "Milk Run." The design and types of conveniences within the huts was limited only by the ingenuity and initiative of the occupants.

However the new crew did not jump into the business of house building immediately. It was only after a few cold and wet nights in their pyramid tent that they decided the next order of business had to be a stone hut.

Standard procedure for new combat crews upon reaching a theater of war was more training. There would be a short term of indoctrination to operational flying, mainly local familiarization flights, before Darden, Lamar, and the rest of the gang went into combat. This left some time for them to become familiar with the base and its environs.

The small village of Poggiorsini was about a mile south of the base, but they were advised to stay out of it because many hardened fascists still lived there. True or not, they believed the reports and none of the Darden crew ventured into nearby towns except for Spinazzola. The weather was changing. One day it was warm enough for T-shirts, the next day they needed jackets. The four officers immediately after arrival organized a trip to the post exchange, located in Spinazzola, and all the officers bought long, wool overcoats, since it was clear that the winter even in southern Italy would be very cold. Reynolds also bought new shoes.

Darden, Craig, Reynolds, and Lamar were quick to learn who to avoid and who to cultivate. The one most avoided was the mail officer. If they were in their tent when he arrived they could expect to get a huge sack of uncensored, outgoing mail dumped on the cots in their tent. This was mail written by enlisted men. Regulations required that it be censored by an officer, who put his name on the outside before sealing it and sending it on its way to the addressee. It seemed intrusive and demeaning to the enlisted men, since officers were allowed to censor their own mail. Most learned to scan the often embarrassing details contained in private letters to girlfriends or wives, and to key on information regarding locations and targets. Still, it was onerous, and the flight crew decided very quickly that it was best not to stay around your tent if you were not flying. You would be put to work.[10]

Corporal Robert Cutler from squadron operations, usually seen driving his jeep through Tufa Town, was someone else to avoid. Not because he had any great character flaws; he was, in fact, a personable young man. But when the officers were not on a mission, Operations would send Corporal Cutler with orders for them to perform what they regarded as busy work. There was no telephone system anywhere in Tufa Town, so if the corporal could not locate the officers they felt perfectly justified in doing what they wanted. Later, on operational flying—combat missions—it was the unfortunate Cutler who was sent into each hut to awaken individual officers and stand by until he could verify that the flier had actually placed his feet on the floor. This was dangerous work, he had learned the hard way; sleep-deprived flight crew often swung their fists at their nighttime tormentor.[11]

The officers of the Darden crew would soon meet the corporal on official business in the pre-dawn darkness of that late Italian summer.

Chapter 8

First Combat
September 1944

Sleep came late, long after midnight. This day would bring the first combat mission, the first true test of all of the training, of the equipment, and of themselves. After dinner in the officers' mess hall, and an evening of letter writing, card playing, and reading, the four young residents of the drafty pyramid tent—Darden, Lamar, Craig, and Reynolds—had lain awake in their bunks and talked about anything but the upcoming mission. Girls, home, after the war, sports. The mood had been a curious mixture of giddiness, bravado, and soberness. Finally someone, Reynolds perhaps, had said it was probably a good idea to get some sleep, and the lantern had been turned down and slowly, impossibly it seemed, sleep had come to each of them sometime long after midnight.

But for what seemed like an eternity they had lain awake silently, each knowing by the breathing of the others that no one was really asleep yet. But if it wasn't time for sleep, it was certainly the time to think the thoughts of a young man far from home, from family, from the comforts of peace, to contemplate mortality and try to imagine the coming day. There was curiosity, eagerness, and fear. There was, to be sure, a certain fascination and trepidation as each contemplated the possibility of his own early death. But that was not the primary fear. There were worse things than dying, they knew that. To a man, combat fliers years later always said their greatest fear was not performing, of letting their buddies down, of causing the deaths of others. And so they quietly drifted off, their breathing becoming deeper, bunks jerking occasionally when a dream caused someone to flinch. Gentle snoring filled the night air.

At long last, a light shone somewhere in the blackness of the tent and Lamar was aware of the whispered calls to arise. Corporal Cutler, sent to awaken these young warriors, was wary and discreet. He had been punched and shoved and sent flying backward when he had too abruptly shaken the shoulder of a young flier who was to go on operations that day. Now, the gentlest of prodding, the most deferential of whispered greetings, a respectful distance kept from the flailing arms and the sometimes violent jerks. The corporal knew his job, now. He had a list of names, a diagram of the sleeping arrangements. He refrained from jocular small talk, he kept his voice low, respectful, but authoritative. "Lieutenant Darden, sir? You're on for today. Good luck, sir." Then withdraw a few feet, ensure that the awakened young man actually placed his feet on the floor. On to the next one.

Lamar heard Darden's bunk creak, saw the form of the big pilot emerge from the wool blankets, his bulk formless and ethereal in the muted light of the corporal's flashlight, the cone of bright illumination dimmed by the enlisted man's fingers placed over the lens. Darden was sitting now, and so it was on to the next flier. "Lt. Reynolds, sir?" The enlisted soldier repeated his greeting, his hope for good luck. What did good luck mean to the corporal, wondered Lamar. Coming back to base intact, with no dead or wounded, no holes in the aircraft? Dropping the prescribed number and type of bombs squarely on the target, whatever it might be? Finding the weather clear, the flak gone, the fighters non-existent? Did it mean a perfect flight there and back, a greased landing, a beer in the officer's club after debriefing? Did it mean, perhaps, a canceled mission? A stand down while wretched weather obscured the target? There was no way to tell what good luck to any individual might mean. Invariably in war, one man's good luck was another's misfortune.

"Lt. Craig, sir?" And the third officer was rousing himself. Lamar lay still, listening to the mostly good-humored cursing, the shuffling of bare feet on the rough floor. He felt a separation, a distance between him and the others that he had never experienced before.

It was the first combat mission for the crew, but not for Lamar. Standard procedure for a new crew was for a veteran pilot, a seasoned flier, to take the place of the co-pilot to ease them through the strain of the first mission, to act both as judge of their conduct as well as to serve as fount of knowledge. It was a good system, one that allowed a new crew the settling assurance of someone who knew the ropes, and a kind of assessment of newbies for the rest of the squadron. It was a good system for all but the co-pilot.

Combat crewmen had trained in various places across the country, pilots largely in Texas and California and Kansas, bombardiers in New Mexico, navigators in Texas or Louisiana, gunners in Texas or Arizona. They then were assembled in a variety of combat crew centers, where they trained for two months to fulfill exactly their individual and collective duties. They knew they needed each other, and that their buddies would not let them down. They would fly their missions together, go on leaves together, complete their tours together. They would fly—in the Fifteenth Air Force in Italy—fifty missions, and go home together.[1]

But it seldom happened that way. Crewmen became ill or were wounded and missed missions, which they had to make up. Pilots might be assigned to another crew for a mission or two until a replacement arrived. Bombardiers or navigators or gunners might be needed for wounded or ill crewmen on another plane or for special training in a new technique or updated instrument. Then, if they were to rotate home with their original crew, the missions would have to be recouped in some way.

For Lamar, the first mission for the Darden crew was excruciating. He arose with them, went to breakfast, then had to sweat out on the ground the bombing mission to Budapest, where they were to strike an oil refinery. Six hours and thirty-eight minutes, Lamar waited. Six hours, thirty-eight minutes of mental agony, wondering if "his" boys would be coming home, or whether a military policeman would be assigned to guard the door of the green tent until the personal effects of Darden, Craig, and Reynolds could be inventoried and sent home. He wandered around Tufa Town, meandered back to his tent, moseyed up to the operations hut, strolled to the officers' mess hall for lunch. He wrote letters. He tried to read the B-24 flight manual for the hundredth time, but realized after a half-hour that he hadn't turned a page. Finally, he walked the half-mile to the flight line to await the returning bombers.[2]

Of course, they did return, and in deference to the fear and agony and frustration that Lamar endured, the crew sympathized and bestowed a new nickname. Lamar became Skippy.

"You skipped the first mission, Lee." Reynolds looked at Lamar and laughed. "So, Skippy, did you stay safe while we heroes were up winning the war?" And the nickname stuck.

For the rest of the crew, the mission had been largely uneventful. After an early breakfast, they had gone to a converted barn for a mission briefing, been transported by trucks to the flight line, taken off at 7:45, formed up in tight defensive formations and flown to Budapest. They had flown six and a half hours, with Gideon Jones, a veteran pilot, sitting in Lamar's right seat. Over the Budapest/Magyar Oil Refinery, they had released their two-and-a-half tons of bombs, and headed for home. En route they had been escorted by American P-38 fighters, seen one twin-engine ME-110 German fighter and six ME-109 single-engine fighters, and experienced flak for the first time. A crewman in another bomber had been wounded, and they returned to Spinazzola at 1435, or about 2:30 that afternoon.[3] Lamar was there waiting, and he watched as the giant four-engine bombers broke out of formation and entered the traffic pattern over Spinazzola, their long tapered wings giving them a curious grace that was absent when they squatted level on the ground. The planes were a mixture of bare aluminum and dull olive drab. The Darden crew, being new, had been assigned to one of the older ships, which still wore a chipped and faded coat of olive green paint. Months earlier, it had been determined that the camouflage paint was largely unneeded now, so newer replacement aircraft arrived shiny and bright as a newly minted dime, bearing just the star-and-bar insignia of the U.S., and army serial number on the tail. Colorful group insignia were added to the tails, and individual artwork (normally focused on scantily-clad young women) graced the noses of old and new aircraft alike.

Throughout their tour, the Darden crew was customarily assigned one of the older aircraft.

So now they all, except for Lamar, had experienced war. They knew the sights and sounds and smells of combat. More importantly, they knew how they individually had reacted to other humans attempting, however impersonally, to kill them. None would ever grow accustomed to this feeling, none ever accept unquestioningly that another woman's child was trying to take their lives. But they did know now that such a thing was possible to survive, that they could perform what they had been asked to do, and not let down their buddies or themselves. They had been tested, and they had passed.

All except Lamar could record in their individual logs that they had flown a combat mission, that they only had 49 to go, and that they had received credit toward an Air Medal, the blue and gold ribbon which would be pinned below their silver wings and would mark them as a veteran flier, an experienced combat crewman. Award of the Air Medal generally required completion of five combat missions; subsequent awards for more missions were noted by small bronze oak leaf clusters that attached to the medal ribbon bar. The medals themselves were virtually never worn, but the ribbons denoting the award were usually discreetly present. They were one of the marks of a veteran.

The next morning at 6:31 exactly, thirty-one heavy bombers of the Black Panthers rose ponderously into the air to attack a railroad bridge in Hungary. The Darden crew had checked the Fly-No Fly list and learned they were not flying that day. But the following day, September 19, they were on the "fly" board, and Lamar arose with the others, glad to finally get his chance. Once more, sleep had been elusive, but he felt a surge of adrenalin that purged his body of any trace of tiredness. As they stepped out into the chilly early morning, Craig looked up at the black sky and noted the absence of any stars. A low, thick cloud layer obscured the sky, and a few puddles were evidence of rain during the night. Lamar was careful to leave his billfold and all identification with his clothing in the tent. He would be carrying only his dog tags during the mission. Those gave his name and serial number. That was all the information they were supposed to give the enemy in case they were shot down and captured.

The four young men went to breakfast at the officers' mess, dubbed the Panther's Lair, where they downed French toast, or chipped beef on toast—always referred to as SOS or some other less presentable name—and all but Lamar drank several cups of coffee. With his absence of smell he had never developed a taste for the drink, which was lucky for the bladder of a combat flier.

Then it was off on a footpath through a grove of olive trees to mission briefing, held in a large, tile-roofed, sandstone barn that also was the base theater when not being used to brief combat crews. As Lamar and the others filed into the large room, which could hold up to 200 men, he noted the crude benches and metal bomb fin crates set up in rows facing a low dais, upon which was a large screen, now covered with a curtain.

There was something exciting, slightly mysterious, and perhaps a bit melodramatic about the layout. The boisterous young fliers found seats, usually with others from their crews, and sat down amid a buzz of quiet conversation, muted laughter, and jostling. On the dais were several chairs to the left of the large, covered board, and Lamar recognized the weather officer. There were a couple of others whose faces he had seen but whose job in the bomb group he did not yet know.

One of the men, with the twin silver bars of a captain, rose and fiddled with some cords that restrained the cover on the board. He glanced at his watch, then looked down the central aisle as the door opened once again. He straightened, and in a surprisingly deep voice that belied his slender frame, called "At-TEN-shun!" In a well-practiced routine, all the officers rose as the Group commanding officer, Lt. Col. Harold C. Babb, strode down the canyon of leather-and-olive clad fliers.

Babb had become acting CO at the beginning of the month. The first commander, Col. Robert Crowder, had been killed in April, shot down on a mission to Bucharest after leading the first nine combat missions of the 460th. He had been a no-nonsense leader who insisted that a commander's place was always in the number one position of the first box on every mission. A German fighter had made a head-on pass on Crowder's plane, and the heavy bomber suddenly nosed up and then fell back tail first, trailing flames and smoke. Two men survived and were captured, later repatriated.[4] The Deputy Commander, Lt. Col. Bert Harrison, like Crowder a West Point man, assumed command after Crowder's death. A boxer at the academy, he likewise brought a serious demeanor to his leadership, and had instituted the tight-formation regimen that was the order of the day when the Darden crew arrived. Tight formations were grudgingly accepted by the crews as necessary to survival in preventing fighter attacks on the formations. What was generally viewed as Army chicken shit was Harrison's insistence that while one-half of the pilots were busy practicing formation flying, those not in a cockpit would be performing close-order drill on the base parade ground.

Lamar and the rest of the Darden crew had missed much of this, however, as Harrison had been promoted to Executive Officer of the 55th Wing, and Babb became the acting CO on September 1. He seemed to be well liked by the crews, but everyone knew it was not a permanent slot for him.[5]

Babb strode to the dais, turned to the assembled crews, and nodded once, a short, abrupt downward slash of his head. "At ease." The young officers sat down, and the group chaplain, always known as Padre, asked the blessings of Almighty God on the young fliers preparing to fly into the shadow of the valley of death. The captain, the group intelligence officer, pulled back the curtain that covered the large area map. A red ribbon ran from Spinazzola north into Germany.

"Men, this morning we will take the war to the Germans in Blechhammer. The Krauts have a synthetic oil refinery there that we are going to remove. We are beginning to hurt them, by reducing their ability to produce oil and keep their machinery running. We have bombed the refinery at Ploesti several times and it is now in Allied hands, and the Germans are feeling the pinch." Darden and Lamar glanced at each other. For most fliers, Ploesti was still seen as a major mistake, when on the first mission, several hundred low and slow B-24s were sent in at treetop level to bomb the famed oil plant. Several hundred American fliers were lost, shot down, or consumed by the billowing fires that erupted as the storage tanks were blasted.[6]

There followed a briefing by the group weather officer, who advised of low clouds and high winds en route, but predicted that the target area over Blechhammer would be clear by the time they arrived. The operations officer displayed several aerial photos of the area around Blechhammer, and took pains to point out that several Allied prisoner-of-war camps were sited around the synthetic oil plant. "Ensure that you are able to identify the oil plant. If you cannot visually see the target, you are to proceed to your secondary target." Each airman understood the horrible consequences of unleashing bombs that might fall on Allied soldiers, perhaps even downed airmen. Next, the intelligence officer spoke again. Flak in the area was expected to be moderate, which the seasoned fliers among them knew meant heavy, and fighter opposition could be expected. Once more, he reminded them that northern Italy was still in German hands, and if they had to crash-land or bail out they should hide their parachutes, lie low until the end of the second day, and then try to establish contact with friendly groups who could help them evade capture and return to Allied-controlled territory.

Times were given for engine start, for take-off, and assembly, and Darden and Lamar made careful notes. After the briefing, Lamar and the other co-pilots each checked out ten escape kits to be handed out to each crewmen at the start of each mission. They were collected and turned in when the aircraft returned. The kit was small, designed to fit in the leg pocket of a flight suit, and very basic: silk maps of the region, printed on both sides (silk meant they could still be used if wet, and could serve as bandages if necessary); a dime-sized, brass-cased compass; a short saw blade; and 48 gold seal U.S. dollars (the gold seal was unique to the war zone, and was more acceptable to non-Americans, it was explained. It also served as an unmistakable flag to banks in the U.S.: the notes were not to be used except overseas. It would do no good to try to "borrow" them for later use in the States).[7]

They climbed into the back of a six-by-six truck and were driven to the flight line, stopping in front of their designated bomber for that day. As a replacement crew and not one of the original members of the 460th as they shipped overseas early in the year, the Darden crew flew what was available.

Carrying their kitbags, they jumped off the truck and began suiting up for the mission before beginning their individual routines and rituals.

Darden and Lamar spoke to the crew chief. They signed off on Form 1-A, indicating that all was fine and that they accepted the ship. The Liberator had been armed during the early morning, and the lethal cargo of 500-pound bombs was visible in the open bay doors, two sets of corrugated, hinged metal covers that slid up the side of the fuselage when opened. They were a bit like old roll-top desks, except that each door panel had a single piano-style hinge that ran horizontally about six inches from the outside edge. That was enough for the door to roll on its tracks and slide up the outside of the aircraft body.

The B-24 was a very complicated machine, with hydraulic systems, fuel lines, electric circuits, and manual controls, each with dozens of individual monitors, checks, switches, locks, fuses, and levers. The malfunction of any of these could imperil the ship and her crew, so a system had been developed that, if followed faithfully, would reduce the likelihood of overlooking a critical component. The pre-flight check had been standardized, and it comprised several printed pages of specific instructions, beginning with an exterior examination.

Pilot and co-pilot did the walk around together, starting with the inboard section of the right wing, below the fuel cell, checking for leaks. Next they inspected the right main landing gear, the supercharger of the number three engine, looked for loose cowl fastenings in the nacelle of the same engine, moved on to the outboard engine, and then to the leading edge of the right wing to look over the de-icer boots. They quickly moved to the nose of the bomber, insuring the nose turret was locked in forward position, and inspected the pitot tubes for blockage that would cripple their airspeed and altitude instruments. A small fire extinguisher behind a door on the right nose was checked, and then the left wing and its systems, including the flaps and ailerons. The fliers moved around the fuselage, inspecting the tailskid, the antennae, tail section, and the ball and tail gun turrets. Then it was time to climb into the cockpit, ensure the ignition and master switches were off, and signal the engineer to begin pulling the mighty propellers through a full six blades to assure the engines would turn freely and to check for leaks.

All of that took about five minutes for an experienced team, longer if discrepancies were noted. But discrepancies were rare, because the Crew Chief had already checked these items and reported to the Operations Office that the aircraft was ready for the mission. That was his full-time job. When the aircraft returned from a mission, if it could readily be made fit for another mission, the Crew Chief would get it ready, even if he had to work all night. He could call on other specialists for help if needed: mechanics, metal workers, electricians, machinists. Most Crew Chiefs did their job well, and the flight crews learned to love and respect them for their dedicated, unsung hard work.

Once seated in the cockpit, the preflight procedure continued, with Lamar reading from the long printed checklist while Darden responded. Lamar was comfortable now, the routine of the pre-flight erasing any chance for jitters or stray thoughts. The cockpit was an old friend, as familiar as the front seat of a family car. They unlocked the controls, and Lamar began calling out each item. There were twenty-six items to be verified before even starting the engines.

The first item was "Form 1-A?" Had the pilots checked it for anything written up by previous pilots? Despite the routine of minutiae, both pilots were crisp in the ritual.

"Check." Darden's voice was clear and strong.

"Loading?" Lamar kept his finger on each item listed until hearing from Darden. This point was to ensure that the pilot had checked the weight and balance of the aircraft. Too heavily loaded, they would never be able to take off. If the weight were distributed wrong—for example, too much weight in the rear of the aircraft—disaster awaited.

"Check." And so on down the list through wheel chocks, pitot covers, flight controls, auxiliary power unit and hydraulic pump, brake pressure, gyros, auto pilot, intercoolers, cowl flaps, de-icing equipment, and more, establishing that each switch and lever was in the proper position. Only then were they ready for the engine start procedure, an event that had its own check list.

Finally the green flare went up from the control tower, which was the signal to start the aircraft engines. Both pilots could not miss that signal.

"Ready to start?" Darden looked to Lamar, who nodded and flipped the page to the required list. Starting each of the four engines was a complicated procedure in itself.

"Clear!" Both pilots shouted through the open side windows. The propellers would quickly slice and dice anyone in their arc, and "clear" was a universal signal on any flight line that an engine was about to be started. Lamar held up three fingers to the ground crew, indicating that number three engine—the inboard powerplant on the right side—would be the first started. The engine-driven hydraulic pump operated from that engine, so it was always fired up first. "All clear, guard posted!" One man stood by with a fire extinguisher, while another stood where he could easily see the the pilots' hand signals.

"Ignition switches?"

"Ignition switches all on." Lamar answered this one himself, as he flipped on all four ignition switches.

"Throttles?"

"Throttles cracked!" Darden's right hand was on the four levers in the center control console between the two seats.

"Booster pump?" These pumps started the fuel pressure for priming. Lamar's duty here was to turn on the pump switch, check for pressure, and announce "Booster pump on!" He pressed the primer switch for one second before releasing it, repeating this two or three times.

"Start engines!" With his left hand, Lamar continued priming number three, and with his right he meshed the starter switch and held it in that position until the engine began turning the blades. Slowly, agonizingly slowly, the props began to turn, the engine popping like a giant motorcycle engine with no muffler. A large cloud of blue-gray smoke shot from the exhaust, and the roar of a single 1,200-horsepower radial engine ricocheted off the metal hardstand in a deafening staccato of popping and growling. Each crewman could feel the vibration, a visceral trembling that resonated through the entire fuselage. Lamar brought the mixture control back to auto-rich and turned off the booster pump, and the engine smoothed out to an even symphony of raw power. He checked the oil pressure gauge. "Oil pressure coming up," he called out.

"Number three started." The same procedure was followed to start the other three engines.

For the next several minutes, the heavily loaded bombers sat in their hardstands, while crews in each made last-minute checks of all the equipment. Once more, there was a checklist to complete before taxiing.

"All instruments?" Lamar read the first item. Darden then called out the status of several key instruments, beginning with the directional gyro, which he checked by caging, spinning, and quickly releasing the locking knob. The indicator stopped spinning, and called out "DG checked." The pilot then moved on to report on the manifold pressure, tachometer, fuel pressure, oil pressure, oil temperature, cylinder head temperature, carburetor air temperature, hydraulic brake accumulator pressure, landing gear warning light, free air temperature, and compass. "All instruments checked!"

While the pilots were doing this, each crewman was running through his own checklist, ensuring the bombsight was functional, navigation gear in order, gun safeties on, and radios operational, a list of frequencies ready.

"Vacuum?" Lamar questioned the flight engineer. Webb turned the vacuum selector valve and called out "Engine one," and Darden checked his own gauge. The needle indicated the safe zone of 3.75 to 4.25 pounds, and affirmed. "Checked." Webb nodded. "Engine two!" Darden checked that engine, and affirmed once more.

"Altimeter, time." Lamar checked his own watch against the wind-up clock atop the instrument panel. Darden then set the altimeter to the field elevation and affirmed, and checked his own watch as well as the aircraft clock. Each pilot confirmed that the chocks on his side were away from the wheels, and reported their removal. It was finally time for the bomber to begin to move.[8]

Finally another flare went up indicating it was time to taxi into position for takeoff in order along the taxiway. Darden applied power to the four radial engines to ease the heavily loaded bomber from its space on the hardstand. There were 30 nearly identical bombers, and the roar of 120 of these huge engines, each producing 1,200 horsepower by way of 18 cylinders as big as five-gallon paint buckets, was deafening. Everyone standing behind the prop wash of any one of the behemoths was forced to clamp his eyes shut tightly, grasp his headgear, and bend forward slightly to keep from being tumbled backwards on the hard steel mats. Dirt, sand, small bits of metal shavings, all were blown by the mechanical cyclone into the face of anyone unfortunate enough to be stationed behind the armada. It was a sandblasting. And thus began the ponderous, slow movement along the taxiway of what surely were some of the most awkward-appearing machines of war ever devised. The noise of a single B-24 taxiing is prodigious—loud creaks and groans as the massive, whale-like body rocks slowly on its landing gear, squeals of protest as brakes are applied, the revving of engines on one side as they turn—and that collection of squeals, clunks, and roars swells to an unholy cacophony as a line of lumbering Liberators queues up for takeoff. Anyone who has watched film of a line of elephants, trunk to tail, awkwardly soldiering on through a wind storm, has a mental image of the taxi routine of a B-24 heavy bombardment group.

To expedite the launching of thirty or forty such heavy bombers, they follow each other closely, the front gun turret only a few feet from the tail of the ship preceding it. Occasionally, accidents happened, when an inattentive pilot or faulty brakes or a sudden lurch or unexpected stop meant the equivalent of a rear-end collision. Sometimes this was minor, but it could also mean catastrophe as whirling propellers severed gasoline lines. Thousands of gallons of high-octane aviation fuel and a full cargo of high explosive bombs are a dangerous mixture at any time. They could become both cause of death and funeral pyre for an entire crew in the blink of an eye.

Any combat crewman from World War II will tell you about takeoffs: it is the most dangerous part of any mission. The overloaded, groaning bomber, filled past capacity with bombs and fuel and guns and ammunition and equipment and men, very vulnerable, very fragile men in the very real physical sense, slowly, too slowly, beginning to move down the runway, the crew sitting with their backs to a bulkhead praying silently or looking out a window at the outside world moving past in slow motion or gripping a religious medal or a token given by a sweetheart while the thunderous howl of the four engines makes conversation impossible and the vibration of the entire 30-ton contrivance is felt clear to their bones, while two pilots in the cockpit are trying to coax the power of every last horse corralled in those engines—"c'mon, c'mom, c'mon!"—the pilot with his hands on the four throttles, the copilot's hands on top to ensure they don't move, pilot watching the far end of the runway that despite the agonizingly slow speed of the insane beast they are riding seems to be coming up too soon, the copilot intently watching the airspeed indicator and calling out the critical numbers, then both of them heaving back on the oversized wheel on its pedestal and the nose coming off the ground but the rest of the bird seemingly stuck on its main gear and then imperceptibly rising a few inches and settling back down then repeating the teasing acceptance of flight and finally, at last, the ship staggering into the air, the rough slapping of the wheels on tarmac or steel ceasing and everyone praying that the beast will stay in the air.[9]

Repeat that dozens, perhaps hundreds of times for all of the bombers on any mission, and you can perhaps get an understanding of how much terror was felt by so many on any given day. Yet they kept on each day at hundreds of bases across Europe and the Pacific.

Lamar strained forward, keeping his eyes constantly moving left to right, up and down, while raising the landing gear (first tapping the brakes to stop the wheels from spinning), adjusting the propeller pitch and power settings, all on the tense commands of Darden. Lamar knew the feel of each lever, each control, and after finding it was able to confirm visually that the lever was the correct one with just a quick glance.

After takeoff, forming up the thirty bombers into combat boxes was a slow motion aerial ballet, and on any given mission similar procedures were followed at many bases as each bomb group joined an ever-growing armada of aerial ships. Since the aircraft took off in the order they were to fly in their assigned box, the squadrons assembled reasonably quickly in their assigned airspace south of Spinazzola. Such sorting out had its own precise procedure to minimize the inherent dangers in bringing so many bombers together in such a small cube of sky, and the air over southern Italy would crackle and buzz at times from the droning of several hundred bombers. It took about an hour after takeoff for all of the 460th Bomb Group to be in position and then to form up with other precisely formed boxes.

Lamar was relaxed now, the first combat takeoff behind him. He and Darden resumed their routine from their combat crew training days and took turns flying for fifteen minutes; during their down stint, they rested while keeping a watchful eye on the planes around them. This day, vigilance was especially important as they climbed up in formation through the cloud cover.

They were at 21,000 feet, on oxygen, still slicing through wisps and swirls of cloud, occasionally being smacked by large rain drops that dissolved into tiny beads that crawled upward on the windscreen. Lamar turned the radio switch to intercom and pressed his throat microphone.

"Crew, copilot. Oxygen check. Call in."

"Hey, Skippy. Bombardier, oxygen fine."

"Yo, Skip. Navigator okay."

And on through the rest of the crew, the gunners and radioman and engineer reporting that their oxygen supply and system were working. Oxygen deprivation was serious business in an unheated, unpressured airplane. At these altitudes, where the outside (and inside in most of the aircraft that was unheated) temperature was 20 to 50 degrees below zero, saliva and moisture from exhaling could freeze in the regulator and halt the flow of air to a crewman who was completely unaware of his lethal predicament. Within a couple of minutes he would pass out; a few minutes later he would be dead. Since his experience in the barometric chamber in his cadet days, Lamar was always watchful of the oxygen supply to each crewman. Every quarter hour each man reported in, while squeezing the oxygen hose to crush any buildup of frost or ice.

Turbulence on top of the cloud layer was bad, and that, combined with the circular, tornadic, swirling turbulence set up by each plane in the tight formation, made flying a physical contest, the pilots constantly wrestling the yoke and rudder pedals to keep the bomber in position in the combat box. They would be over Germany soon, and even in the clouds they could expect to be bracketed with flak as the antiaircraft artillerymen sought to send up enough exploding munitions to damage or down the bombers. Lee checked his watch. They had been airborne nearly two-and-a-half hours.

When he thought about the reason they were airborne, that within an hour or so they would be releasing their bombs on an enemy target, he experienced a twinge, a slight tightening of his stomach muscles. But it was what he had volunteered for, it was the reason for the months of training, and most of all, he knew, it would contribute to an early end to a miserable war.

The engineer came forward, calling attention to engine three, the inboard engine on the right wing. It was trailing a fine black mist of oil, and a check of the temperature confirmed that the engine was indeed overheating. The decision was made to shut it down; they feathered the prop. Clearly they could not continue to target; they would have to leave the formation. It was not necessary to notify the lead that they would be leaving. Radio silence was vital since the enemy could monitor the same frequencies. It was obvious they had lost an engine. They simply eased the aircraft very slowly out of the formation, made a 180 degree and headed home.

Lamar stared straight ahead. He was crushingly disappointed, but that could wait. Now, they needed to get this bird safely back to Spinazzola. When they landed, they were informed that the entire group would soon be arriving. The mission had been canceled due to weather in the target area.[10]

That day, a frustrated Lamar recorded four hours, fifteen minutes of flight time. It was classified as "Combat–non-sortie." No one on the crew would get credit for a mission that day in spite of all their efforts. His flight time was building, but he still had not received credit for a single combat mission.

That was about to change.

Chapter 9

Finally . . . Mission Countdown
20–24 September 1944

Lamar listened to the briefing officers as they described the mission, the target, weather, expected opposition. He noted the times for start-up, takeoff, assembly, and entry at the Initial Point, the position at which they would begin their bomb run. Finally, all the young men hacked their watches—pulled out the stem to stop the second hand, set the minute hand at the direction of the briefer, and counted down: "Five, four, three, two, one, Hack!"

Today, maybe. After the crushing return the previous day from his first scheduled operational mission, today's briefing seemed routine and anticlimactic. Corporal Cutler's early wake-up, the oblation of splashed water on his face, a quick shave, dressing in layers, and breakfast in the Panther's Lair, all part of the ritual offering to Mars. He had been through it once, for nothing, as it turned out. He was not going to get overly excited today.

The mission was to the railroad marshaling yards at Hatvan, thirty miles east-northeast of Budapest, Hungary. Railroad centers were often targeted, since the destruction of such transportation hubs disrupted the flow of arms and materiel, the routing of oil from Romanian fields, and the movement of German troops.

The men filed out of the big barn that had been converted to a briefing area and climbed into the backs of trucks. They were driven to the equipment hut, where they picked up their high-altitude flight gear, parachutes, and oxygen masks.

In the early days of the war, high-altitude flight clothing was primarily sheepskin. Crew stuffed themselves into pants, jackets, boots, gloves, and helmets with the wool, up to three-quarters of an inch long, on the inside. The insulating qualities of the sheepskin were wonderful, but the resulting awkwardness of movement was less desirable. Fliers shuffled around like the Michelin

Man, bound and trussed by the heavy clothing. It was also expensive, and the personal equipment laboratory, clothing branch, at Wright Field, Dayton, continuously tried new gear that would be efficient and less expensive. The equipment was tortured, ripped, strained, and put through a battery of exacting tests aimed at eliminating failure of the equipment. It didn't always work out that way. Early on, electrically heated flight suits proved unreliable, as heating wires broke at points of movement, initially often shocking the airman and rendering the suit useless.

Temperatures at seventeen thousand to twenty-four thousand feet, where the Darden crew would be flying for most of their missions, were frigid. Even in the summer or late fall, when the air was quite pleasant on the ground, combat fliers had to be concerned with frostbite. Standard temperature lapse rate is three degrees F. per thousand feet, so if it were sixty degrees on the runway, it was zero at twenty thousand feet. As winter approached, the temperatures aloft were correspondingly much colder.

By September 1944, a new, improved electric flight suit had been issued, and it generally performed much better than the initial issue. Now, each crewman donned long underwear before putting on a layer of wool—trousers and shirt—and then slipped into a rayon-and-cotton electrically heated jacket and bib trousers, with connections for heated gloves and boot inserts. Over this went a regular wool or cotton flight suit. An eighteen-inch pigtail wire in the electric suit connected to a cord in the aircraft, and the temperature was adjustable by means of a rheostat at each crew station. Tests at Dayton had shown that men wearing the suit in temperatures of minus sixty F. had suffered no discomfort after eight hours, while a volunteer wearing the heaviest sheepskin combination had had to withdraw from the test after two hours because of the danger of frostbite.[1]

In addition to the electric flight suit, crew members normally donned a yellow Mae West life preserver, pneumatically inflated by pulling cords that tripped cartridges of compressed carbon dioxide, and over all of that went the heavy cotton web harness of their parachute. Parachutes, too bulky to be worn inside the aircraft, were stashed inside along with the flak helmets, steel affairs with hinged ear pieces to fit over radio headsets, which were only worn when over the target.

Out to the hardstand, to await the green flares that signaled start-up, and later for taxi. While they were still on the hardstand, a jeep drove by and the driver tossed out 10 packs of K-Rations, a packaged utilitarian meal. Some were prepared for breakfast, some for lunch and some for dinner. It was always a mix of the various kinds. It was usually a scramble for each crewman to get his favorite. The crew kept the packs near their combat station and opened them just after leaving the target area.

The crew went through all of the same strict procedures for preflight inspection, engine start, taxi, takeoff, and assembly that they had employed the day previously. By 0735, thirty-one Liberators from the 460th bomb group were droning north, escorted by P-51s and P-38s as fighter protection.

The armada had done a slow-motion series of turns which kept the bombers away from Budapest and its ring of flak batteries, and now approached Hatvan.

From 12,500 feet, the railroad marshaling yard didn't look very dangerous, and as it turned out there was no flak opposition. Lamar watched from the cockpit as bomb bay doors opened on planes in front, and then sticks of 500-pound bombs began falling from the entrails of the bombers. It was so much like training that this mission had no particular sense of danger to him, and after Reynolds reported "Bombs away!" and then "Bomb bay doors closing," the trip home proved entirely routine as well.

All thirty-one Libs returned to Spinazzola, landing at a mean time of 15:10, or a bit after 3:00 P.M. The crew slowly, stiffly, climbed down from the aircraft where they were greeted by the crew chief, who was pleased to note no battle damage or reports of any malfunctions.[2] Hot coffee and donuts were distributed, they were debriefed by an intelligence officer, and they turned in their flight gear. Lamar recorded 7 hours, 25 minutes in his flight log, had dinner at the Panther's Lair, and went back to the tent. Lying on his bunk, listening to Darden, Reynolds, and Craig tease and joke with each other, Lamar stared at the dark canvas roof of the tent and relived the mission. His first, only forty-nine to go. Piece of cake.

The procedures for mission credit were a bit arcane, subjective, and subject to change. When crews first began flying missions out of England over Fortress Europe, without fighter protection, they averaged more than ten per cent losses on each mission. Commanders decided that twenty-five missions would be sufficient for a tour of combat flying. This was a goal that proved very, very difficult in the first year of the war. Later, when Jimmy Doolittle, following his famous raid on Tokyo, was made CO of the Mighty Eighth Air Force, he raised the number to thirty, and later to thirty-five. This was in response to changing conditions: the Luftwaffe was badly weakened, and long-range P-51s were able to escort B-17s and B-24s to Berlin and back. Overall, the yardstick for determining whether a flight counted as a mission was whether or not bombs were dropped on a target. In Italy, where the Germans had been pushed back into the northern third of the country, and where losses were comparatively light, the missions began at twenty-five, but by the time the Darden crew arrived the magic number was fifty. However, that didn't necessarily equate to fifty separate bombing sorties. Instead, some missions over well-defended targets such as Vienna, Ploesti, or Munich meant double mission credit. And of course, being called back short of the target meant no credit at all, despite the obvious dangers of foul weather, mechanical glitches, or mid-air collisions in the tightly packed combat boxes, as well as the one constant for all missions—the incredibly dangerous takeoffs with maximum fuel and live bombs. If they were attacked by enemy fighters or encountered intense ground fire during a recalled mission, credit could possibly be given. Joseph Heller, a B-25 bombardier in Italy, in his iconic novel *Catch-22,* bases much of the disconnect felt by his characters on the constantly changing required number of missions.[3]

The next day, the Darden crew again took off, but the mission was aborted because of bad weather. The following day, September 22, two days after Lamar's first mission and the crew's second, they were scheduled for another combat operational flight, this time to the heavily defended industrial area of Munich. Here, they would learn why double credit was awarded for certain missions.[4]

Once more, thirty-one Libs of the 460th group took off about 0800 and joined up with other groups to form an aerial armada, an aluminum river that extended for miles. The sheer numbers of American bombers that were able to launch strikes against Germany and her allies was impressive even to those who were part of it. On one occasion, while resting in the right seat after his turn on the controls, Lamar counted more than two hundred bombers in the long line ahead of him. He had no idea how many more were behind.

To discourage German Focke-Wulfs and Messerschmitts, the bombers flew in tight defensive boxes, drawing together even closer as they entered enemy airspace. Here Darden and Lamar learned just how difficult formation flying was when they were preceded and surrounded by dozens or scores of other bombers. It was far more difficult than in their training days, harder even than the practice formations when they arrived at the squadron. The turbulence created by so many propellers on so many engines—four for each bomber in the case of the B-24—was violent, disruptive, and nerve-wracking. They could see planes around them rise and fall, swerve sharply to left or right, as the pilots fought to stay in formation and not slam into anyone else. It might be compared to driving an eighteen-wheeler in a tight convoy on a three- or four-lane expressway, with trucks close ahead and behind and on both sides, roaring at breakneck speed while the road itself bucks and heaves. But the trucks would have an advantage: brakes. At the best of times, it was no picnic.

Now, as they entered the defensive perimeter of Munich, a sprawling urban center, Lamar experienced truly spirited defense. They were ducking in and out of clouds, which added to the stress of maintaining their position, and then ahead he could see the clouds of death that signified flak explosions. They were black, with red or black or white centers, and they seemed to fill the entire sky through which they had to fly. Their concussive explosions further added to the turbulent air, and Lamar could see around them planes that had obviously been hit hard.

German flak batteries were hard to eliminate. They could be mounted on rail cars and moved quickly, and their crews were motivated and highly skilled. The guns were massive: an 88 mm flak cannon weighed 11,534 pounds, with a barrel 16.6 feet long. Impossible to avoid, the bigger guns—88 and 105 mm— hurled an explosive shell higher than any Liberator could go, up to 42,000 feet in the case of the 105s. The explosive shells weighed 33 pounds (20 pounds for an 88) and were set by the gun crew to detonate at a particular altitude, which was often radioed in by fighters who stayed just out of range of the bombers' defensive guns.[5] When they exploded, red-hot fragments of jagged metal easily pierced the thin aluminum skin of the bombers and the far more fragile skin of their crew. It was not uncommon for a bomber to return with several hundred holes punched in the wings, fuselage, and tail, holes which were patched overnight by the intrepid ground crews. Crew members were not so easily repaired.

"Bomber at 11 o'clock, going down." The report from the gunner in the nose turret was flat, emotionless, metallic over the headset. "No 'chutes."

"Come on, guys, jump!"

Lamar cautioned his crew to keep radio discipline. Very soon, they were in the flak field themselves, and they could feel and hear the thumps of exploding shells and the rattle of flak on the fragile aluminum skin of the Liberator. To Lamar, it sounded like gravel being thrown against the metal roof of a farm shed.

They were on the bomb run now, with Reynolds peering through his Norden bombsight to be ready when it was time for "Bombs away". But he reported no clear view of the target because of low level cloud cover. Apparently the lead bombardier could not see the target either. Standing orders of American Air Force commanders were that no bombs were to be dropped blindly. The formation swung slowly to the northeast, still bracketed by heavy flak. The secondary target, another industrial area of Munich, was visible, and they released their 500-pounders. Lamar felt the sudden lift of the big bomber as it was freed of the burden of four tons of bombs.[6]

"Okay, guys, we just did our job for Uncle Sam. Now we're flying for ourselves." It was a common saying, and it became a mantra for bomber crews everywhere, whether thought or spoken aloud. Lamar followed the formation as it wheeled left in a huge and complicated turn for home. At 23,150 feet, each of the bombers was leaving a trail of condensation in its wake as the heat from the engine exhausts met the frigid air. To Lamar, they looked like they were plowing the sky, leaving furrows of white in the blue air.

It had not been an easy mission. They had been in the air for seven hours, forty-five minutes. Nineteen of the thirty-one group aircraft returned with flak holes puncturing the skin or with other, more serious damage. Two failed to return, having been shot down over the target. The Darden crew, having been at Spinazzola just nine days, did not know the other crews well, but they recognized the guards at the tents and stone houses that appeared shortly after they had returned to the area.

Blue W for William was from their squadron. It had been hit just as "Bombs away" had been called, and witnesses had seen it smoking as it descended while still apparently under control. Later, it was learned that all the crew had been captured near Tittmoning, in Bavaria. One of the crew, Rubin F. Harkey, had been shot and killed by German soldiers. The rest were prisoners of war.[7]

The other missing plane, *Red N, Naughty Nan*, of the 761st squadron, had been hit after the bombs had been released. After the war, pilot Bill Kristen told the unit historian what occurred:

> On the rally we were at low altitude so we started a left turn, about a forty to forty-five degree bank. I noticed there were "sticks of four" bursting to the left of me all the time and they kept "walking in" so I slid out, sure enough they went in between me and the lead. I slid back in and picked up one in the side of the bomb bay. It went through the number one and two main tanks, took the life rafts with it, and turned us over in the formation—we recovered. I left the formation. . . . I think we feathered one engine at that time and then decided that we didn't have enough fuel to get back to Italy so we decided to go to southern France. Well, about halfway across Switzerland, two Morane Saulniers (Swiss fighters) . . . picked us up. Wilkey, our tail gunner, said: "Willie, he blinking his flashlight." We had already dropped our guns and everything overboard. Then he led us down into the 2,000 foot strip at Dubendorf.

Kristen later escaped and rejoined the 460th in Italy.[8]

There were injured crewmen after this mission, and one aircraft of the 760th squadron was hit particularly hard. Each squadron in the 460th had different identifying colors—red, white, blue, or yellow. For the 760th, the engine nacelles were blue, and a large letter in blue on the rear fuselage identified individual aircraft. *Blue M for Mike,* flown by the Ray Wells crew, had been savaged in the raid. The left elevator had been nearly blown away, and the aircraft had more than two hundred holes throughout it. As the Darden crew climbed down from their Liberator, they saw an ambulance parked by *Blue M for Mike.* Lamar and the others walked over, carrying their kitbags and parachutes. They knew it was the first mission for the Wells crew.

Lamar watched, as crewmen and medics gently, tenderly almost, passed the limp body of the tail gunner through the side gunner's window of the airplane. The gunners of his own crew recognized Stanley Mayo, whom they had just met in the enlisted men's mess. For several minutes, out of respect for Mayo and out of a realization of their own mortality, they stood silently as the body of the young airman was wrapped in a blanket and loaded aboard the olive green ambulance.[9]

They received double credit for the mission. But silently, Lamar wondered if any of them could survive fifty missions. He was profoundly touched by this first sight of the dead of war.

He did not have long to think about it. Two days later, September 24, they were sent to bomb the west marshaling yards in Salonika, Greece.

Once more, the group left Spinazzola with thirty-one aircraft, but three returned early for a variety of mechanical ailments. No fighter escort for this mission, and the only opposition was expected to be light flak, which fighters could not quell. The bombers began their run at 23,400 feet.

But the Germans apparently had moved in many of their railroad flak guns, mounted on train cars which could easily be shifted for maximum defense of a variety of locations. So once more, the flak was intense, accurate, and heavy. Lamar watched as the black, lethal clouds began to fill the sky before them, and once more felt the shock waves of exploding ordnance. He held on as the Liberator jerked and bucked in the turbulence. Ahead of them flew many more bombers from other bomb groups, all close together in a seamless stream of Allied air strength.

Darden was at the controls, and Lamar was watching the planes around them as well as silently noting the uncountable number of flak bursts. Then, a plane from another group just ahead and to the left of the Darden ship was hit. The 88-mm antiaircraft shell must have struck the main fuel tanks or the bombs themselves, because in an instant, the aircraft was transformed into a giant ball of flame. Only the wing tips and the double tail were visible beyond the fireball, and as Lamar watched in silent horror, the wings slowly buckled as the searing heat burned through the main spar. The entire plane, now only a molten amalgam of steel, aluminum, and human flesh, plunged to earth like an unholy comet.

Lamar was stunned. He knew that ten families would be getting telegrams they all hoped would never come, and that ten young men would never again hug their loved ones or smile in joy or cry in sorrow or love or laugh or simply live their lives in quiet anonymity or public approbation.

The group received single credit for the Salonika strike, but for Lamar it was one of the most emotionally challenging missions he flew. For days, he was haunted by the image of the doomed bomber. He wondered whether the crew had experienced pain or terror in the seconds before they were embraced by eternity, whether death had been quick or, in the manner of someone in a car wreck in which seconds seems to last minutes, had been agonizingly slow. At one point, Lamar was unsure that he could continue flying combat, and he worried that his preoccupation might put the crew—and other crews—in danger.[10]

Chapter 10

It's Not All Combat . . .
October–November 1944

The Darden crew had started flying their combat missions in the number seven position, often called "tail-end Charlie," at the extreme back end of their box. They flew about as close to the other aircraft as they had practiced back in the States. No one had criticized their formation flying, and they had been moved farther up in the formation to where they were generally flying in the number three position on the left wing of the lead aircraft, so they assumed their formation flying was satisfactory. However, they were somewhat disgusted when early one morning Corporal Cutler came by their tent just as they were preparing for a lot of work in connection with the building of their stone house.

Cutler looked uncomfortable as he delivered the news. They were scheduled for a practice formation at 1030; be sure to be on time, because Major Mason was going to be personally leading the formation. More close order drill.

Lamar turned to Darden. "Darden, I don't know about you, but I am getting mighty tired of this practice formation bit. If we don't know how to fly formation by now, we are never going to learn. Let's fly so close to Major Mason today that he will be afraid to fly in the same formation with us again."

Darden grinned. "Okay, Partner. We can do that, for sure."

Airborne, Darden and Lamar eased their heavy bomber alongside the left wing of the lead bird flown by Maj. Keith Mason, the 760th Operations Officer. Over the radio came the call to "Close it up, close it up. Keep it tight." They grinned at each other, and finessed the cumbersome 24's right wing to within ten feet of the fuselage of Mason's Liberator. They were not flying high enough to require oxygen masks, so Lamar could easily see the expression on Mason's face. Lamar remembered he usually had a smiling face, but today he was not smiling.

They saw the pilot look over his left shoulder, and continue to do so for the next two and a half hours as they made large, ungainly turns in the bright blue air over southern Italy. They chuckled and snickered in gleeful appreciation of his discomfort at always finding them glued to the same hair-raising distance. Eventually, the formation spread out to land back at base, and the two lieutenants anticipated the call at debriefing for more air between the aircraft.

But for several days, Lamar heard nothing from Mason. Finally, he asked Darden if he had heard anything from the ops officer about what they considered the foolishly close formation flying.

Darden shook his head. "Not really. I did see him over at the Panther's Lair the other evening and he said to me, 'Do you fellows like to fly that number three position?' I told him as far as I was concerned it was all right with me. He said, 'Fine, we will leave you there, you are the only crew that can fly it right and we will just leave you there.'" Lamar was deeply disappointed. Fortunately, that was the last practice formation he and Darden were to fly. They were given other, more enjoyable, flying jobs.[1]

For a week and a half after the Salonika mission, the 460th Bomb group had a bit of respite. Weather and other factors kept the heavy Liberators on the ground for the most part. The Darden crew picked up some new flying duties, tasks which built up their flying time without exposing them to the hazards of combat. Presumably, every hour in the Libs increased their proficiency, their familiarity with the myriad systems of the complex airplane, and ramped up their odds of survival.

It was a good theory.

Darden and the crew were assigned to test-hop arriving replacement aircraft. This was not bad duty. Since the airplanes had essentially been test-flown for many hours from the U.S. across the Atlantic and North Africa before arriving in Italy, it was largely a pro forma task. Each system was tested, the engine performance noted and recorded, and the suitability for combat judged. Minor discrepancies were listed on the Form 1-A. All in all, routine work but enjoyable. No mission credit, but they were never shot at, either.

A more enjoyable new duty to which they were assigned was the weekly "bus run" from Spinazzola to Parmiglianno, a British-run airstrip near Naples. As crews completed twenty-five missions—halfway point of their tour—they were sent on R & R (rest and recuperation leave) to a camp on the Isle of Capri, in the Bay of Naples on the Tyrrhenian coast.

The area was a longtime tourist oasis, set on the sparkling Tyrrhenian Sea, famous for its deep blue color and warm waters in the summer. The white walls of the small towns up and down the coast were brilliant in their intensity, contrasting with the emerald foliage and rocky escarpments. Rising above everything was the towering Mount Vesuvius, a dramatic backdrop to the beckoning scene.

For centuries, even millennia, the area had been a favorite of the mighty and the humble alike. The Roman emperors Augustus and Tiberius had palaces built on Capri, and it was by common assent the home of the Sirens of Greek mythology, who tempted Ulysses and his crew. A rugged rock face still holds the Phoenician Steps, carved by the Greeks, that connect the Marina Grande to Anacapri, and a picturesque, large castle has been called Barbarossa Castle since the Turkish pirate set fire to it in 1535.

Now, it was a place for American bomber crews to get away from the stress and terror of combat, to relax, to stroll around the small towns, sprawl on the beaches, explore the caves and grottos that dotted the rocky coastline. Lamar understood the need for it, after the horrific explosion of the bomber just ahead of him, but for now, he became the bus driver for those going on R & R. Each week, a lucky crew who had finished twenty-five missions was loaded aboard in Spinazzola—the gunners and bombardier from the Darden crew excused from the flight—and flown to Parmiglianno, to Naples by truck, and from there transported by boat across the bay to Capri.

Darden, Lamar, and the skeleton crew waited in Naples while a boat took the crew out to Capri and returned with the crew that had just completed their rest tour. Those who had been to Capri were easy to spot: virtually every flier on leave there sported a tiny silver bell hanging from the collar hook of his leather flying jacket, a replica of the bells of San Michele, reputed to be good luck. Many returned with handmade leather squadron patches or paintings of their aircraft on the backs of the jackets. The souvenirs of war provided local artisans with a lively trade.[2]

On this day, 10 October, they were taking a crew that had flown several missions but not the usual twenty-five. The story was that the pilot, a 1st lieutenant, was exhibiting signs of what then was called combat fatigue. In an effort to restore him, the crew was going on rest leave early. Lamar empathized with the pilot.

The assembled crew reported to the war-weary Liberator "bus" in their best dress uniforms, silver wings above a line of colorful ribbons. They were happy, a bit self-conscious, at times giddy and then abashedly low-key. They knew that they were getting this break early, and they had mixed feelings about it. After pre-flighting the old bird, Darden and Lamar invited the passenger crew to sit in the radio room and the waist while they climbed into the cockpit.

It was one of those perfect autumn days in the Mediterranean, a high blue sky holding a bright sun that warmed the heart equally with the earth. The good spirits of the R & R crew were contagious, and Darden and Lamar grinned at each other as they went through the checklists, taxied out to the metal-planked runway, and lifted off easily. The combined weight of the additional ten men did not approach the gross weight of the bombs, fuel, guns, and ammunition that had to be wrestled into the blue for each mission. Today, the old Liberator was almost nimble, effortlessly rising through the chill air and turning quickly for the west coast. It was the kind of day that brings out exuberance in fliers, a time to express their exhilaration at being alive and blessed with the gift of wings. Flying in formation at twenty thousand feet is a job, a dirty and dangerous job that must be done with precision and timing and a certain amount of luck and a maximum amount of skill. There is never the opportunity to see much of the landscape, or to appreciate cloud formations or a glorious sunrise or a brilliant, azure sea. But today, on a crew-ferrying flight, they could fly low. They could swing inland or cruise through valleys or skim the waves or do any of the other thousand things that peacetime pilots can do in the wonder and joy of finding themselves aloft.

They flew low, often below villages that were perched on the sides of the Apennines mountains. Lamar could see villagers—children, probably—wave as the big, olive-drab bomber thundered past at eye level. They arrived at the coast and turned north. Just to the west, off the tip of Point Campanella, was the Isle of Capri. Point Campanella jutted from the Italian mainland and formed the southern rim of the Bay of Naples, and just to the east they could see Salerno, where the first wave of Allied troops had waded ashore in the bloody invasion of September 1943. The Germans had known the time and place, and had sited machine guns and artillery to greet the landing craft. Despite the slaughter, Allies had entered Naples on 1 October.

Lamar thought of the terrible sacrifices and horrific loss of life that had occurred barely a year earlier. Despite the dangers that accompanied the job of piloting a bomber, he was glad once again that he had chosen to enter aviation.

A slight dip in the ridge that marked Point Campanella drew the bomber like a moth to flame, and Darden pointed the Lib toward the depression. They skimmed the cut by only a few feet—Darden was still feeling exuberant. Lamar looked at the earth rushing by on both sides, shook his head, and grinned at Darden. He too was feeling a kind of immortality this day. They popped into the air over the Bay of Naples and circled to approach the airfield at Parmiglianno.

The airstrip had been in use before the Allied invasion. It had a single, short macadam runway which had been extended a few hundred feet by the use of Marston mats. Destroyed hangars from pre-invasion bombings lent it an air of decrepitude. It wasn't much of an airfield, really, but it served for lightly loaded aircraft on bus runs. Still, Lamar had never particularly liked it. There was no room for error of any sort.

They contacted the tower and a distinctly British voice directed them to enter the traffic pattern for the east runway. This brought them over some high ground, and Lamar involuntarily craned his neck to see the earth below. The Liberator, with Darden at the controls, crossed over the approach end of the runway high and slightly fast, it seemed to Lamar. The bomber landed hard on the paved runway, and the Lib raced down the strip at an alarming rate. Both Darden and Lamar stood on the brakes, but they quickly overheated and faded. The plane entered the steel plank extension of the runway, still going far too fast to stop by the end. Lamar looked ahead and saw the burned-out shell of an airplane that had slammed into a stone wall beyond the limits of the runway, and realized they were about to do the same thing.

But, as they left the end of the steel mat runway, the nose wheel collapsed. The pilots felt the jolt as the nose of the bomber dropped and began to plow the earth. Sometimes small disasters prevent larger ones. Such was this case. The increased friction and drag of the aircraft nose converted to a plow succeeded in stopping the Liberator short of the stone wall that had been the demise of another warplane. Even as it slowed, Lamar was throwing electrical switches off and shutting down the fuel system to prevent a possible explosion and fire.

When the groaning, protesting troop carrier née bomber finally stopped, the silence in the plane was nearly total. It didn't last long, however, because Lamar was unbuckled and out of his seat in about one heartbeat. He twisted out of the right seat, jumped through the cockpit doorway into the engineer's cozy space and hence into the radio room, preparing to exit through the overhead hatch there. As he pushed open the small metal door into the radio room, he came face to face with some of the crew headed to rest camp. They were standing around the tiny quarters, and the pilot was looking overhead at the hatch.

"If you don't want to get out of here, get the hell out of the road and let someone out who does!" Lamar was furious at the benign acceptance of the mishap; he recognized that the bomber might still become a funeral pyre for them all. He undogged the hatch and climbed out, followed quickly by the rest. He ran along the top of the fuselage toward the nose turret and jumped. He looked back to see the rest of the flight crew and R & R crew following. As they exited, a crash truck came skidding to a halt beside the damaged bomber.

Lamar, somewhat in shock by what had happened, walked slowly to the rear of the plane. He saw the deep furrow plowed by the heavy nose, and the twin ridges of soft earth that had been thrown up on both sides of the ditch. He stood in the furrow and extended his arms horizontally. The tops of the ridges came just below his outstretched arms.

The men who were assembled around the disabled plane looked up as the steady roar of another four-engined bomber split the silence. A B-24 was replicating the flight pattern of the Darden "bus," and they watched in amazement as it too hit the runway at a speed that was far too fast. The pilots of this second bomber saw—too late—what had happened to Darden and Lamar's craft, and the men on the ground heard the anguished scream of the brakes as they sought in vain to slow the ship before they too ran out of runway. Thinking they might be able to avert catastrophe by turning off the runway onto a taxiway, the pilots miscalculated their speed, and the Liberator slid sideways. Unable to withstand the lateral force, both main landing gear collapsed, leaving the bomber on the pavement resting on the underside of the fuselage.

There were now two crews, still dazed and not quite comprehending what had happened, standing around two wrecked aircraft. Crewmen of the second bomber were in their best uniforms. They had just completed their tour of missions and had expected to head home without delay. They were clearly upset by what they now expected would slow their rotation to the States.

As the young airmen gaped across the runway at each other, the growl of yet another set of radial engines drew their attention skyward. A C-47 Dakota transport was also going to land at Parmiglianno, but this aircraft was landing in the opposite direction.

In a flash, they understood. They had been directed to land downwind! Normally planes take off and land into the wind, which both increases lift and slows the ground speed. If an airplane normally lands in calm wind at 120 mph, by landing into a 20 mph wind it effectively slows the speed to 100. Landing downwind in that case would mean a ground speed of 140, which is evidently what happened to Darden and Lamar, as well as the second B-24. They looked around, but could see no sign of a wind sock.

The pilots rode the crash truck back to the control building and climbed the outside staircase to have a chat with the controllers. They were four very unhappy fliers.

"Well, if you did not want to land in that direction, why did you?" The British controller looked at them in astonishment.[3]

The next time they landed at Parmiglianno, Lamar noted that a new wind sock fluttered in a position easily seen from the control tower as well as by pilots overhead.

Their "bus" was obviously not flyable in the near future—as it turned out, it apparently never flew again—and the skeleton crew thought they might have a day or two to explore Naples. But the group had flown a mission that day to the Piave-Susegan highway bridge, and there they had encountered fierce antiaircraft resistance. Two bombers were lost, with the crews bailing out, and fifteen suffered flak damage. Several crewmen had been wounded. Darden received a call that his crew was listed for a mission the next day, and that they would be picked up that evening at Parmiglianno and returned to Spinazzola.

They expected at the least a royal chewing out and a mountain of paperwork over the damaged Liberator. But there was a war on, bombers were expendable, and it had been seen as war-weary and a pain to keep flying. No one was happier than the ground crew chief when he learned of the accident. Nothing was ever said to either pilot about the loss of the "bus."

October was a time of administrative change. Two weeks after the Darden crew arrived in Spinazzola, the group received a new commander, a West Point graduate in his mid-thirties. Col. John M. Price was a bull of a man, a former All-American tackle on the 1930 team and the '31 team captain. Since his commission twelve years earlier, Price had graduated from pilot training at Kelly Field, served three years in the Canal Zone, and been a flying instructor and head of a flying training station. He was a no-nonsense officer, but he was considered absolutely fair. Lamar later would learn just how fair his commander was when it came to flying personnel.[4]

Winter was fast approaching. The combination of wet, cold weather and the hardpan below the few inches of earth in Tufa Town proved a winning combination for igniting in Darden, Lamar, Craig, and Reynolds the fires of desire for better quarters. The hardpan prevented stakes securing their tent to be driven very deep, with the result that several times in the few weeks they had been at Spinazzola they woke in the middle of the night—sometimes in the short night before a raid—to find their tent had collapsed around them in a downpour. This meant a couple of hours of miserably trying to erect the tent once more, in the dark and soaked to the skin, with inadequate tools and while standing ankle deep in mud. They were more than happy to contribute up to fifty dollars each and hire a local contractor to build a rather comfortable hut they would call "Casa Mañana"—House of Tomorrow.

When the contractor—a well-known local man dubbed "Humbliago" (this might have been a play on Umbriago, Jimmy Durante's mythical sidekick about whom he sang)—agreed to build a house if the Americans provided the material, the four young men traced in the earth the layout of their dream home, in full scale *in situ*.

They borrowed a six by six truck, with GI driver, to haul the tufa stone from a nearby quarry, and scrounged the executive officer's jeep and driver to pull a trailer filled with sand from another local quarry. They found a truck driver who had liberated some four by six timbers from somewhere along his regular run to Bari. The contractor had a hatchet and rusty saw for shaping the soft stone, a hoe for mixing the concrete, plus a plumb bob, pick, shovel, and trowel. With three assistants, he set about constructing Casa. Things went fairly steadily, but it took four attempts at constructing the fireplace before the Americans accepted it as anything that looked like fireplaces with which they were familiar.[5]

In a letter to his sister Thelma on 31 October 1944, Lamar described the house and its progress: "We have our house almost built now. The Italians still have to finish the plastering and put in the tile floor. Also put in the doors and windows and we will be ready to move in. Shouldn't take more than four or five days. It may not have all the modern conveniences but it sure as h___ will beat a tent."[6]

Included in the letter was a sketch of the exterior with the notation "Red tile roof and white stone walls," and a floor plan that revealed a living room, closet, and wash room. A single door and four windows were noted, as was a fireplace.

In a 4 November letter to his sister Mildred and her husband, Norman, the strain of flying combat is evident, despite Lamar's attempts to ignore the daily grind. As he closes the three-page letter, he admits

> I'm rather tired tonight. Flying over here gets rather tiresome. Darden and I used to fuss over who got to fly. Now we fuss over who gets out of flying. We settle it by taking 15 minute turns. So now we keep one eye on the clock to see when our fifteen minutes is up then after fifteen minutes we reach over and slap the other to wake him up.[7]

Neither regulations nor Lamar's quiet and protective temperament would allow him to describe the hell that some of the missions had become.

But the missions continued.

Chapter 11

Mission after Mission after . . .

"It was bad, Skippy. I can't get the sight of it out of my head." Bernie Sturtz, the little tail gunner for the Darden crew, always had an unobstructed view of where the bomber had been. He was often kidded about going into battle backwards: "You always see where we've been, but you never know where we're going," Lamar teased. "Do you back up to the pay window, too, Bernie?" On this mission, however, there had been little levity.

Lamar and Sturtz were walking slowly around the wind-swept perimeter of the base at Spinazzola, collars of their leather jackets pulled up around their ears. Lamar regretted that he had not thrown on his heavy wool overcoat, but it hadn't seemed that cold when they started out, and Sturtz seemed anxious to talk. Three hours earlier, they had returned from a long and rough mission to bomb railroad switchyards at Rosenheim, Germany. En route to the target, while still over the Adriatic, two Liberators flying just behind the Darden crew collided.

One of the bombers, possibly trying to lose some airspeed to maintain position in the cramped combat box, had raised its nose. Varying the pitch attitude of an aircraft is a common and accepted way to control airspeed: slowly raising the nose causes the underside of the wings to offer more drag as it resists the wind; lowering the nose slightly increases the airspeed. In formation flying, however, that almost always was a recipe for disaster, so pilots of the heavy bombers constantly jockeyed with the throttles.

On this mission, one of the bombers had climbed into the belly of a bomber slightly ahead and above, and the propellers of the right engines of the top bomber had sliced the lower plane in two just behind the wings. Sturtz, in his lonely, rearward-facing battle station, had seen the entire incident. The higher, lead plane and the lower one had both nosed up about forty-five degrees after the collision, and then the entire back half of the lower Liberator suddenly fell away.

"Three guys bailed out of the first Lib, Skippy, but there wasn't no way to get out of that second one. I saw a couple of planes suddenly stand on one wing to get out of the way, there was junk all over the sky. Then I watched as this half airplane, the front half, headed straight down."

Lamar listened as the sergeant, struggling against his emotions, sucked in the raw October air. He didn't feel like a counselor, or even an officer at that moment. He and Sturtz were friends, had been since combat crew training in Pueblo. Lamar knew that witnessing the deaths of other airmen was a powerful, lonely, and soul-searching event. He felt helpless, not knowing what to say. But he sensed that sometimes the best thing was just to listen, and so he did. Lamar didn't tell the gunner that the three men who had bailed out of the top aircraft had not been found, that they were probably dead from exposure in the cold sea. For all combat fliers, seeing the white blossoms of parachuting crewmen was hope, visual proof that survival was possible. It would do no good to puncture that balloon.

"That Lib went straight down, straight down, all four engines still running but they were just getting those poor bastards down quicker. It hit the sea dead vertical, and I can see it yet. Those four props sent out eddies, four of them, like if you'd thrown four rocks at once into a pond. The waves from all four engines collided with each other, started canceling each other out, and then the next sea wave rolled through and then . . . then there was nothing. Like it had never been there. Just the sea rolling over their graves."[1]

There was nothing more to say. The two friends, sergeant and lieutenant, walked slowly against the wind, hands in their pockets, each lost in thought. They came to a point where the enlisted gunner would head one direction to his tent, and the pilot would head off to his hut on the other end of the quarters area. Lamar put his hand on Sturtz's shoulder and squeezed. Neither said good-bye.

Bombing missions out of southern Italy were not the scenes Lamar and his flying buddies had earlier viewed in newsreel clips in theaters around the country. Nearly everything they had seen in those black-and-white, grainy strips had been shot in England, where the 8th Army Air Force was pounding Germany from bases across the island nation. There, crews trooped out to waiting B-17s and '24s, ran a gauntlet of fighters and flak, and returned to base near a small village, where they could relax over a pint in the local public house. Here, in Spinazzola, Lamar and the crew seldom left the base, and never to drink or get an authentic Italian dinner in some picturesque inn. They were advised that even a year after the Allied invasion, fascist sympathizers were still abundant and would be a threat to individual fliers wandering around.

So that left flying missions, occasional test-hops of new aircraft, and the weekly "bus run" to Naples. The men were tired, and the strain of combat was beginning to show for most of them.

October had not been a good month. Two days after the accident at Naples the Darden crew was among 34 Liberators of the 460th that took off from Spinazzola to bomb the Bologna ammunition dump. They faced fierce antiaircraft fire over the target and again at the rally point near the coast, and twenty-one bombers suffered flak damage. But strangely, despite what must have been a routine arming of the bombers, thirteen Libs experienced technical difficulties: bombs simply refused to drop. One of the thirteen was that of Darden and Lamar.

The bombs that day were of the 100-pound fragmentation type. Two were mounted on one bomb shackle with a loop of cable. When Reynolds toggled the bomb release over the ammo dump that was the target, only the top bombs in each shackle released. The cable held the lower bombs fast, and blocked the upper bombs from going down. This prevented most of the released (and armed) explosives from dropping. The result was a bomb bay full of live armament, scattered in disarray in the belly of the bomber.

They had made the bomb run from north to south, and the delay in releasing the bombs meant they now were over their own ground troops, which were arrayed just south of Bologna. Darden and Lamar knew immediately that something was wrong when they didn't experience the sudden climb of the bomber after Reynolds called "Bombs away!"

"Skippy, I'm going to go back and see what the heck just happened," Reynolds said over the intercom only seconds later. Darden always monitored frequencies among aircraft and base, while Lamar kept his headset and throat microphone set to crew intercom.

"Let me know what you find out," Lamar said. Two minutes later Reynolds reported.

"It's a mess, Skippy. Damn bombs everywhere, they didn't all release. I'm going to need some help pushing them out of here."

The pilots nosed the plane out toward Ravenna and the Adriatic, while two gunners joined Reynolds on the narrow catwalk in the bomb bay. They wrestled each bomb out of the pile of released and partially shackled explosives and shoved them out the bay to drop into the sea far below them. It was nerve-racking and backbreaking labor, leaving the men gasping as they struggled in the thin, air sucking oxygen from the walk-around bottles they tucked into their Mae Wests.

Six hours and forty minutes after taking off, the weary crew landed at Spinazzola.[2]

On 23 October, three days after the mission that so upset Sturtz when he witnessed the fatal mid-air collision, they were back in the air to bomb the diesel engine factory at Augsburg, Germany. It was one of the largest efforts of the 460th since Lamar and the crew had joined the group five weeks earlier. Forty-six

Liberators took off at 0715, formed up, and linked up with other groups to head north. They were met by P-38s four hours later, and the twin-engine fighters furnished cover over the target and during withdrawal.

As at most targets of industrial and military importance inside Germany, the flak was heavy, the black bursts presenting a field of death through which the bombers stubbornly advanced, a phalanx that could not vary its path until the bombs had been released. Each member of each crew silently prayed, many going through a ritual that they hoped would bring them through safely. They touched religious medals, or glanced at a photo of a girlfriend or wife taped near their battle station. They muttered mantras—"oh god, oh god, oh god . . ." silently, or sometimes not so silently. They crossed themselves, or touched the pocket of their flight suit where they had tucked a small Bible. They brushed fingers over their wrists, to feel the silver identification bracelets given them by loved ones.

And then, they heard the magic words "Bombs away!" They rejoiced as they felt the upward surge of the bomber, and hundreds of voices joined an aerial choir that sang the same tune. And then the familiar shibboleth: "We finished our job for Uncle Sam, now we're flying for us."

The bombers turned for the rally point, eager to get away from the rings of antiaircraft fire that always seemed to target each Liberator individually.

The strike against Augsburg was one of the longest flown by the Darden crew, eight hours fifty minutes. Six aircraft, low on fuel, were forced to land at friendly bases north of Spinazzola, but none were lost to flak or fighters. They received double credit for the mission because of the heavy opposition and long flight.

And still there were the aborted missions, flights that drained the men of all emotion but for which they received no credit toward their tours. On 29 October, they were launched after the usual early wakeup, tense breakfast, and businesslike briefing. They went through the process of donning their flight gear, checking out the airplane, sweating out the signal flares, bracing for the always unnerving takeoff with full bomb load and fuel, the forming up, and for a couple of hours they had fought to stay in position in their combat box. Then they received the code word to return. The mission was canceled. Lamar recorded flight time of four hours ten minutes.

The one bright spot, if so small a lessening of darkness could be called bright, was the refreshment tent on the flight line that awaited crews when they landed. Here, for a few minutes before heading to interrogation, crews could grab a cup of hot coffee and a doughnut and visit with their crew, or the crews of other bombers, and shake their heads over a loss or complain bitterly about unforeseen resistance or miserable weather. They could laugh grimly, or celebrate giddily when a mission proved to be a milk run after they expected the worst. A photo taken after an unidentified mission shows a crowd of airmen, standing on steel planking outside two large open tents, still in parachute harnesses and flight suits. Darden, wearing his overseas cap, and Lamar, wearing a crusher hat, stand with a third man, all of them with their hands in their pockets. It is impossible not to read in their casual stance their relief at finishing another one. The photo of course is silent, and what they are saying is gone forever. But the picture needs no words. There is joy in simply still being alive.[3]

November arrived on a chill wind. On the second and third, the Darden skeleton crew—usually absent the bombardier and gunners—test-hopped newly arrived aircraft, replacements for the Liberators that were lost or shot up or simply worn out with the grind of missions. On the fourth, they set out to bomb the benzol plant at Linz, Austria. The weather was awful, and the group ducked in and out of clouds for virtually the entire haul. Over the target, a solid layer of undercast obscured the plant, but they were able to bomb by means of a new technique and device called PFF, a kind of radar coupled with terrain-reading ability. Because of the severe weather, the crews received double credit for the seven hour, forty-five minute mission.

The following day, they set out to bomb troop concentrations at Podgorica, Yugoslavia, east across the Adriatic. It was a small mission in terms of the number of bombers deployed: seven launched, and all returned. An additional thirty-one bombers headed for the Florisdorf oil refinery near Vienna. One suffered flak damage then was attacked by German fighters, and it crash-landed in Yugoslavia. Partisans picked up the crew, and a week later they were back in Italy.

Yugoslavia represented a different kind of war for the fliers of the 460th. The country, a kingdom on the east coast of the Adriatic across from Italy, had been invaded by Germans and Italians in April 1941. Nearly immediately, several groups of irregulars had arisen, some to collaborate with the occupiers, others to resist and fight.

The politics of the region were less important to the airmen than the very real consequences to them should they have to bail out over the country. One group, the Ustashi, were pro-Nazi and utterly ruthless to downed Allied airmen, they were told. Combat crews being briefed before a mission over Yugoslavia were advised by intelligence officers: "Men, if you are surrounded by Ustashi with rifles and machine guns and you have only your .45, might as well shoot it out. They are going to kill you anyway, and turn in your body for a reward."

Word on the two remaining groups—the Partisans and the Chetniks—was largely the result of fierce lobbying by the leaders. The largely pro-Communist Partisans, led by Josip Broz Tito, gained the support of the Allies at the November/December 1943 Tehran Conference, a decision that meant they would be given considerable materiel and weapons for the course of the conflict. The Chetniks, led by Draza Mihailovich, were accused of collaborating with the

Germans, and there were sometimes pitched battles between the two guerilla groups. The occupying Axis troops, meanwhile, instituted draconian measures to stamp out the fires of resistance. It was announced that for each German soldier killed in Yugoslavia, 100 civilians would be executed; for each soldier wounded, 50 would be killed. After the war, some accounts indicated that the Chetniks—loyal to King Peter II—had been as anti-German as the Partisans, but preferred attacks on German rail centers and similar targets far from their home territory so that local retribution would be less likely. Partisan guerillas were not popular with local villagers, because retaliation for Partisan raids fell on them. And it was Mihailovich who arranged for the mass evacuation of more than five hundred downed Allied fliers in late 1944, the largest such effort during the war. Word was not leaked to airbases, however, because leaders did not want to jeopardize possible future rescues.[4]

Regardless of the ultimate truth about the charges and countercharges that flew back and forth between the resistance fighters, the result for Allied fliers was this advice: shoot it out with the Ustashi. Chetniks would probably take your boots, and may or may not turn you over to the Germans. Partisans would help you escape. In fact, so strong was the belief that Partisans were the main source of Allied help that barrels were set up in the mess halls of airbases in Italy. Crews that had finished their tours left uniforms and boots there, to be dropped to Partisans in Yugoslavia. Of course, no one told the fliers exactly how they were to distinguish one irregular soldier from another. And none asked.

Risks were something they accepted, and certainly the risks of dropping down among enraged civilians in Germany or Austria were probably higher than for Yugoslavia. It had been reported and confirmed that many downed fliers had been killed by civilians who considered the bomber crews murderers and terrorists as their bombs fell on nonmilitary population centers, whether by design or poor target identification.[5]

On 6 November, Lamar and the rest of the Darden crew suited up for Vienna. As they sat in the briefing room and the map was unveiled to display the red ribbon of the flight path that ended at the heavily defended Austrian city, there were groans from the assembled officers. This was a mission they dreaded. Vienna was the second most heavily defended of the Third Reich cities, second only to Berlin itself—"Big B" in bomber parlance—and the young fliers hated the trip. It usually meant a big effort, with hundreds of aircraft slotted to pound the target, and that meant a hazardous, close-formation echelon and fighting wake turbulence for hours. They had already seen their own ships collide in such formations, with the resulting empty chairs in the mess halls and the guards stationed at the doors of huts and tents. And that was the easy part. Then they had to mentally check out for several minutes as they flew through a blizzard of flak bursts, each man going someplace better than where they were at that moment, but still keenly aware that a single antiaircraft shell in their bomb bay meant instant oblivion for everyone in the bomber.

They were not disappointed. The seven-hour, twenty-minute round-trip flight was as bad as they thought, with pilots exhausted at the end by constantly fighting the heaving air and dodging rising and descending aircraft. When they arrived over Vienna, a low cloud layer obscured the target—the Vienna South Ordnance Depot—so they once more bombed by radar installed in the lead bomber. The good news was that while they could not see the target, antiaircraft gunners could not see them, either, and the usual solid layer of black flak was absent. All the aircraft returned, with no casualties or damage, and the crews still received double credit for the mission.[6]

On 8 November, the group was assembled for an awards ceremony. They were to receive the Distinguished Unit Citation, given to all members of the group for their collective superior work in dismantling Hitler's dream. The servicemen stood in rows in their best uniforms while Major General Nathan Twining, commander of the 15th Air Force, read the citation and attached a silk battle streamer to the unit colors. Thereafter, each member would wear on the right chest a blue ribbon in a gold metal frame, a group award given only in combat.[7]

Later that day, Lamar and the crew were assigned to test-hop a new Liberator, and while they were suiting up in the equipment shack Hank Alder began teasing Lamar.

"Skippy, I think you got the best go on the crew." The little ball-turret gunner's Tennessee drawl was distinctive and slow.

"What do you mean?" Lamar asked in his own distinctive deep bass. He was struggling into the electrically heated flight suit that was necessary now for all flights as winter approached.

"Well, I'm always workin', ever' mission. Always spinnin' that Sperry around, checkin' out the guns, hangin' out there with nothin' but glass between me and the ground." He had pulled on his electric flight suit, and was reaching into the open cubicle that bore his name for his harness and parachute. "And you? What's a CO-pilot do, anyway? I mean, that's not even a job. You don't see any CO-gunners, do you? Or CO-bombardiers?" Alder was shoving his flight helmet and oxygen mask into his kit bag, along with gloves and boots.

"Really, Skippy, I swear that all you do is ride along to get some more sleep and draw your flight pay, while all the rest of us are busy winnin' this war." With that, Alder grabbed one of Lamar's boots, which he had removed to pull on his flight suit, and tossed it into one of the highest open equipment bins. He ran out the door of the equipment shack, laughing.

Lamar grabbed his boot—it was not very high for a tall man—and hurriedly stuffed his remaining gear in his own kit bag. He headed for the door after Alder, in high spirits. Dashing through the door, he ran smack into Gen. Twining and Col. Price, who was showing the general around the Spinazzola air base. Mortified, Lamar snapped a quick salute, then marched away at double-time before the astonished senior officers could reprimand him. He caught up with Alder at the hardstand. The gunner had seen Lamar's clumsy exit, and was laughing hysterically.

"Laugh at an officer, Alder? I'll show you!" Lamar grabbed him around the neck, and they rolled to the pierced steel planking of the hardstand, where Lamar pretended to work him over. The rest of the crew chuckled at the sight. They all knew that the caste distinction between officers and enlisted men was artificial, and for a combat crew simply didn't exist when they were around their airplane. Such roughhousing was good for morale, and a good release for many of the tensions that were building with each mission.[8]

For the next few days, there was little flying as weather socked in the air base, or obscured targets across Europe. On 12 November, Lamar went to the Link trainer to practice instrument flying, and recorded one hour of simulated flight.

The next day, another test-hop, this time in an aircraft equipped with a new navigation system, called Loran—an acronym for long range navigation. The new system employed radio signals from two separated stations, with special equipment that measured the time differences in the two signals. This was then plotted on a chart, and a second set of signals from two more stations would pinpoint the position of the aircraft. This was a sophisticated system, and the next day, Mike Craig was sent to Bari, Italy, for training on the new equipment.[9]

On 15 November, Darden, Lamar, and the "bus run" crew flew to Naples once more with a crew headed to rest camp on the Isle of Capri. However, a high wind made unsafe the boat trip across to the island, so the returning crew was stuck on Capri for the night. The Darden crew at last got to spend a night in Naples, where they took in the sights and ate a leisurely dinner. The next day, they flew back to Spinazzola with the returning combat crew.

A long mission—the longest the Darden crew would fly—was scheduled for 17 November. The results were to prove significant to the crew for the 18 November mission.

On Friday, 17 November, the Darden crew climbed into an olive-drab Liberator, *Blue J for Jig*, an aircraft they had flown numerous times. It was a veteran plane, a J model equipped with a rotating nose turret. It was flown by several crews, mostly new or recent arrivals who did not yet merit an individual ship of their own. A previous crew, now long ago rotated home, had christened her *Bottoms Up*, and commissioned a squadron artist to paint a pig-tailed blonde, on her back with her rump saucily in the air, on the left nose of the bomber below the pilot's side window. The painting was only slightly risqué, since the young woman was wearing shorts and a blouse, unlike many of her sisters who flew naked into battle.[10] Forward of the iconic nose art was the standard white square with a snarling black panther, the 460th emblem which graced every aircraft in the group. As on all 760th bomb squadron airplanes, the nacelles of *Bottoms Up* were blue, as were the tips of the propellers, and the individual aircraft identifier—*J*—was also painted in blue. The twin tails were painted to clearly mark her as a member of the 460th: the top half of each vertical stabilizer was painted yellow around a large square of olive drab, indicating the 55th Bomb Wing; the lower halves were olive drab and featured a large yellow circle, marking the 460th Bomb Group. Each group of American bombers (or fighters) anywhere on the globe had its own unique paint scheme displayed on the tail, to assist fliers in identifying their organization while forming up in the air for a strike. Also painted on the tail was the army serial number: 42–51926.[11]

On this day, the mission was to the Blechammer south oil refinery, deep inside Germany, and *Bottoms Up* was filled to capacity with six thousand pounds of bombs and the maximum twenty-seven hundred gallons of fuel. Lamar, upon learning that the lead force was a particular bomb group, groaned.

"What's up, Partner?" Darden leaned over to Lamar during the briefing.

"Those guys always go too darn fast and don't conserve fuel. Happens every time they lead," Lamar said. "I don't like following them. Not that we have a choice."

Darden gave a philosophical shrug of his shoulders. "Nope. We don't."

Once more, gremlins struck at the bomb release mechanism. The bombs refused to drop over Blechammer, and the fully loaded *Bottoms Up* was falling behind the rest of the formation as they rallied for the return flight. Hurston Webb, the flight engineer, and some of the gunners climbed onto the narrow catwalk—they were getting used to this—and without oxygen masks began to pry the bomb release mechanism until all of the bombs at last fell through the open doors. Freed of the weight of three tons of bombs, once more the plane rose as though unchained from shackles and the pilots began to think they could pour the coals to the Liberator and catch up with the formation. For now, they were all alone and sitting ducks for any roaming German fighters.[12]

Those hopes quickly sank. Glancing behind them at the sight glasses that were the fuel gauges, two vertical tubes in the radio room on the forward bulkhead of the bomb bay, they knew that was impossible. They had left Spinazzola with twenty-seven hundred gallons of aviation gas. Now, only four hundred gallons were registering in the sight gauges.

This would mean fuel conservation, and subsequent low speeds, if they were going to get home at all. Reluctantly, Lamar carefully reduced the RPM of each engine as much as he dared, and pulled each mixture control back until that engine coughed. Then he pushed the lever forward a notch. The mixture control allowed the pilots to control the air-fuel mixture at various altitudes and temperatures. In older carburetor-equipped automobiles, with a constant pre-set mixture of air and fuel, the car would lose power as it ascended mountainous terrain, because the air became thinner while the fuel remained constant. In airplanes from the earliest days, pilots had been able to reduce the amount of fuel to keep the ratio constant with the decreasing air as they climbed through altitude.

With that done, he told the flight engineer to carefully monitor the temperature in each engine, as leaning the mixture could sometimes result in higher cylinder head temperatures. The temps appeared to be holding constant. Next, Lamar set the autopilot to gradually bring *Bottoms Up* down, at a very slow rate, so that when they arrived over Spinazzola they would be—theoretically, at least—at traffic pattern altitude and not have to waste fuel climbing or doing otherwise fruitless maneuvers.

The crew was aware of the predicament, but largely stayed off the intercom. There was very little to say. That ended when they reached the coast of the Adriatic. The Liberator was droning along at what seemed like a snail's pace, and the flight engineer was constantly checking the fuel gauges to report on their progress. It seemed a gamble to cross the open sea with so little fuel. None of them wanted to ditch a Liberator, notorious for breaking up, and no one wanted to bob around in life jackets or even the rafts during mid-November. Reynolds was particularly unhappy.

"Skippy, dammit! This is crazy. What are you guys thinking up there? Stay over land, for God's sake!"

"Reynolds, we're doing our job here. We need to get this bomber back if it's going to continue to do its job." Lamar was terse, but he was also aware of an unregistered reserve of 100 gallons of fuel. It was a gamble, but not a fool's choice. They headed across to Italy.

They reached the Italian coast, and soon saw an Allied base, which Reynolds, in the nose, quickly pointed out. When Lamar said he thought they could continue on to Spinazzola, Reynolds came unglued.

"This is idiocy!! We are passing up a perfectly good landing field, and for what?!" Reynolds was now in the radio room, staring at the two glass tubes, which by now registered nearly zero. "For Gawdsake, Lamar, land! You aren't going to make Spinazzola, we will all have to jump and this plane will be lost for good. What are you going to say to Col. Price then?"

Lamar felt a twinge of doubt, and looked behind him once more. There Reynolds pointed emphatically at the fuel gages. "Empty, Lamar. Dry! NO MORE FUEL!" Lamar turned back to the instrument panel and ignored the frantic bombardier.

Bottoms Up came through the final approach window at Spinazzola and landed without incident. They were the last plane to land, and Lamar entered nine hours flying time in the aircraft log. It gave four hours thirty minutes of first pilot time and four hours thirty minutes co-pilot time to each pilot. The crew quietly unloaded and threw their gear into a truck that drove out to pick them up. Lamar stayed behind while the bomber was refueled, curious about how close he had cut it. There were 35 gallons left in all tanks, enough for about ten minutes of flight.[13]

But now, if needed, *Bottoms Up* would be available for a mission the next day. She and the crew would have to be taken off the board if they had landed elsewhere, so Lamar was certain he had made the right decision. He did admit to himself that it was a bit closer than he would have wanted.

They missed the donut truck, the interrogation, the noisy group transportation back to quarters. But for Lamar and the boys of *Bottoms Up*, the rattle of the steel Marston mat runway had been all the welcome they needed.

That evening, they learned they were on for a mission the next morning, and they would be flying *Bottoms Up* once more. Mike Craig had returned from his Loran training, and upon learning the crew was on the fly board, went to ensure that he was listed as the navigator. He didn't want to miss another mission.

While he was at Bari being trained, Craig had received four packages from home. None of the other three in "Casa Mañana" had received any boxes, although a few letters had gotten to them that spoke of packages mailed. Now, Craig opened his goodies and passed around the homemade cookies. The crew was in high spirits, augmented by the treats from home, and Reynolds's resentment toward Lamar had disappeared as soon as they landed. With Craig's return, they were back to being the complete crew.

Tomorrow, they would fly their twenty-first credited mission. After today's marathon, it was sure to be easier. In spite of the long flight and the difficulties encountered, they did not get double credit for today's trip to Blechhammer. Of the last ten trips to a target, however, they had received double credit for all but three. Soon they could be going to the rest camp at Capri instead of just flying the air bus for other lucky crews.

Lee Lamar as an aviation cadet during basic flight training in 1943. He is on the wing of a Vultee BT-13 Valiant. (Lee Lamar collection. Used with permission.)

Newly-minted 2nd Lt. Lee Lamar in February, 1944, at completion of his flight training and commissioning as an officer in the Army Air Force. (Lee Lamar collection. Used with permission.)

(Opposite top) The officers of the Darden crew in front of their tent at Spinazzola, Italy, in late summer, 1944. Left to right: Lee Lamar, copilot; Don Reynolds, bombardier; Mike Craig, navigator; Randall Darden, pilot. At 23, Lamar was the oldest. (Lee Lamar collection. Used with permission.)

(Opposite bottom) Two Vultee BT-13 Valiants in formation. Known disparagingly by cadets as the Vultee Vibrator, the all-metal basic trainer was flown by Lee Lamar and thousands of other young men in the second phase of their flight regimen during World War II. The Navy designation was SNV. (Lee Lamar collection. Used with permission.)

(Above) An aviator in high-altitude gear. His outer clothing is sheepskin, with the wool side inward, and he is wearing a sheepskin helmet with radio headset, goggles, oxygen mask and walk-around oxygen bottle, necessary when bailing out at high altitudes. He is also equipped with a backpack parachute. (United States Army Air Force illustration.)

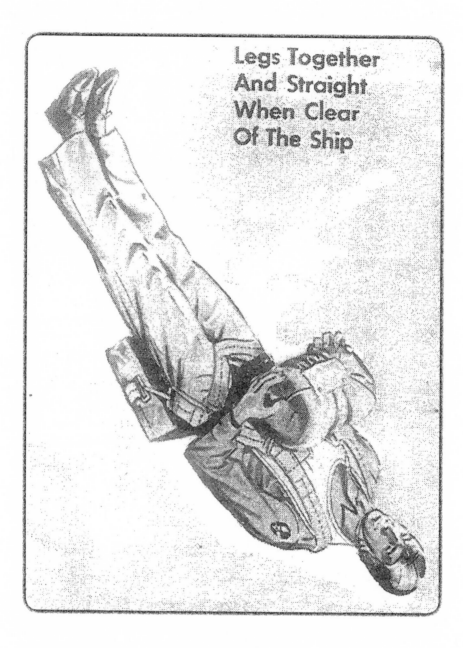

Legs Together
And Straight
When Clear
Of The Ship

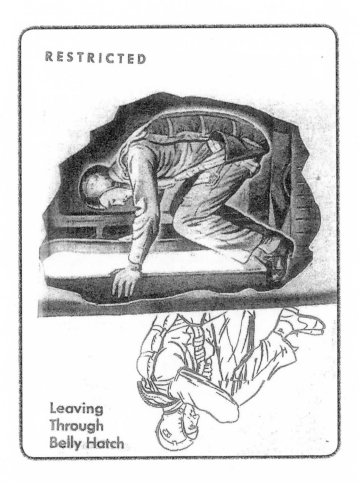

Leaving
Through
Belly Hatch

These illustrations from the Pilot's Manual for the B-24 Liberator indicate proper technique for bailing out from the rear hatch of the bomber. Lee had neither enough time nor altitude to conform to the book: he pulled his ripcord as soon as he jumped and hit the ground immediately after his canopy deployed. (United States Army Air Force illustration.)

Ploesti – "Flak" Romania

(Opposite top) *Bottoms Up* was graced with a painting of a provocatively posed young woman as well as the Black Panther of the 460th Bomb Group. An older bomber, it also wore the olive-drab paint commonly used before mid-1944, when it was decided that camouflage was no longer necessary for Allied aircraft. The pilot is believed to be Lt. Col. Harold C. Babb, group commander of the 460th for a time. (Lee Lamar collection. Used with permission.)

(Opposite bottom) The Darden crew following completion of Combat Crew Training. The bomber in this photo, taken in July, 1944, in Topeka, Kansas, is not *Bottoms Up*. Standing, left to right: Lee Lamar, copilot; Randall B. Darden, pilot; Wade Moore "Mike" Craig, Jr., navigator; Donald Reynolds, bombardier. Kneeling, left to right: Oren Bozarth, flight engineer; Henry L. Alder, ball-turret gunner; John Nordback, nose turret gunner; Joseph Betine, assistant engineer and waist gunner; Bernard Sturtz, tail gunner; and Swante Norlund, radio operator. Bozarth was injured in a shooting accident just days before the crew left for combat in Italy and did not deploy with the crew; Betine was ill on the mission of 18 November 1944 and was replaced by Mario Briganti. (Lee Lamar collection. Used with permission.)

(Above) B-24s of the 460th Bomb Group flying through flak over an enemy target. On the bomb run until bombs were released, the Liberators had to fly straight and level, and flak exacted a heavy toll. (Courtesy of Keith Mason. Used with permission.)

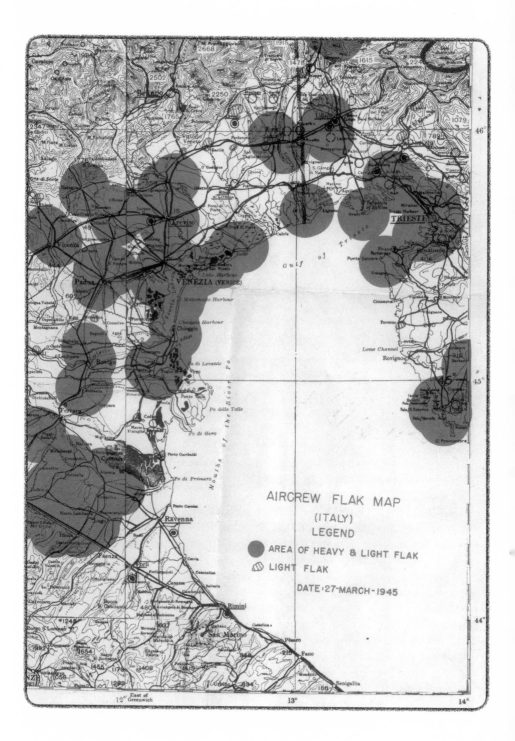

AIRCREW FLAK MAP
(ITALY)
LEGEND

● AREA OF HEAVY & LIGHT FLAK
◐ LIGHT FLAK

DATE: 27-MARCH-1945

(*Opposite*) This Aircrew Flak Map of northern Italy was carried by B-25 pilot Lt. John Morris. It depicts known German flak batteries, including those around Pula. Lamar's crew did not carry a flak map, reckoning that all of the major cities were ringed by anti-aircraft batteries, and knowing that the Germans had many mobile flak guns mounted on railroad cars. (Map courtesy of Terry V. Morris. Used with permission.)

(*Above*) This small watercolor painting of the last minutes of B-24J *Bottoms Up* depicts bursts of flak over Pula. Both left propellers of the bomber have been feathered, and the Liberator is clearly struggling. "Last Haul" was painted for Lee Lamar in Stalag Luft I by a fellow prisoner of war, Frank Hokr, who considered himself well-paid by the half chocolate bar offered by Lamar. While the painting depicts a silver-colored Liberator, *Bottoms Up* was an older bomber and was sprayed olive-drab. (Lee Lamar collection. Used with permission)

(Opposite) Photo from the original prisoner of war record of Lt. Lee Lamar, issued at the Dulag Luft at Frankfort-en-Main. Lamar and other prisoners were able to recover the documents after their German captors abandoned the camp near Barth to flee ahead of the advancing Russian army. (Lee Lamar collection. Used with permission.)

(Above) The first clue. This twisted and torn fragment of aluminum, clearly bearing instructions in English on starting an aircraft, was the first bit of *Bottoms Up* kicked up by archaeologist Luka Bekic in the fall of 2005. Bekic and his team uncovered more than 3000 pieces of Lamar's bomber, and they searched for more than a year to learn the fate of the crew. (Photo by Luka Bekic. Used with permission.)

(Opposite top) In Pula, archaeologist Luka Bekic examines a scale model of the B-24J *Bottoms Up*, a gift from Lee Lamar. Left to right: Lamar, Bekic, Ronald Wright, and the author. (Photo by Sharyl Wright. Used with permission.)

(Opposite bottom) Luka Bekic (left) shows the author a detail on one of the thousands of fragments he and his team from the Croatian Conservation Institute recovered from the crash site of *Bottoms Up*. Lee and Bonnie Lamar look on, both clearly moved by the collection of detritus that formerly had been Lee's bomber. (Photo by Sharyl Wright. Used with permission.)

(Above) Returned at last to the country where he was shot down and captured during World War II, Lee Lamar and his family pause on the stone pier at Rovinj, Croatia. Left to right: grandson Kraig Hufstedler, Lamar, wife Bonnie, son-in-law Kirt Hufstedler, granddaughter Katie Hufstedler, and daughter Kathy Hufstedler. (Photo by Ron Wright. Used with permission).

(Above) In Piazza San Marco, the central square of Venice, in August, 2007. Lee La-mar and the group accompanying him to Croatia stopped over in the Italian city before proceeding to the site of Lee's shoot-down and capture. Left to right: Sharyl Wright, Bonnie Lamar, Ronald Wright, Lee Lamar, and the author. (Photo by Jeanette Okerstrom. Used with permission.)

(Opposite top) Lee Lamar (fourth from left, front row) at the Croatian Air Force base near Pula, August, 2007. Behind him are Croatian fighter pilots; to his right are three Partisan veterans; to his left is the base commander, Maj. Stanko Hrzenjak. The com-mander asked that pilots not be identified. (Photo by Luka Bekic. Used with permission.)

(Opposite bottom) These reenactors, in a World War II Jeep in front of the Collings Foundation B-24J, dressed in authentic period flight gear as they prepared for the film-ing of a documentary on Lee Lamar's experiences as a bomber pilot and prisoner of war. (Author's photo.)

Lee Lamar and the author in July, 2007, in front of the Collings Foundation B-24J *Witchcraft*. The foundation generously offered to fly them in the last B-24J, from Fort Collins, Colorado, to Kansas City. It was a heady and emotional flight, the first time Lamar had been back in a B-24 since bailing out of *Bottoms Up* in 1944. (Author's photo.)

Chapter 12

18 November 1944

It was 3A.M., and the faithful Corporal Cutler was gentle but insistent as he shined his flashlight in Lee Lamar's eyes.

"Lt. Lamar, sir. Time. Breakfast at 3:45." He stood back, and when Lamar threw the blankets back and swung his feet onto the cold tile floor of Casa Mañana, he moved on to roust Craig and Reynolds. Darden was already sitting on the side of his bunk, rubbing his eyes and running his hands through his hair.

It was the 18th of November, the 1,904th day of the world war, and the 73rd day since the four officers of the just-completed tufa-stone house at Spinazzola had arrived in Italy. For Darden and Reynolds, today would be their twenty-second mission credit. For Lamar it would be his twenty-first. Craig had missed the Blechammer mission while undergoing training for Loran operation, and this would be his twenty-first also. Just twenty-nine more to go after this one.

Lamar scraped the blond stubble from his face. Shaving to go drop bombs from an unheated airplane from twenty thousand feet might have seemed an extravagant waste of energy to a casual observer, but the fliers had learned early on that rubber oxygen masks strapped tightly to their faces for six to eight hours would rub their faces raw if they didn't shave. Slowly, with little conversation, the young officers pulled on long johns, woolen shirts and trousers, and ankle-high boots. They grabbed jackets—most left the mild-weather leather A-2 jackets and opted for alpaca-lined service coats—jammed crushers or overseas hats on their heads and headed to the Panther's Lair for breakfast. Sleepy-eyed men shuffled into the mess hall in a variety of uniforms, the variety itself giving lie to the word "uniform," and stood in line for trays of eggs, bacon, toast, and coffee.

They took their time. Craig went back for more coffee, and Reynolds wanted more eggs. The mess hall was not full, but it seemed to exude good cheer as some of the flying men spoke loudly, or not at all, as was their wont. There were a few newbies, men for whom this mission would be their first, but for most the early rising and breakfast were now routine. It's what they did, these bomber boys, and in exchange for dropping bombs on people who would try to kill them, the army gave them dry quarters and warm beds, mess halls and a ticket home that didn't require that they lose a limb or eye or go totally crazy. As jobs in war go, most agreed, this was a pretty good one. That is, if you could ignore the guards that quickly appeared at the tents and huts of crews that did not return after most missions. Few of the dead in the air war came home to die. As Howard Nemerov, a two-time poet laureate of the U.S., wrote many years later, the dead stayed out there in this, the clean war.[1]

Lamar and his buddies headed off for the latrine before going to the 0500 briefing. They had sat through these sessions before with full bladders or insistent bowels, and they learned quickly that leaving a briefing to attend to private business was not done.

Lamar, Darden, Reynolds, and Craig filed into the briefing room and found seats together. The décor of the large room was still Wartime Scrounge, a mixture of rough benches and bomb fin boxes, recycled after having served their original purpose. The quarters for the men had improved, but the administrative areas were still very primitive. The only possible upgrades were a few chairs scattered around.

"You going to tell them to just half fill the bird today, Lamar?" Reynolds grinned at Lamar. "I mean, shoot, let's have some real drama, huh?"

"Already did that. Going to try it today with a thousand gallons max. We can save Uncle Sam a ton of money. Too much waste." Lamar deadpanned and looked serious. Craig, who had not shared the anxiety of the day before, snickered. Darden shook his head.

"Ten-HUT!" The assembled officers rose as Col. Price, the ex-football player, marched down the aisle to the dais in front. Lamar, still embarrassed about slamming into his commanding officer and Gen. Twining while chasing Alder, always looked away when the colonel entered, afraid he might be recognized.

"At ease, men." The assembled fliers sat. "If you got 'em, smoke 'em." The war had become very much a cigarette war. Smokes were everywhere, given free in Red Cross packages, sold for nearly nothing in post exchanges, lit up in crowded briefing rooms, even at times in the airplanes, verboten only during fueling operations on the flight line. Young men who had never smoked before the war, who had been lean, hard athletes pure in body and mind, now reached into shirt pockets and tapped out cigarettes. Zippo lighters were passed around to ignite the rolled tubes of tobacco, smoke was sucked into lungs, and clouds of white smoke were exhaled into the room to gather in a hazy layer below the rough ceiling. At longer briefings, the smoke overcast slowly lowered, until it seemed that all the fliers would have to go on instruments just to navigate out of the room. For most, lighting up had become a way of relaxing, a ritual shared after a mission, a way to calm jangled nerves. Smoking would become an addiction for many, still holding them hostage long after the war. Lamar, true to his Methodist upbringing, did not indulge.[2]

After the opening prayer by the padre, the colonel addressed the crowd in the room.

"Men, we still don't have photos of yesterday's strike because of the clouds, so I can't talk about your effort at Blechhammer. I know most of you think the cloud cover was good, since we didn't lose anyone to flak, but our job is to hit our assigned target and if we can't see it that's not a good thing." Col. Price, the West Point man, always stood at parade rest when briefing the group, his arms behind him, back straight.

"I have had reports that some of the formation flying got a bit ragged, and I don't have to remind you that a loose formation is just an invitation to those Luftwaffe fighter boys to fly through and take some of us out. Let's do better today, or we will all be practicing close formation flight anytime we're not on operations. I want waist gunners to be able to touch wingtips of your box mates! Tighten it up. Do I make myself clear?"

A crisp "Yes, sir!" erupted from the group of fliers. They had learned to play the army game of exuding enthusiasm when threatened.

"Okay, let's talk about today." The colonel nearly smiled and looked almost relaxed. He looked to the group intelligence officer and nodded.

The officer pulled back the cloth cover to reveal a large map of Italy, the Mediterranean, and southern Germany. A red ribbon stretched from Spinazzola to a point just above the top of the Adriatic, a location still in Italy.

"Our target for today is the German air base at Udine."

The fliers smiled, and a sense of ease permeated the now stale air. "Oh, baby!" someone said above the murmurs, and this was met with quiet laughter.

"In this area are four German fighter bases. They normally do not give us much of a problem. They do not come up and attack us when we have good fighter escort. But they keep a close watch for anyone out of a tight formation. When they see one of our planes out of formation, especially one with an engine out they come up and pick them off. We think that if we bomb these four bases and make the runways unusable we will be free of this problem. We do not think the enemy will repair those bases just for the purposes they have been using them for. We will not be flying with the rest of the 15th AF today. The four bomb groups in this wing will each be bombing a target in northern Italy."

The intelligence officer tapped the pointer tip against a series of overlapping red circles representing known flak batteries. "There should be no more than thirty-three guns in the target area, and flak is expected to be Medium concentration, Accurate, and Heavy caliber—probably 88 mm."[3] MAH was the norm for most missions, unless of course they were going to a major German city, where the red circles overlapped in dozens upon dozens of well-placed antiaircraft batteries that ringed important targets. Thirty-three was nothing to sneeze at, but it didn't warrant much concern, either.

"Fighter escort will be P-51s. They'll pick you up at the coast and stay with you through the rally." Lamar looked at Darden, who nodded. Maybe it would be the black pilots of the 332nd fighter group, the so-called Red Tails, who, it was rumored, had not lost a bomber to enemy fighters since they began flying escort in July.

"Weather should be pretty good, with a few clouds in the area of Udine but nothing to obscure the target. Pilots, pick up your flimsies, take-off at oh seven thirty. Col. Price is leading the mission today. Capt. Martin of the 762nd will lead the second attack unit. Break for individual briefings."

From here, pilots, navigators, and bombardiers would go for briefings that included information specific to their jobs. Darden looked over the flimsy, a summary of the mission to Udine that was typed on onion-skin paper. As usual, it was labeled "Secret," and would be returned by the pilots at the interrogation at the end of the mission.

For pilots, the war was a blizzard of numbers, numerals that changed for each mission, and the flimsy was vital to keep track of the bewildering information thrown at them each briefing. On one side, typed single-spaced from top to bottom, was a wealth of details starting with a list of times: Breakfast, briefing, transportation, stations, start engines, taxi out, take off, depart assembly area, depart Altamura, rendezvous, target time, and time of return. Details of who would lead, the deputy leader, and the second attack leader followed, and then particulars of the rendezvous (groups and order of placement, place and time of meet up). The order of flight was spelled out, and the route with specific checkpoints and map coordinates was detailed. Fighter escort information was given—type of fighter and place of rendezvous, and the point of climb to mission altitude stated. Bomb type and fuel load were noted, and specific details of the bomb run were laid out for both primary and secondary targets should the first be obscured. The rally procedure (forming up after the bombing attack) was specified, and the route back to base written out. Radio procedures and air-sea channels were included, as were squadron call signs, as well as call signs for bombers and fighters, and the recall code word was there as well. Non-standard procedures were noted at the bottom of the page, such as the carrying of chaff (to confuse radar signals) and procedures for the use of IFF (Identification Friend or Foe) devices. The back side of the flimsy had diagrams for the position of each ship in the formation, labeled by pilot, and a final checklist to refer to before take off: parachute, oxygen mask, life vests, escape kits, winter flying equipment, navigation equipment, steel helmets, flak suits, bombing tables and target maps for the bombardier, proper flimsies for the radio operator, and the last item, "Entire crew has proper knowledge as to their destination."[4]

Darden and Lamar sat through the pilots' briefing, which was essentially an oral run-through of the flimsy, and then Lamar went to the intelligence shack next door to check out escape and evasion kits, one for each crewman. They were more properly evasion kits, since there was little to be relied on in the event of capture, and certainly were not survival kits since they contained no food or emergency gear. Still, they were better than nothing, but many also carried their own version of a survival kit. This usually consisted of some kind of canvas bag containing some extra socks, a half-dozen chocolate bars, maybe an extra pair of underwear or handkerchief and anything else they thought they might need if they managed to evade capture and were trying to get back to friendly territory. Many sported large hunting knives sent from home or purchased locally. Lamar's Aunt Myrtle had said in a recent letter that she was sending him a knife, but it had not arrived yet. A few carried pistols. Darden had a large .45 revolver, like a true Texan, but Lamar did not carry a handgun.

Prior to the Darden crew's arrival in theater, combat fliers routinely carried side arms everywhere they went. But a few incidents involving armed young men in strange places convinced the brass that the pistols needed to be gathered up and checked out only for combat missions. By now, only a few bothered. Figuring they could not possibly shoot their way out of Germany, they climbed into their bombers largely unencumbered by personal weapons.[5]

They took the six-by-six to the flight line and there learned they would again be flying with a substitute crew member. They met Sergeant Mario Briganti. Mario would be the assistant engineer and waist gunner replacing Joe Betine, who had been grounded by the flight surgeon for some minor ailment that prevented him from flying at high altitude. Briganti, from Waterbury, Connecticut, was new to the 760th, arriving just recently, but at nineteen years old was already a veteran of missions with the 8th AAF in England. He had joined the Caterpillar Club (its members had all bailed out of an airplane in trouble) there when his crew had been forced to abandon their bomber over England. This would be his first mission out of Italy, and of course the first with the Darden crew. He seemed competent and eager, and Darden and Lamar welcomed him to the team.

They all trooped to the equipment shack to don their flight gear. There, the individual equipment for each combat crewman was kept on open-front shelves, labeled by name. Leather helmets, oxygen masks, life vests, and parachute harnesses, as well as the packed canopy itself, were stored there to be retrieved before each mission. Some gear was pulled on in the shack, but kit bags were used to carry much of it to the aircraft to pull on later.

At the hardstand, each crewman walked up to the perky blonde gracing the nose and patted her bottom for good luck. The standard procedure for pre-flight inspection of the aircraft was quickly completed, with Lamar climbing to the top of the fuselage through the radio-room hatch and then out on to the wings to check the fuel tanks and ensure the caps were down and locked. Missions were dangerous enough without the hazard of leaking high octane fuel through a loose or missing cap. After coming home with only thirty-five gallons remaining the previous day, he was especially cautious—he wanted to see fuel all the way up to the cap. He climbed back through the hatch and moved forward to the cockpit, where he and Darden went through the litany of the pre-start checklist.

At last came the signal to start engines, and at hardstands along the taxiway of the long, single runway, propellers began to turn, slowly at first, then faster, before settling into fan-like whirling discs as clouds of blue-gray smoke belched from the innards of the huge radial engines. Four times for each bomber the procedure was repeated, and the chorus of barking, bellowing engines once more split asunder the quiet dawn of the Italian countryside. The Darden crew eased into position for the lumbering nose-to-tail taxi to the runway, all with their headsets on which dulled the clamor of all those engines, as well as the counter-pointing squeals from the struts of the landing gear that protested each sway and bounce of the heavily-loaded beasts.

As they slowly taxied, creaking and groaning, toward the takeoff end of the runway, Lamar remembered a mission that began badly. They had been ready to taxi when the engineer discovered one of the engine electronic devices was malfunctioning. The crew chief climbed aboard and made a substitution from a spare unit aboard. They could have departed that way, but the conscientious chief did not want them to fly without a usable spare unit. While they were taxiing out, Lamar watched the man sprint across the field to a mechanic shack to exchange the malfunctioning unit for a good one. Then he ran to the end of the runway to hand the unit up through the open bomb bay door to Webb, who put it in place while Lamar and Darden were rolling *Bottoms Up* out on the runway for takeoff. Lamar had always felt good about the quality of their ground crew, but this demonstration of concern punctuated the dedication he had often observed.

There were two Liberators ahead of them now; they were third in line to take off. Lamar made a last check of the myriad of gauges to assure himself that everything was running perfectly. Halfway down the runway, with a full load of fuel and bombs, was a poor time to discover an overheated engine. He recalled another mission when they were just ready to taxi onto the runway to take off with fully loaded B-24s in front and behind them. A mechanical glitch had been discovered that would prevent them from making the mission. They radioed their problem and were told to fast taxi to the other end of the runway and return to the hardstand. They applied power to all four engines, taxied at nearly take-off speed to the far end of the strip, and watched as Liberator after Liberator took off just over their heads. The crew chief climbed aboard and worked feverishly to correct the problem. After almost an hour he had it fixed. Lamar and Darden concluded that the formation was probably still in the assembly area south of Spinazzola. They made a fast takeoff, initiated a climbing left 180-degree turn, and headed south. After gaining several thousand feet of altitude, they began to see black specks in the distance. Soon they were seeing B-24 bombers by the hundreds, and they scanned for the markings on the vertical tail surfaces that distinguished the 460th Bomb Group. Finally they spotted the familiar yellow circle-and-square, and they looked for the number three position just off the left wing of the lead aircraft. It was still empty. They made a quick 180-degree turn to the left and slowly eased their plane into position, waving to the pilot of the lead aircraft as they did so. Lamar had grinned to himself. They would not have to worry about fuel that trip. The delay had saved them about an hour of fuel. Sometimes things have a way of working out.

On this day, after the interminable aerial ballet of forming up, the group at last headed for Udine, no more than a couple of hours north. As missions went, this would be rather small and relatively short. They welcomed a truncated mission, all of them still feeling the strain of the long and anxiety-plagued flight of the previous day.

The armada cleared the coast, and Darden gave Lamar the signal to check the guns.

"Gunners, check your shooters. Try not to shoot down any good guys." It had happened before, though not to the Darden crew, and surely would happen again to the careless. The relative calm—if the roar of four radial engines and wind howling through the open sides of the gunner ports could be called calm—was quickly shattered by the explosive reports of ten .50-caliber machine guns. On ships across the formation, gunners had charged their weapons and squeezed off several rounds to ensure they worked and were ready if needed. The racket, even with headsets pressed firmly against their ears, was shocking, and the recoil could be felt at each station in the bomber, a pounding as though a crowd were beating against the airplane with sledgehammers.

It was, truthfully, satisfying for the gunners and even a bit fun. Few of them now got to fire their weapons at German aircraft, for the Luftwaffe was largely absent from Italian skies, and fighter escorts usually kept enemy fighters out of their defensive boxes. In the waist, Briganti and Swante Norlund grinned at each other. It was good to be young, alive, and in command of a .50-caliber machine gun.

For the two hours to the target, Darden and Lamar took turns flying the bomber in the churning sky of the combat box, fifteen minutes on, fifteen off. They reached the IP, the initial point, and by longstanding agreement since

Lamar was flying when they reached the start of the run he would continue flying until they released their bombs.

The formation made a slow right turn and headed toward the air base south of Udine. Lamar's eyes were glued to the lead aircraft so he could keep *Bottoms Up* tucked tightly in formation, but he could not help but see another formation of bombers in front and below him making a bombing run. He could see the bombs being spaced evenly along a runway making it completely unusable. But he could also see bursts of flak—somehow the briefing officer had convinced him, or he had convinced himself, there would be none—but no one had bothered to tell that to the Germans.

Shortly afterward, Lamar felt the sudden upward leap as the load *Bottoms Up* had been carrying was released. He heard Reynolds call out, "Bombs away." In a few seconds, they would turn to the rally point and head for home.

Wasn't to be.

The explosion cut off in mid-sentence Reynolds's routinely calm announcement that bomb bay doors were closing. As the 88-mm shell blasted through the left wing, Lamar felt *Bottoms Up* stagger, and was almost immediately aware that the two engines on the left wing were winding up into ever faster RPM's. In spite of Lamar and Darden's combined efforts, *Bottoms Up* immediately began to lose altitude, falling headlong from the sky. They plummeted fifteen thousand feet until Darden and Lamar were able to bring the Liberator back under control. Throughout the freefall, there was no panic, no frantic screaming in the intercom by any crewman. But surely each man considered that this was it, this was the time they would leave the bomber if they could, before they were pinned by centrifugal force against a bulkhead, waiting only for the final collision with an unyielding earth.

But the pilots struggled against the disrupted aerodynamics and ruptured fuel lines and shattered hydraulic systems and gaping holes in the wing, doing what they could to achieve some stability. All of the flight controls seemed to work, and the feathering buttons on both left engines still functioned. They managed to shut down both engines.

By now, they were far behind the rest of the bomber formation—it did no good to expose everyone to continued fire simply to circle around a single crippled bomber. Those were the lonely facts of war in the air, and they accepted them without bitterness. They, too, had been forced to leave wounded bombers and their crews to luck or death on previous missions.

Lamar found himself surprisingly calm, given the circumstances. But he had always figured that in this line of work, the odds were good that he would be hit pretty hard before fifty missions were up. They were now almost across the Adriatic Sea, hobbling through the air at five thousand feet.

"Everyone okay?" No reports of injuries, although Norlund had been wounded in the arm. It was broken, but he said nothing, and most of the crew wouldn't learn about it for many years. The pilots ordered the crew to throw everything out, including guns and ammunition, to lighten the stricken bomber.

He and Darden agreed on a plan, and Lamar explained to the crew over the intercom what they hoped to do.

"We're going to try to make Vis, but we are going to keep to the Yugoslavian coast as long as we can, staying just out of range of any flak guns on the coast. If we have to bail out, we will turn left and jump out over land." The little British-held island of Vis was a familiar checkpoint to the crew on previous missions.

He called the navigator. "Mike, I think that's Pola up ahead. Keep us out of the flak box around that place."

The islands of Brijuni were the first sizable islands in the northern approach to Pola, and it was home to several German flak batteries. The low and slow Liberator must have seemed like a gift; it was a target they could hardly miss, and flak gunners were rewarded with leave each time they brought down an Allied aircraft. They quickly opened fire, bracketing *Bottoms Up* with evil black clouds that seemed to squeeze out of the air itself all thoughts of freedom or escape. Darden and Lamar tried to fly an evasive action, flying only a short distance before turning left or right. It took the efforts of both pilots to make the mortally wounded bomber respond, each standing with both feet on the right rudder to make it turn to the right. Banking left was easy, but they lost altitude with each turn, altitude they could not squander. Wham! Another shell exploded in *Bottoms Up,* and the elevator was rendered inoperable. They now had no control of the up and down position of the nose, which virtually eliminated any possibility of a landing. Lamar thought to himself, "I wonder how far we can fly one of these things without the elevator?"

More shells took out the rudder pedals, leaving them just the ailerons. It was time to leave, and they did so methodically, calmly, with a deliberation that belied the dry throats and pounding hearts of ten young men. Most of them were able to drop from the crippled bomber with relatively little work, although their egress from the war machine was not paramount to its designers. There were no ejection seats, no detachable pods complete with survival gear and floatation rings. Instead, the means to their salvation were hatches to drop through, and tunnels to crawl through, and then the empty air as they stared down at the earth, now far too near.

For Lamar, the horrifying trip over the twin bomb bays, where he was held fast by the steel claws of the stanchions supporting the catwalk, was particularly wrenching. He knew how W. B. Yeats's Irish airman felt.[6]

As he stared down at the earth, now alarmingly close, Lamar thought once more of his parents. He didn't know if his parachute would deploy, since the rip cord had been pulled loose during his struggles in the belly of the beast. But there were no options. He launched himself through the photo hatch head first.[7]

Chapter 13

What Hath God Wrought?
Faucett, Missouri, 02 December 1944

When Samuel F. B. Morse, a sometime art professor and inventor, petitioned Congress for the award of $30,000 to construct a telegraph line between Washington and Baltimore, he had begun a revolution in communication. In 1844, when the line was completed, Morse set up shop in the old Supreme Court chambers in the Capitol, and before a crowd of congressmen and news reporters, sent the first official message by the newfangled electric machine.

"What hath God wrought?" he tapped on the key in a series of dots and dashes in a code he had invented, a code that was later to give fits to Lee Lamar and a generation of aviation cadets.

The message had been suggested by the young daughter of a friend, who had selected a verse from the book of Numbers, 23:23. Later, the short experimental telegraph line was expanded from coast to coast and across the Atlantic. It was by telegraph that Mark Twain was able to cable from London that the reports of his death were greatly exaggerated. The telegram became an icon of personal communication, and because it was expensive compared to posted letters and charged by the word, a new syntax was used that eliminated what were deemed unnecessary words. A famous story made the rounds about a journalist who wanted to know Cary Grant's age, and sent a telegram: "How old Cary Grant?" The reply was predictable: "Old Cary Grant fine. How you?" Perhaps the shortest telegram, by two parties who needn't have worried overly about the cost, was one reported to have been sent by the author and playwright Oscar Wilde, curious about how his latest work was doing. "?" he telegraphed his publisher. Not to be outdone in minimalism, the publisher replied: "!"

There was something dramatic in the delivering and receiving of a telegram, a certain flair that spoke of important matters that couldn't wait for the plebian mail.

But the novelty of the nearly instant communication had worn off in the hundred years since Morse sent that telegram from the Capitol. By 1944, it had become the means of notifying families across the U.S. of something serious regarding their loved one in the service. Telegrams went out across the country, to small towns, to farmhouses, to city apartments, to rich and poor and in between, carrying phrases like " . . . regret to inform you." Americans learned to hate the telegram, to dread the knock at the door of a Western Union messenger bearing a windowed envelope.[1]

On 2 December 1944, Urvie Lamar opened the barn door into the barnyard at his small farm outside of Faucett, where he had been doing the morning milking. Coming through the gate into the barnyard was Mr. Bleavens, the Faucett grocery man, where the family traded. Blevens did not normally call on his customers and certainly not this early in the morning. He had a yellow envelope in his hand.

Urvie's suspicions were raised. "It's Lee, isn't it." It was a statement, not a question.

"Yes, Urvie, I'm afraid it is." Lamar's father grimly accepted the envelope. The telegram had been delivered to the postmistress at Faucett. Western Union did not deliver in the country, but the postmistress was a friend of the Lamars; she understood the implications of the telegram, and despite the rationing of gasoline found someone willing to deliver the message so it would not end up in the mailbox at the end of the driveway.

Urvie walked into the house and laid the envelope on the kitchen table. He sat down and began to shake. Nannie arrived from the front room. It had been several weeks since they had heard from their son, which was not unusual. But Urvie was sure he knew what a telegram meant.

With trembling hands, Lamar's mother opened the envelope and the couple slowly read the telegram. It was addressed only to Mr. Lamar, but neither bothered with the oversight. Women in 1944 had long ago become accustomed to being ignored in officialdom. But certainly the message in the telegram could not be ignored:

THE SECRETARY OF WAR DESIRES ME TO EXPRESS HIS DEEP REGRET
THAT YOUR SON SECOND LIEUTENANT EDGAR L LAMAR HAS BEEN
REPORTED MISSING IN ACTION SINCE EIGHTEEN NOVEMBER OVER
ITALY. IF FURTHER DETAILS OR OTHER INFORMATION ARE
RECEIVED YOU WILL BE PROMPTLY NOTIFIED.
    (signed) WITSELL ACTING THE ADJUTANT GENERAL [2]

It had taken more than two weeks before the heart-stopping telegram was sent.

Such are the messages that break the hearts of parents during wartime. The Lamars had no way to deal with this news, although neither could claim they had never considered it a possibility. Urvie, in fact, had as much as told his son that combat flying was more than a little dangerous, and he would probably be killed. But there is a complete universe that separates death in the abstract from the very real pain of believing that your youngest child has in all probability died before you. The telegram was difficult to assess, since "missing in action" was not the same as "killed in action."

There was hope, but how much hope should parents hold? Was it crueler not to know, perhaps never to know, or to be faced with the most horrible words that the wonders of electricity could send?

Neighbors heard, of course, and many dropped by to offer encouragement to the Lamars, to pray with them in the parlor, to bring in food.

Three days later, Lamar's father sat down and wrote one of the few letters he had written to his son since joining the Air Force. It is the simple, unpretentious epistle of an unsophisticated man in great distress.

> Dear Lee, just a line to let you no [*sic*] that we are all OK and hope and pray you are the same. Mildred and Thelma is here and Rich is having a good time it has rained the last 3 days here. Lee we had a telegram Saturday saying you were missing over Italy. We have all the hope in the world we are praying day and night for you. Lee just as soon as you receive this letter ans it as soon as possible for you no how we feel Charlie and Shorty is OK Lee tell us if your crew is all right I have been stripping tobacco, and almost done I have 8 or 9 of corn to shuck yet. Well Lee as it is getting late I will close for the time and hoping and praying to hear from you in the next mail so ans soon and be a good boy.
>
> With lots of love,
> Dad

It was returned days later. Undeliverable. Addressee MIA.[3]

The day before the elder Lamar penned his note, the letter writers in Washington had typed a follow-up to the telegram, although it was several days before the Lamars received it.

The term "missing in action" (the letter said),

> is used only to indicate that the whereabouts or status of an individual is not immediately known. It is not intended to convey the impression that the case is closed. . . . Experience has shown that many persons reported missing in action are subsequently reported as prisoners of war, but as this information is furnished by countries with which we are at war, the War Department is helpless to expedite such reports.

Permit me to extend to you my heartfelt sympathy during this period of uncertainty.

It was signed J. A. Ulio, Major General.

The War Department letter was official, and while it offered some hope for Lt. Lamar the tone was distant and impersonal, despite the closing sentence. Hundreds of similar letters no doubt went out each day.

A flurry of letters then followed. On 7 December, a brigadier general wrote from the War Department and added a detail that was ominous in its implication:

"A report has now been received that he (Lamar) became missing in action over the Adriatic Sea instead of Italy."

A letter dated 9 December came from Maj. Gen. Nathan Twining, the commander of the 15th Air Force, the man Lamar had nearly bowled over as he chased little Hank Alder out of the equipment shack. It is bleak, and its stark prose offers little solace:

> Interrogation of returning crews has revealed that Edgar's aircraft left its formation soon after bombs away apparently because of damage from the enemy's anti-aircraft fire. The pilot of the missing plane called over the radio and announced that he had a gas leak in one engine and would fly to Yugoslavia. This is the last contact with the ship.

The general then announced the award of the Air Medal to the missing airman, in recognition of "his splendid accomplishments while on operational flights." The letter, brutal in its efficiency, ends by noting that "Edgar's personal property is being carefully packed and sent to the Effects Quartermaster in Kansas City, Missouri, who will forward it to his designated beneficiary."

The family was heartsick. They had sent a son off to war, and now only his clothing, albeit carefully packed, would return. Lamar's mother, instinctively recognizing the need for the mothers of all the missing aircrew to make more human contact than the sterile letters from the War Department, requested the names and addresses of the young men who had gone down with her son. Earlier, she had experienced the anguish of another mother whose son was missing, when she heard from Mrs. Munn. Her son, Kenneth, had been at the University of Missouri with Lee, and joined the Air Force a month or so before him. Both young men went through the same training bases, but Kenneth always was a class ahead, and Lee never was able to contact him. He was sent to Italy to fly with the 15th Air Force and was shot down. Mrs. Munn, learning that Lee was in Italy, had written Mrs. Lamar in the hope that Lee might learn something. Of course, that was not possible, and by the time Lamar arrived, Munn had been returned safely to his base and sent back to the States.

The Lamars received a reply to the request for information about the crew in a letter from Headquarters, Army Air Forces, in Washington. It was dated 16 December, and addressed to Mr. William Lamar.

"Due to necessity for military security, it is regretted that the names of those who were in the plane and the names and addresses of their next of kin may not be furnished at the present time."

Once more, the letter closed with a paragraph that was well-intentioned but offered little comfort:

> Please be assured that a continuing search by land, sea, and air is being made to discover the whereabouts of our missing personnel. As our armies advance over enemy occupied territory, special troops are assigned to this task, and all agencies of the government in every country are constantly sending in details which aid us in bringing additional information to you.

So, with a cold winter approaching and with chilled hearts, the Lamars prepared for Christmas. It would be a haunting and depressing holiday, filled with sadness despite the presence of Lee's brother and sisters and new little ones. A small tree was decorated in the parlor, but it seemed only to emphasize their loss in war while the world celebrated the birth of the Prince of Peace.

On the 23rd of December, Urvie and Nannie Lamar sat down to a quiet dinner. Darkness came early now, and outside the Missouri countryside was somber, cold, and gray. The old dirt road that went by the home place had been upgraded, and now carried the designation of U.S. Highway 71. But with gasoline rationing, it didn't carry much traffic, and in the quiet of this winter day the sounds of motor vehicles could be heard long before they hove into sight. Urvie turned his head at the whining of tires on pavement, and then frowned slightly as the car slowed. It turned into the gravel drive of the Lamar place. Urvie got up to go to the door.

His heart sank as he recognized Mr. Beavens again. It was too close to Christmas to get more bad news. Urvie Lamar took the envelope in to the kitchen. There could be no hiding it from Nannie.

"You open it, Urvie," his wife said, in a voice so soft he didn't recognize it. More than five weeks had dragged by since their son had gone missing in action, and although they outwardly expressed hope, they knew that the odds were long that he would be found safe now. With trembling fingers, he tore the end from the envelope and pulled out the telegram. Together, they read the latest message from the War Department, and burst into tears.

WILLIAM U. LAMAR
FAUCETT, MO

REPORT JUST RECEIVED THROUGH THE INTERNATIONAL RED CROSS
STATES THAT YOUR SON SECOND LIEUTENANT EDGAR L LAMAR IS A
PRISONER OF WAR OF THE GERMAN GOVERNMENT. LETTER OF
INFORMATION FOLLOWS FROM PROVOST MARSHAL GENERAL.

Tears of joy.

Chapter 14

"Vor You, Der Var Iss Ofer"

Bottoms Up was in the last few seconds of her life as an airplane. Running now on just two engines, with her controls shot away and headed for earth at 180 mph in a great sweeping left turn, the huge bomber was soon going to become a pile of burning scrap. Lamar realized he had no time to think about what he had to do. Standing at the front of the photo hatch in the back of the mortally wounded plane, he dropped head-first into the void.

From his first ride as a student in a Piper J-3 at St. Joseph's Rosecrans Field, Lamar had assumed that this day would come, sooner or later. So long as he was a pilot, particularly a military pilot during wartime, he always thought that he would have to rely on his parachute. Although pilot and aircrew training did not involve the actual use of a parachute, he had sat through countless intelligence briefings advising airmen on what to expect if they had to bail out of their stricken aircraft, actions to be taken in the air and once on the ground.

Those briefings came back to him now as he began the prescribed tuck-and-roll, essentially turning a somersault in the air. The recommended procedure was a full roll, and a count to ten before pulling the ripcord to release the white silk canopy of the parachute.[1] This delayed deployment would allow the airman to avoid getting struck by the airplane, or getting a 'chute tangled with some part of it, it and would also mean being less of a target. It was not unheard of for airmen coming down, helpless beneath the canopy, to be shot as they descended.

For about the first third of his forward roll, Lamar thought about the delayed count. For the next half second, or the second third of the roll, he realized that he was far too low to delay pulling his ripcord. He jerked hard on the D-ring, ignoring the fact that the metal wire cord had pulled out once during his struggles to get past the bomb bay and might not function at all.

The result was stunning, in a very physical sense. The 'chute, no doubt aided by some propeller wash, snapped open with a vengeance, the G-forces resulting

144

from the collision of speed and rapid deceleration slamming Lamar's head to the right. Just as the canopy blossomed, he was able to look over his shoulder. He saw *Bottoms Up* in a nearly level attitude just clipping a line of trees perhaps a half mile away. At that instant he hit the ground, hard. It had been just seconds since he jumped.

He looked over in the direction of the crash, where a plume of dense, oily black smoke was already boiling up from the shattered bomber, smoke fed by fuel, oil, tires, and a host of other flammable items aboard. He could see a white strip, a parachute that looked as though it had only partially deployed. "Must have been Webb," he thought to himself. "His 'chute didn't open, poor guy." Lamar quickly gathered his own canopy in both arms and looked around for somewhere to hide both it and himself. Intelligence officers had advised aircrew to hide their 'chutes and try to hide out until the end of the second day. The Germans would probably have stopped looking for them after that. Then, they could try to evade capture and work their way back to Allied territory.

Lamar had landed in a field bounded by low stone walls, coming down hard on an exposed layer of worn rock at the apex of a low hill that commanded a view of fields and patches of trees all around. There had been no time to prepare for the impact, and now he found that his right knee would not support his weight unless he locked it in a straight position. His arms were full of the white silk parachute canopy and the long nylon shrouds that connected the canopy to his harness, and he awkwardly hobbled down the hill toward the intersection of two stone walls. There he pushed aside a tangle of sticks and leaves that had been swept by wind into the angle. He clawed at the earth with his bare hands, able only to scrape a small depression in the hard dirt. Lamar threw in the parachute and harness, and pulled the Mae West over his head to add to the pile. He covered the equipment with leaves and sticks until there was no sign of the glaringly bright white of the 'chute or the yellow of the life jacket. Then he crawled over the wall.[2]

The land sloped quickly into a kind of sink hole, one of the many karst depressions that pocked the area. He walked a few steps, struck by how the rolling terrain and brushy patches of scrub oak reminded him of home in Missouri. Dropping to one knee—his left, with his right stuck awkwardly to the side—the young farmboy-turned-pilot dug below the layer of decaying leaves to the dirt below. Here, the soil was rich and black, the result no doubt of being carried to the depression by decades or centuries of rain. Lamar scooped up a handful and let it trickle slowly through his fingers. It was strangely and unaccountably comforting to make contact with the most basic of things.

He rose stiffly and stumbled back up the hill to the wall. He was twenty-three years old, a serious young man with a strong religious faith. He was also dazed, hurt, unarmed, and alone in a land occupied by men with guns who had just tried to kill him and his crew. A half-hour before, he had been the well-trained pilot of a colossal flying machine, a four-engine bomber capable of carrying four tons of bombs. Now he was alone, a stranger in a strange land. But he was not frightened, not cowed by his circumstances. That might come later, but for now, he was simply glad to be alive. Only minutes earlier, caught in the bomb bay with the bomber in its last throes, he had been nearly resigned to his own death.

Lamar stopped at the stone wall and again dropped to his left knee, clasped his hands together and closed his eyes.

"Lord, I'm kind of in a spot right now, and I could sure use some help." He gave thanks for being alive, and asked for His watchful eye through the rest of the war. Later, he regretted not stopping his prayer there. Instead, he says in chagrin, he laid out details of exactly what needed to be done, including linking up with Partisans. Not a good idea to tell the Lord how to do His work.

When he finished the short prayer, he heard the growl of aircraft engines, and looked up to see two American P-51 fighters swoop low over the area of the crash. He stepped into the open and waved both arms, but with little belief that the pilots had seen him. Their eyes were focused, no doubt, on the burning bomber. But the sight of the fighters was comforting, nonetheless.[3]

Lamar crawled over the fence and headed east toward a small patch of scrub oak, scraggly and stunted, perhaps six feet high. The leaves were brown and sere but still largely on the branches. He crawled into the thicket, took a few deep breaths, and realized he was exhausted. A few hours of herding the Liberator always wore him out, and now that physical exertion was coupled with the stress and terror of being shot down and bailing out. After several minutes, Lamar pulled the escape and evasion kit from the leg pocket of his wool flight suit. It was mid-November, but the temperature was fairly mild, and his coveralls and cloth field jacket were more than enough protection at the moment.

A dime-sized compass in the kit looked promising. So did a map of the area, and Lamar studied it carefully. He knew he was somewhere close to Pola, which was claimed by the Italians but still inhabited mainly by ethnic Croates loyal to Yugoslavia. He needed to head south to link up with Partisans and—he hoped, at least—be repatriated to Italy within a few weeks. Other items in the kit he was not so sure about. Forty-eight gold-seal U.S. dollars might be useful. The small saw blade looked impractical.[4]

Lying on his stomach, Lamar looked back toward the field in which he had landed. A movement caught his eye. His heart beat faster, and he involuntarily held his breath while sliding a fraction deeper into the thicket. Seconds went by, an eternity in which his heart pounded in his ear drums. Then he saw Darden flop over the stone wall near where he had crossed and head toward his area of concealment.

When the big Texan was within twenty feet or so, Lamar gave a low whistle, and Darden spun toward him. Lamar waved an arm, and soon the two pilots were side by side in the thicket of scrub oak.

"Man, am I glad to see you. I thought you were still in the plane when it hit," Lamar said quietly, in a voice softer than a whisper. "I saw another 'chute laid out, so I guess Webb's 'chute didn't open, he didn't have enough altitude."

"Nah, partner, I was right behind you. That was my 'chute you saw. Webb left long before us, I'm sure he's fine along with the rest of the boys." Darden was in reasonably good spirits, considering the situation. They shared a kind of giddiness about finding themselves alive when just minutes earlier they could not reasonably expect to be.[5]

Strangely, and to Lamar's later regret, he and Darden never talked about their experiences in escaping from the crippled bomber. They were too happy to be alive when they first landed, had no opportunity after being captured, and "war stories" were frowned upon at the Stalag. Lamar believes Darden might have been able to kick open the bomb bay doors and jump out.

The young men studied the area map from Lamar's escape kit. To reach Yugoslavia from the Istrian peninsula would mean heading southeast for a couple of days. There, they might be able to link up with Partisans who would guide them through the countryside until they could contact a boat to take them across to Italy. The other alternative was to head northeast, hoping to walk around the head of the Adriatic and perhaps all the way to southern Italy. They took stock of their equipment. It wasn't much. Darden had an identical kit to Lamar's. In addition, he had a large .45-caliber revolver, his personal weapon. Darden was a proud Texan, and he was not going to stop carrying his revolver. God created man, but Col. Colt made him equal.

Neither man had anything to eat, but lunch was the furthest thing from their minds.

"Let's get going. Those Jerries are going to head straight toward that crash site, can't miss it with all that smoke, and we better be long gone by then." The two men rose. They worked their way through the thick brush and stunted oaks to a slight ridge, still in cover, that overlooked a shallow valley. Darden started to step into the open. Lamar grabbed his collar and jerked him back into the thicket.

"You better look before you start out." He pointed to the hillside opposite them, perhaps a quarter-mile away. A line of gray-clad figures was slowly advancing, spaced at intervals of about ten feet or so. Each carried a rifle at the ready, clearly visible.

What the two pilots had not known was that a large contingent of Germans had been assigned to the area. Those troops were now carefully combing the area below the flight path of *Bottoms Up* for crewmen who had bailed out and any equipment that might have been thrown out of the crippled bomber. The plane, which had been headed south, had slowly swung to the north after the last hits over Pola, pulled in a left turn by the two engines still working on the right wing. To get to Yugoslavia, Lamar and Darden would have to hide and wait out the searching Wehrmacht troops, then work their way through enemy lines.

The two pilots retraced their steps and crawled back into the dense scrub oak.

Lamar looked at the big frontier-style revolver that Darden had strapped to his waist. The sight of the long line of German infantrymen advancing methodically toward them was still in his brain.

"Darden, you're going to get us killed with that six-shooter, you know that?"

"What do you mean?" Darden looked at him through narrowed eyelids.

"I mean just that. It's big enough to see a mile away, and those Germans are going to shoot first and then ask questions. Get rid of it!"[6]

For a long moment, Darden seemed to ignore Lamar, refusing to look at him or acknowledge his co-pilot's concern. Finally, he pulled out the long-barreled revolver, crawled a couple of feet out of the thicket, and slid it under a layer of leaves.

The afternoon passed slowly, with both men keeping very quiet. They could see little, but occasionally Lamar thought he could hear faint shouts. Too far away to be distinct, but they sounded German to him. The cold sun began to slide down the western sky, and soon long shadows crept across the bit of field that he could see in front of him. He was beginning to feel hungry, but one more search of his field jacket revealed nothing to eat. He knew it would not. His right knee was beginning to throb. Lamar ignored it, thinking instead of his folks and the family and Thanksgiving in Faucett.

Night closed over the area, and the two downed pilots scraped together leaves that had fallen and were held in the thicket. They pulled some over themselves, nestled into the rest. Their parachutes would have been handy to build a shelter or wrap themselves in, but the stark white of the canopy would have been instantly visible. Strangely, Lamar felt no particular fear or even discomfort. The stunted trees surrounding him reminded him of the second-growth oaks on his parents' farm. There was a familiarity about them that painted his actual situation—perilous at best—in a wash of the ordinary, a pale, translucent film of surreal equanimity.

Although it was mid-November, the night was not overly cold. Proximity to the Adriatic no doubt contributed to the mildness. In any event, Lamar and Darden both woke often throughout the long night, sometimes with sudden jerks as dreams of being trapped in the falling bomber played in color in the theater of their minds. An occasional groan, a spasm that caused dry leaves to crackle, and once, far away, the barking of a dog, were the only sounds that night. It was strange, Lamar pondered, the things he thought about in the waking moments between fitful bouts of sleep. Cookies. The boxes of cookies sent by Mike Craig's family that the four officers had shared the night before. They would be finished by others, now. Too bad. Great cookies. Casa Mañana. They had only gotten to live in the stone hut about a week. What would happen to it now? If they were able to get back to Spinazzola, would they have to reclaim the house, or start over with another? He tried to think ahead, to picture the next several days and weeks, but the uncertainty of even the next few hours pulled a curtain across any visions of the future.

The gray wolf of false dawn, a full hour before the sun would climb above the furthest hill, provided Lamar with just enough light for his eyes to turn traitorous. Distant bushes began to move stealthily, far away trees assumed the exact outlines of Wehrmacht troopers, complete with rifles and bayonets. In the absolute silence he could clearly hear the pounding of his own heart as he looked out of the thicket, straining to discern details that the night was not ready to yield. He was keenly aware of his stomach clamoring for food. The crew had eaten breakfast about twenty-four hours earlier, and nothing since. He settled in to wait, but for what? Lamar was under no illusions about their chances.

At noon, the game was up. Darden and Lamar had both seen the tops of the first distinct "square-head" German helmets as a line of young soldiers slowly advanced up a slight rise toward them. They instinctively crawled further back into the small thicket of scrub oak, but they both realized the futility of the move.

Two soldiers entered the scraggly grove, moving cautiously one step at a time. Others, perhaps a dozen, remained just outside or moved around the edges. A shouted command, in a loud and excited young voice, alerted Darden and Lamar that they had been found. The two Americans slowly, stiffly, rose with their hands up, and were immediately confronted by the muzzles of Mauser rifles, with bayonets attached. Through gestures and prods, they understood that they were to move out of the thicket toward the rest of the German squad, now all of whom were aiming their weapons at the pair. As Lamar started to take a step, he dropped a glove he had been holding and bent to pick it up. The response was immediate, loud, and very definitely threatening. Screams of "Nein, Nein!" and "Pistole!" were followed by a violent shove from one of the infantrymen. Bewildered, Lamar looked down. He saw Darden's revolver nearly at his feet, clearly visible to the Germans. He straightened slowly with his hands displayed above his head.

Shaken, he looked at Darden, who was wide-eyed in alarm. "Told you your damn six-shooter was going to get us killed," Lamar said to the Texan. "Or me, anyway."[7]

One of the soldiers picked up the revolver, and the Americans were marched out of the thicket, where they were quickly and roughly searched. The Germans took their watches and personal other items, as well as their escape kits. One of the young Germans spoke very limited English.

"Where is Sturtz?"

Bernard Sturtz was the tailgunner, one of the three crewmen who had been working on dropping the ball turret when Lamar finally made it back to the waist section. Later, Lamar found out that the gunner had struck his mouth, hard, on the lip of the photo hatch as he dove through, and his dogtags had been torn off. Whether the Germans recovered the metal tags from the crashed bomber or found them on the ground below the last flight path of *Bottoms Up* he was never able to learn.

Lamar and Darden indicated they had no idea of the location of the crewman. Another of the German soldiers tried to question Lamar on the whereabouts of his parachute, using a combination of sign language and an occasional word. He knew exactly what the man was asking, but was determined that the enemy soldiers would not make use of his parachute. The silk or nylon canopy was highly desired for trading for a variety of things useful to soldiers, including, perhaps, female companionship. Lamar pretended not to understand anything the German was trying to convey.

"He wants to know where you hid your 'chute," Darden added, helpfully. Lamar scowled at the pilot, and continued to display complete incomprehension. Finally, they were pushed ahead, and the squad continued to search for other crewmen for some time.

They came to a small, wooden schoolhouse and stopped for a break. The soldiers all carried rucksacks, and they pulled out bread and a spread that resembled butter and began to eat. One of the Germans, about Lamar's age, held out a slice of the dark bread to him, with an almost wistful look.

"Vor you, der var iss ofer," he said softly. Lamar pushed his hand away and refused the bread. The German shrugged his shoulders and ate the bread himself. Lamar was very, very hungry. He regretted his angry rudeness.[8]

Later, they were taken to a road where a convertible awaited them to transport the Americans into Vodnjan, a small village not far out of Pola. They were placed in the back seat with armed Germans in the front and back.

Don Reynolds, the bombardier, had bailed out of *Bottoms Up* shortly after being knocked unconscious by the shell that blew out the rudder pedals. He awoke to hear the bail-out bell and immediately dropped through the nose-gear door. Now, he was hiding, alone, in a wooded area alongside a road. He saw Darden and Lamar being driven by in the olive-drab convertible. He continued hiding until later that day before heading out, hoping to avoid the same fate.[9]

Chapter 15

Interrogation and Isolation

The wooden door on cell 88 slammed shut with a haunting echo, followed by the metallic clicking of a lock that mocked all thoughts of freedom. Lamar listened as the footsteps of the German guards rattled off the walls of the long hallway, fading into the distance. He looked around the tiny cubicle in the wooden edifice known as Dulag Luft, the interrogation center for Allied fliers. There was little to be seen except a cot, with a single thin blanket on a hard mattress. The walls were bare wood, still smelling new despite the thousands of prisoners who had come through this dreaded place just outside Frankfort en Main.[1]

But even in the darkest of hours there can be tiny rays of light, Lamar quickly discovered. There, on the wooden frame of the utilitarian cot, were two pairs of freshly laundered GI socks. No doubt they had been left there by a previous prisoner who had not been allowed back to retrieve them before being sent on to a prisoner of war camp. Lamar had packed his own personal escape kit with extra socks and underwear, a few candy bars, and other items not included in his official kit, but in the urgency to bail out he had left it in the cockpit of *Bottoms Up*. Knowing he would need them for the upcoming winter in Germany, Lamar sat down, removed his boots, and pulled on both pairs of socks, covering them with his own original and now dirty socks. He silently thanked the unknown flier who doubtless would have cold toes through the freezing winter. He also was grateful that the guards had not discovered them and confiscated the socks for themselves.

It had been an eventful week, a full seven days since Lamar and the rest of the crew had bailed out of their Liberator.

At the small village of Vodnjan, a short distance from Pola, Lamar and Darden were reunited with Mike Craig, the navigator. In a short account written many years after the war, Craig recounted that he had landed in a field where a farmer was working, and the man had quickly taken him into his house. He spent the night there, but the next morning he was captured by German troops. A trio of Wehrmacht non-coms was assigned to escort him on the long train ride to Frankfort and the Dulag Luft. Then they would go on leave.[2]

Reynolds would later recall that Craig had been captured rather quickly after bailing out, as he tried to make his way to the crash site. Whatever the events, the trio of Darden, Lamar, and Craig were to be sent north by rail out of the Istrian peninsula. They were told that if any of them tried to escape, the others would be shot. Events played out that they never had the opportunity to test the threat.

On the train, late in the afternoon of 19 November, a Sunday, Mike shared the food he had been given for the ride north. It consisted of a loaf of Italian bread and two small tins of meat paste that resembled oxblood shoe polish. The prisoners' rations had not been increased despite tripling the size of the detainees. The airmen checked out the contents of the two tins and decided not to ruin the very good bread by the addition of the mysterious paste. They ate all of the bread, and later left the tins for some lucky passenger to take home. Lamar would come to regret his fastidiousness, as rations were meager at best throughout his time as a prisoner. He thought often of the two tins of meat as his stomach growled at night.

The first stop for the train and the three Americans was Trieste, where they were able to see firsthand the results of their handiwork in attacking enemy installations. In Trieste, the passengers all had to disembark on the south side of the city and walk to the northern reaches; the rail lines had been totally smashed in a raid by the 460th a couple of months or so before the Darden crew was assigned to Spinazzola. Months later, the tracks were still twisted cords of steel and blasted beds of rock and wood. There was a small bit of satisfaction in knowing that the many missions they had sweated out, with little opportunity to see the aftermath of their seeds of destruction, had been worth the effort.

The following night, they stopped in a small town where the prisoners were taken to the local jail so the guards could sleep without having to stand watch over them. Lamar was taken aback by the cleanliness of the civilian cell, with a soft feather mattress and freshly laundered sheets. For the first time in his life that he could recall, he got into a clean bed with a dirty uniform and mud-caked boots, afraid to remove anything in the event that something, somehow, would arise that required his immediate absence. Dreams of escape had not yet died. He knew that chances of escaping and evading recapture would diminish drastically once they were inside Germany, so each in the trio of Americans was constantly on the lookout for any opportunity.

Next stop: Udine, the town whose airfield they had bombed when they first were hit by antiaircraft fire. There they picked up another American prisoner.

They learned that he was a P-51 pilot, but the guards returned and they were unable to continue their conversation. Lamar wondered if his had been one of the escorting fighters on their mission, but he was never able to learn that. The next day, they picked up three more downed fliers. Once more, the presence of a guard gave little chance to exchange the smallest nugget of information.[3]

From Udine, the train had to thread the Brennner Pass through the Italian Alps. One of the only routes between Germany and Italy, the pass itself was the target of American medium bombers flying out of Corsica and bases in central Italy. Many years later, as a member of the Heart of America Wing of the Commemorative Air Force, Lamar would meet Bob Zulauf, another member. Zulauf was a B-25 pilot who regularly bombed bridges and trains in the Brenner Pass. In a conversation about their war experiences, Zulauf recognized that he easily might have bombed Lamar and his fellow prisoners as they targeted every bit of rolling stock through the entire pass. "I take it all back, Lee. I didn't know you were a passenger." The two old pilots laughed grimly at the irony that one might have killed the other in the impersonal business of bombing.

On Thursday, Thanksgiving Day for the Americans, they were somewhere in the Brenner Pass, where they had to make a train transfer requiring a waiting period. The guards took them to a small barn not far from the railway station to wait. Shortly the guards showed up with a large pot of soup. It was something dark and unrecognizable, but they managed to get a fire going in a wood-burning pot belly stove in the barn and heated it. There was plenty of it; the guards had secured it from somewhere. They didn't know exactly where they were, and they were under armed guard, but the day still seemed special in some unarticulated way. Even with the self imposed silence among them, the downed fliers held their bowls of soup, cheered by the warmth and the smiles they flashed each other. It was a holiday Lamar would always remember. It was one of the few meals they had on the trip.

The guards themselves were obviously distrustful of each other. The Americans quickly learned that when alone with a single guard, the German soldier was invariably decent to them. When together, they resorted to shouted orders, rough treatment, and a mien of disdain toward the prisoners. None dared be accused of a lack of enthusiasm or loyalty to der Vaterland.

One of their escorts was a young boy, no older than seventeen and possibly younger. He spoke English quite well and the only guard to do so. He was also the easiest for the Americans to get along with. While waiting at a station for the next train, an announcement came over a loudspeaker that made the assembled civilian passengers groan loudly. Lamar was near the boy soldier and out of earshot of the other guards. He asked what the announcement had been.

"A delay. A bridge has been blown up." The young man spoke softly, and Lamar had to strain to hear him.

"Germany is going to have to be careful or it will not have any bridges left in the country," Lamar said, just as quietly. He expected a sharp retort.

"Ya. You are so right." It was evident to all, even this young soldier, that the war was lost for Germany. It was only a matter now of when and how the end would come. And how great would be the destruction to the country.

In Munich, Lamar had one brief opportunity to escape, a tiny window that quickly slammed shut. The party of prisoners and guards had stopped for the night in a bomb shelter to await transport out of the city in the morning. Lamar and several prisoners had gone to sleep in a small room adjacent to a larger central hall with a wood-burning stove. Sometime in the night he awoke to find himself alone in the room. He stepped out into the central hall, where he could see the other prisoners and two of the guards, all asleep, huddled around the stove. Should he climb the stairs and try to get away, even though he knew the chances of escaping a major German city were slim? Before he could take a single step, however, the third guard appeared at the top of the stairs and shouted for everyone to wake up and move out. It was the only chance, however slim, that Lamar ever had for escape.

And so on 25 November 1944, they arrived in Frankfort. The dreaded Dulag Luft, with its wooden wings of cells that stretched for what seemed like a city block, was something every flier over Germany had heard about. Intelligence officers had told them often what to expect, and the Americans entered the gates armed with knowledge that would mitigate but not eliminate the fear and isolation they were about to endure.[4]

Darden, Lamar, and Craig were separated immediately. Lamar was led to a nearby holding cell, where a half-dozen prisoners were sitting on the floor. As he entered, one of them put a finger to his lips and pointed overhead. Lamar understood, and there was no conversation for the next hour or so. Finally, he was called out and photographed, while with Teutonic precision the details of his status were recorded on an official form. The photographs, like any modern police mug shots, were taken full-face and in profile. The head-on photo shows a clearly sullen young man, glowering into the camera, disgusted with his situation and obviously in no mood to smile. It is a handsome face, and the black-and-white print could be mistaken for a Hollywood publicity pose for an upcoming movie about the war. It is not the picture of a smiling and confident young cadet, nor does it display the proud demeanor of a brand-new officer and pilot. After the photo session, Lamar was led to his cell. For the next week, he would get used to the call of "88" as he would be led out to face his interrogators.[5]

German interrogation of allied fliers was done almost exclusively by the Luftwaffe. It was a serious business, and could be terrifying, but the German air force officers usually relied more on gaining the trust of a prisoner, or cajoling a bit of "meaningless" information from an unsuspecting detainee, than on physical abuse. Prisoners who had been through the Dulag Luft and later escaped had been able to give Allied intelligence officers a fairly complete picture of what a newly captured airman could anticipate, and those details were passed on to combat fliers on frequent occasions.

They could expect to be separated from friends, to spend a week to ten days alone in a solitary cell, to be threatened—sometimes obliquely, sometimes overtly—and to be talked to in the most reassuring manner by someone with nearly flawless English. It would be important for the fliers to always give only name, rank, and serial number, even when the tiniest bit of information seemed already to be known by the Germans. And so it was.

A couple of days went by, with Lamar seeing no one, not even guards. A meager meal would be shoved through a tiny opening in the bottom of the cell door, but the door itself was not opened. The food was bad, very bad, and there was very little of it. Lamar continually regretted shunning the two cans of meat paste as they left Pola.

Lamar was summoned from his cell after a couple of days and led to the interrogation room. He was startled to see what appeared to be an undamaged Loran navigation set in the corner of the room. But he was not questioned about the super-secret navigation equipment. He figured it was merely to startle him, to make him believe the Germans already knew everything about everything.

A young German oberleutnant, a first lieutenant, introduced himself. Lamar nodded, determined to resist any efforts to gain information from him.

"Lt. Lamar, in order to classify you as a prisoner of war, we must know about your military unit. If you do not cooperate, and we are not able to confirm your unit, you will be shot as a spy." The German officer stared at him without blinking. But Lamar was unfazed. This was exactly the routine he had been told to expect. The interrogator doubtless already knew the unit to which *Bottoms Up* was assigned. There were markings aplenty on their aircraft to clearly identify the 460th bomb group, the 760th bomb squadron. Reveal nothing, the Americans had been told. Once you do, you will be expected to provide more information. Resist, and eventually the Germans would tire and send the captive to a prisoner of war camp.

The routine continued for several days, and Lamar would be returned to his solitary cell without having said anything more. One day, he was called again to the interrogation office only a few minutes after being returned to his cell.

"Lt. Lamar, we have just discovered that a Lt. Lamar, flying out of Italy, was shot down some months ago and evaded capture. We think you are that same Lt. Lamar." The oberleutnant stared through the American pilot, his face hard. If the Germans really did believe Lamar had once evaded capture, he could expect to be tortured to reveal the names of those who had assisted his eva-sion. Was this a new tack, a different way to break down resistance of recalci-trant fliers? It was not anything he remembered from numerous briefings.

Lamar straightened and looked to the far wall. "Sir, I am aware of another flyer named Lamar. He may have been shot down and evaded capture. I am not that Lamar." This could become very, very rough, Lamar knew. His stomach churned.

The questioning and threats went on for some time. Finally, the German ap-peared resigned.

"Lt. Lamar, you are one of the most stubborn individuals I have ever encoun-tered. You do not have to tell me the answers to these questions. We already know the answers. We just want to properly identify you so we can send you on to a POW camp." Lamar said nothing, and the interrogator turned to a book-shelf and pulled down a thick volume. Lamar could see the cover, a thick pink paper one, on which were printed "460th Bomb Group, The Black Panthers."

"Your commanding officer is Col. John Price. Your squadron commander is Maj. Bob Martin. Your . . ." The German continued to read the names of virtually every officer in the bomb group. But Lamar was unfazed. It was no mean feat to know the names of all the officers, but it would not have been that hard to learn, either, since much information was published in the daily American press. Moreover, he was convinced that the large book was most-ly blank pages, taken down and displayed for effect. The tome was simply too large to be believable, in Lamar's view. There wasn't enough information about the Black Panthers that differed from any other American bomb group to fill a book that size.

As the German junior officer read down through the list of group officers, he came to a lieutenant who had recently been promoted and moved to an admin-istrative position. It would have been understandable to correct a seemingly minor error, to perhaps show the Germans that they didn't know everything. But Lamar resisted the urge; such a seemingly small detail might be useful to the Germans, or it might be seen as readiness to cooperate in apparently harm-less ways. Lamar said not a word.

Eventually, Lamar was moved to another wooden building, along with a number of other prisoners, including Darden. They were not able to talk, but it was comforting to see his crewmate. In this new building, Lamar had a much larger room with a more comfortable bed. He was alone, but soon heard a voice from the adjacent room.

He was able to talk a bit with the prisoner in the next cell, but even then La-mar was keenly aware that the man might have been a plant by the Germans. Perhaps, but he had a heck of a story. The man said he was British, a bomber crewman whose ship had been hit over Germany. The plane was going down, and another crewman's parachute had been lost or destroyed when it was hit. Together, each holding the other in what surely must have been a death grip, the two friends had jumped together with a single parachute. The speaker's leg had been injured in the explosion, and he landed awkwardly on it when they hit the earth and now was in great pain.[6]

Lamar was to meet many fliers in the coming months, some with nearly unbelievable tales of escaping death. But he had witnessed many things, felt himself lucky to be alive, and knew that no situation could be considered beyond the realm of truth in the incredible world of war. Later, he encountered a tail gunner who had ridden the back section of his bomber all the way to earth, the horizontal stabilizer apparently acting as glider wings. The tail assembly landed in trees, the gunner was knocked out and thrown from the wreckage, only to be captured by Germans who verified his incredible luck by finding his unused parachute still in the shattered remnants. Another gunner had jumped from his flaming bomber without a 'chute, had free-fallen for thousands of feet, and landed on top of a deployed canopy. He had slid down the shrouds, and the two airmen had clutched each other to both land safely. It was difficult to sort truth from fiction or exaggeration, and there were enough plainly miraculous escapes to render meaningless the search for exact truth. His own experience of being caught in the bomb bay and pulling out the rip cord without apparent ill effect was hard to understand. Why would he question anyone's account?

Thus far, Lamar knew, he had been confronted by the tactics of solitary confinement to break down his sense of team and community; threats to induce fear of his own death; and the perhaps unintentional sidebars of poor sleeping facilities and even worse food. The bread, he later learned, contained at least 30 per cent sawdust and minced leaves and straw. It was poor fare, but German civilians were not eating much better. The sleeping routine was probably an intimidation technique, a way of breaking his resistance. The bed in his original cell was missing slats, and the thin, straw-filled mattress sagged so badly that sleep was all but impossible. Once when he had tried to sleep on the floor, he had been angrily confronted by a guard who demanded he climb back into his cot.

What was next? Lamar was soon to learn. He was taken the next morning to a large room where a man in civilian clothes (Lamar later learned he was a lieutenant-colonel and an accomplished interrogator) greeted him warmly. It was the classic "good cop" ploy. For what seemed like an hour at least, the man made small talk. He discussed his suit—it was made of wood fiber—and of farming in Canada. He claimed to have raised wheat in America's northern neighbor, and to have done so a full two hundred miles further north than anyone had previously been able to do. Lamar feigned deep interest, but when asked about his own accomplishments he had replied that he found the man's stories fascinating, but was too young to have any stories to exchange. He also knew that the room was doubtless wired to record the entire conversation, and he vividly recalled American intelligence officers warning against the slightest slip. Any shred of information, however trivial, might prove to be important and possibly result in the loss of American lives. Lamar was keenly aware of his responsibility. Eventually, the interrogator tired of the fruitless exchange, and Lamar was returned to his cell.[7]

Late that afternoon, Lamar, Darden, and about forty others—including Mike Craig, whom they saw again for the first time since entering Dulag Luft—were sent northeast to a holding camp at Wetzlar. There they waited until there were enough prisoners to fill a train. The food was a bit better than at the receiving camp, and there was a fraction more to eat. But it was the "Joy Box" that notched the Wetzlar experience a tick above undiluted misery. The box, issued by the International Red Cross, contained towels, soap, tooth powder, underwear, cigarettes, shaving equipment, toilet paper, vitamins, a sweater, and other personal items that made the experience seem like Christmas to the prisoners. Most of them only had what they were wearing when they bailed out of their aircraft, and none had been able to shave or clean up in more than a week. They were now allowed to, and it was a briefly transforming event. The euphoria over the personal items was tempered shortly thereafter, however, when they were given their new German ID tags. They were expected to always have the metal tag around their necks; it was a sobering and humiliating gift from the German government.

Lt. Lee Lamar was now prisoner 6424.

In a few days, the prisoners at Wetzlar were herded onto a train that would take them to Barth, on the Baltic Sea 130 miles north of Berlin, a windswept and bitterly cold place for the coming winter, a winter that would go down as one of the coldest across Europe in centuries.

They were transported in antiquated but regular passenger cars, not the cattle cars of the old Forty and Eight (forty men, eight horses) of the First World War. Still, it was not a pleasant tourist trip. They were crowded eight to a compartment, and would be in these close quarters for several days. There was not enough room for all to sit, nor any place for them all to sleep at night. Smaller prisoners were able to crawl up into the overhead baggage compartment to grab some uneasy and fitful sleep, while the rest rotated between sitting on the two hard wooden benches or standing in the area between them. A little British Spitfire pilot easily slipped into the baggage hold.

They were a sad-looking lot. One of their compartment mates had bailed out over Vienna, landing square atop an air-raid shelter just as the all-clear had sounded. Civilians had beaten him viciously, and he was still recovering from massive head wounds. His hair was missing in large, scabbed-over chunks, several of which were infected. Another was a pilot who had bailed out over Germany from his stricken Liberator, and also had been attacked by civilians. They had captured two of the crew, and he was forced to watch as they beat his crewmates to death. Incredibly, a young boy who had witnessed the capture ran to get his father, who stopped the mob from killing the pilot. His own son, he told them, was a prisoner of war in the U.S., and had written him that he was treated extremely well. (A few years later, Lamar learned, the pilot had been able to return the favor. The German had been arrested for being a Nazi and was to be tried at Nuremberg. He was able to get him released.)

On the night of 6 December, four days after his parents received that first telegram declaring him missing in action, Lamar and his train mates were nearly killed. Ironically, those responsible for their close encounter were the British, although no animosity was involved. Just the odd circumstance, which in later wars would be known as "friendly fire."

Just outside of Leuna, a small town near Meresburg, the train was stopped at the passenger station. Lamar had secured a space on the floor, and he was trying to grab some much-needed sleep. The banshee wailing of the air-raid siren jarred him from his light sleep.

The Allied air forces had settled on a strategy of 'round-the-clock bombing, with the Royal Air Force opting for night bombing and the Army Air Forces conducting daylight raids. The AAF was convinced that precision bombing was possible, and that the heavily armed long-range bombers would be able to devastate any target through repeated raids of hundreds of aircraft. The RAF, which had suffered horrendous losses early in the war during daylight strikes, switched to the safety of nighttime darkness to protect their aircrews. To pinpoint the target, pathfinder aircraft—usually fast, unarmed Mosquitoes—were sent ahead to locate the target and to drop a series of flares to mark the path for the bombers.

The door to the prisoners' compartment flew open. Someone shouted in the darkness, a shrill question that was nearly a scream.

"What does a green flare mean? One just bounced off a car up ahead!"

The little Spitfire pilot, overhead in the baggage hold, was instantly awake. "Hit the deck! That's the center of the target!" He tumbled from the overhead bin to the floor, landing atop Lamar. Instantly, the rest of the prisoners dove onto the pile, covering their heads as the drone of hundreds of heavy bombers filled the evening sky. They could hear the pounding "whoomph" of German antiaircraft artillery opening up on the overhead armada. The barrage quickly became a thundering cacophony, a shattering series of explosions that became an indistinguishable, violent wave of constant assault on their eardrums. Soon the bombs began to fall, and the deeper eruptions of the five-hundred or thousand-pound bombs punctuated the steady roar of the guns. Concussive waves of thick air assaulted their bodies like kicks and punches. Outside, the blasts lit up the darkened city with hellish flashes, and the men in Lamar's train compartment could feel as well as see the brilliant splashes of intense light, followed by the flickering, strobe-like dance of flame and darkness. The explosions were visceral, felt all the way to their bones as the ground shook and the railcar rattled. It was beyond description, the horror and the destructive power unleashed by the overhead bombers, and Lamar was keenly aware of the irony that he might be killed by Allies doing exactly the same job he had done until only days before.

On and on the bombing went. Lamar, on the bottom of the pile of men, could only move his two fists, and finally the constant barrage of noise and light and fury became too much to bear. He began to beat his fist against the floor of the car, crying out to God to direct the next bomb squarely onto their compartment to bring an end to the nightmare.[8]

Gradually, the noise abated, the interval between explosions grew longer, and then there were no more. The silence that followed was complete.

Slowly, the men pulled themselves up from their pile and dusted themselves off. Miraculously, it seemed to them, they were still alive. No one had been hit. And as it turned out, the train was not hit by any of the hundreds of bombs dropped that night.

The next day, the train chugged slowly through the sprawling wreckage of Berlin. Buildings everywhere were in ruins, often reduced to piles of bricks, and many were still burning. The prisoners stared out at the capital of the Third Reich, watching elderly civilians picking through the mounds of rubble, or walking in a daze along littered and shattered sidewalks. For hours, they made their way through the heart of Hitler's Germany, keenly aware that it was the anniversary of Pearl Harbor. They didn't want to go through another bombing, especially one that might be especially vengeful.

Finally, they cleared the metropolis and slowly moved north. The next morning they arrived at Barth, and were marched to Stalag Luft I.

Lamar had survived perilous missions as a pilot, pulled through the interrogation of downed fliers, and lived through a bombing attack. Now he was to endure the hardship of a prisoner of a war. He was now a Kriegie.

Chapter 16

8 December 1944–1 May 1945
Kriegieland

For the next four-and-a-half months, Lamar and his fellow prisoners at Stalag Luft I assumed new identities in a new land. Prisoner 6424—formerly known as Lt. Edgar Lee Lamar—left the community of human beings and became a Kriegie, short for the German word *Kriegsgefangen,* or prisoner. He and the others lived in a parallel universe they called Kriegieland, a place where despair replaced hope, hunger was a constant companion, and fear and anger became normal emotions. Each day was a twenty-four hour cup of time filled with rigid German discipline and procedure but with very little to do. Each was a copy of the day before, with very few exceptions.

Some of the American Kriegies had been there for two years or more. Some of the British fliers had been imprisoned for four or five years. All were under-nourished, surviving on a diet of about eight hundred calories a day, and many had developed nervous tics or other manifestations of stress. A few stared vacantly across the compound for hours, seeing things they could not or would not articulate. For all of them, their weakened bodies were unable to resist colds or infections, and the shortage of showers and sanitary facilities left them filthy and diseased.

But as Lamar and all those who continued to swell the prison camps knew, time was growing short for the Third Reich. They had seen the devastation of the German cities firsthand, and they realized the fragility of the German will to continue the war. The newly arrived Kriegies brought with them a sense of hope that they would soon rejoin the rational world of families and sweethearts and meals and jobs and life instead of death.

Under the protocols originated in the Third Reich for the securing, housing, and treatment of prisoners of war, Hermann Goering, the pompous and obese

161

Reichsmarshall with a penchant for operatic uniforms, insisted that Allied flying personnel would be guarded by the Luftwaffe. Following the strict class
divisions within the German military, officers would be segregated from enlisted men, and the "gentlemen fliers" would not be compelled to work. The
Luftwaffe wanted to foster a sense of an elite fraternity of the air, regardless of
nationality; it was an extension in some ways of their Aryan race mentality, and
the mindset that led to the Holocaust.[1] By the time Lamar reached the gates of
the POW compound north of Barth, however, the responsibility for the prisoners had been shifted to the Gestapo, and life became exponentially harsher
for the prisoners. Punishment was swift for the slightest infraction. This usually meant time spent in solitary confinement, but it might be physical abuse as
well. During Lamar's imprisonment, at least one prisoner was shot and killed
by a guard for inadvertently stepping outside his barrack at the wrong time.

More than nine thousand Allied prisoners called Stalag Luft I their temporary home. After America entered the war late in 1941, there was a steady stream
of downed flying officers marching through the gates of the prison camp, and
soon the original compound was augmented with a second, then a third. A
fourth—North Compound III—was completed just as Lamar and his train com-
panions from Obereusal and Wetzlar arrived. They were the first to occupy the
just-completed prison area.

The camp was situated on a peninsula that jutted into the Baltic Sea, and sharp,
icy winds blew through the compounds and through the flimsy wooden barracks that housed the captured airmen. It was a bleak setting, a gray landscape set against a cold gray sea, with scudding gray clouds blocking the sun
save for infrequent days when it broke through to warm the backs and hearts
of the prisoners. Fine hard snow blew like sand across the open spaces, sting-
ing exposed skin, and the frigid Baltic wind brought tears to the eyes of anyone outside.

The new wooden buildings were as stark and bleak as the landscape. Nine
large residence barracks each housed about two hundred men. Each barracks,
an exact duplicate of the others, was subdivided into smaller rooms, with the
larger spaces holding twenty-four officers. The prisoners slept in three-tiered
bunks; each large room contained a small coal-burning stove, and a rough table and benches. The entire camp was surrounded by a pair of parallel, high
barbed-wire fences, with guard towers situated not more than a couple of hundred feet apart. The towers held shacks about ten feet square, and were manned
by helmeted, grim-faced German troops with machine guns. A single strand of
wire was stretched around the inside perimeter about ten feet from the outer
fences, and marked a killing zone. Any prisoner spotted in this no-man's land,
or even touching the warning wire, could be shot without warning. No one
would ever mistake a Stalag for a resort.[2]

In this desolate and soul-killing universe, Lamar and his "Kriegie Class" learned that Air Force organizational structure had been instituted, a structure that gave a sense of normalcy as well as utilitarian efficiency: a Wing command, under the supervision of the Senior Allied Officer (SAO), had responsibility for the entire camp; Groups—the four individual compounds—were organized into Squadrons, which comprised the personnel of each barrack. Thus, when Lamar arrived, there were forty-six squadrons organized under four groups, all under Provisional Wing X under the direction of Col. J. R. Byerly, a B-17 bomb group commander who had been flying out of Italy until shot down in January 1944.

A week after Lamar, Darden, Craig, and the others of the initiating class of North Compound III arrived, Byerly's position as SAO was supplanted by Col. Hubert "Hub" Zemke, the colorful commander of the famed 56th Fighter Group (Zemke's Wolfpack). The unit was the top-scoring fighter group in the Army Air Forces, having shot down more than six hundred enemy aircraft, and included many of the top aces of the European theater. Zemke himself was credited with 17.75 "kills," including one of the new Messerschmitt ME-262 jet fighters. (The three-quarter kill reflects credit given to several pilots for a single shoot-down). Zemke, whose mother was German, spoke fluent German and was ideal for the top spot. He had become a POW after a violent storm tore a wing from his P-51 Mustang and he was forced to bail out.[3]

The Stalag "Group Commanders" were also a storied lot. Lt. Col. Ross Greening, shot down over Italy while flying a medium bomber, had been one of the original sixteen pilots of B-25s that bombed Tokyo in April 1942, taking off the carrier USS *Hornet* behind Lt. Col. (later Lt. Gen.) Jimmy Doolittle. After surviving the mission—one of the most famous of the war—Greening had been transferred to Europe along with many of the original Doolittle Raiders because of U.S. fears that they would be executed by the Japanese if captured. The other Group Commanders of the prison camp were all fighter pilots, including Lt. Col. Francis Gabreski, the top-scoring AAF ace in Europe, credited with twenty-eight air-to-air kills. He had badly damaged the propeller of his P-47 fighter while making a (very) low level strafing pass on a German air field and had crash-landed. It was scheduled to be his last mission, and of course it was. (Gabreski was later to become an ace in Korea as well.)

Despite being prisoners of the German government, the American and British fliers were self-sufficient to a remarkable degree. Actual operation of the camp—under strict German regulations—was again divided along the Army Air Forces model: S-1, personnel, dealt with the general welfare of the prisoners, including mail, medical attention, and the like; S-2, intelligence, accomplished a great deal despite the watchful eyes of the Germans; S-3, morale, organized games, entertainment, and educational classes for the prisoners; S-4, supply, attended to the distribution of Red Cross materials, rations, clothing, and sanitation.

The arrangement of Allied officers organizing the prisoners relieved the Germans from a host of quotidian headaches, and unintentionally provided the prisoners with a certain amount of freedom to pilfer, harass, and disturb their overseers. From the surface, Stalag Luft I was a well-oiled German machine operated by Allied fliers. Twice a day, prisoners turned out for roll call. But twice a day, the prisoners sought to throw off the count of their guards by switching places, by feigning illness and staying in their bunks, and otherwise causing consternation among the poorly educated guardians of their captivity.[4]

Lamar quickly found other small ways to resist. To hinder possible escapes, the Germans required that any canned food sent through the Red Cross be opened immediately—prisoners were assigned to puncture the tops of canned goods so that they would have to be consumed quickly and not hoarded for a possible escape. Further, all the small packets of pepper in the food parcels had to be discarded under the watchful eye of German guards. The pepper, they believed, could be used to throw guard dogs off the scent of escapees. Assigned the task of aiding the distribution of food parcels, Lamar decided to risk the possibility of thirty days in solitary confinement. He was supposed to open each parcel, remove the packs of pepper, and throw them into a box set nearby. Watching the German guard overseeing the prisoners while not being obvious, Lamar waited until something outside distracted the guard, and then shoved handfuls of the pepper packets into a leg pocket of his flight suit. The pepper, so far as he knew, never aided in any escapes, but it added to the prisoners' enjoyment of the sparse food while giving Lamar the satisfaction of violating the regulations.

Escape from Stalag Luft I would have been very, very difficult. A land route would mean crossing the entire length of Germany, from Barth in the extreme north down to France or another country now freed from German occupation. Food and shelter would have been nearly impossible to obtain, and the movement of everyone in Germany was strictly controlled. With no money and no identity cards, Allied soldiers would be quickly spotted. The best route might be across the Baltic, but the chances of finding a boat and avoiding German maritime patrols would be extremely remote. During Lamar's tour in the prison camp, he never heard of anyone escaping. The difficulty of escape will be apparent to those who have seen the movie *The Great Escape*, which details an actual mass breakout from Stalag Luft III.

Shortly after arriving at the Stalag, Lamar wrote a letter to his family. It was brief, and subject to the strict scrutiny of German censors:

> Dear Mother and Dad and all,
> We had a tough break but everything is OK now. I am not injured in any way and some of my buddies are here with me so I am not too lonesome. They are not

injured either. I hope everyone is feeling fine. Don't worry about me. Everything will be O.K. The Red Cross is taking good care of us. Many thanks to them for the food and clothing. . . . I am not required to work. However we do cook our own food and that gives us something to pass the time away. . . . My letters are limited so don't worry if you don't hear. I'll be O.K. but lazy.

Love, Lee[5]

Lamar wrote regularly, but despite international regulations that required the delivery of mail to and from prisoners, it was the only letter his parents received. A cousin received a single postcard. He received no personal mail during his imprisonment, nor did any others in his barracks. Later, after the Germans left, the POWs discovered rooms full of undelivered and unposted mail. The letters would have been much needed food for their souls. But despite their homesickness, it was actual sustenance that the prisoners missed every minute of every hour. The German food was meager at best; it consisted primarily of vegetables such as turnips, cabbage, and potatoes with very occasionally a bit of meat they suspected was horse. Often the fare was half spoiled, and the heavy black bread that was served often contained bits of glass or splinters and large percentages of saw dust, which they assumed constituted the floor sweepings of a nearby sawmill or carpenter's shop.

The International Red Cross had made arrangements for each prisoner to receive a weekly food parcel, but they arrived infrequently. In fact, from Christmas day to nearly the end of March, very few supplemental food packages arrived. The parcels contained such items as Klim (powdered milk; Klim was milk spelled backwards), coffee, jam, prunes, Spam, sugar, cheese, chocolate bars, and cigarettes. The boxes were much anticipated, and their absence was a sore loss indeed and deeply missed, especially by the Kriegies who had been there for several years. They later learned that the Red Cross food parcels had been regularly delivered to a nearby port, but the Germans said they did not have fuel to transport the boxes from the warehouse to the prison camps. Lamar heard that Americans working through the Red Cross finally authorized a delivery of gasoline to the Germans to allow the food to be carted to the camps.

Included in the original Joy Box given to Lamar and the other prisoners at Wetzlar was a small paperbacked notebook. During his time as a POW, Lamar made notations regularly. It was not a diary or journal, but rather the musings of an inquiring mind striving to stay busy. Countless lists fill the pages—the crew of *Bottoms Up*, the names and addresses of prisoners in his barracks, the contents of a Red Cross parcel, a blazon of army clothing articles he needed to replace, books read in prison camp. One page notes future transactions: one gallon of molasses for figs and candy from R. W. Bell, Sacramento, and another gallon of molasses and two sacks of sausages for H. H. Handley, Jersey City, N.J., in exchange for glazed fruit and maple sugar.

Lamar's orderly, engineer's mind was evident in the transcription of German words and phrases, and the careful, detailed sketches of Casa Mañana, their temporary home in Italy, and in several drawings of houses which he envisioned as home someday after the war.

Shortly after arriving at the prison camp, a new contingent of prisoners arrived, as was the routine until the end of the war. As he watched the parade of new Kriegies march through the gate, he spotted an old friend, David Gross. They had a quick reunion, and Gross told Lamar that Joe Betine, an original member of the Darden crew who was ill on the day they were shot down, had been on his crew when they were downed a week later. So far as he knew, Betine was alive and a prisoner somewhere. A couple of others on his crew had not been so lucky.

A member of Gross's crew who was also a new prisoner recognized Lamar and told him the story of his leather A-2 flight jacket. The jackets, much coveted by flight crews and ground pounders alike, were considered government property, and by 1944 were hard to obtain. A year earlier, the last contracts for leather jackets were filled, and the current contracts called for wool-lined cotton jackets. If an A-2 were among the articles left when an airman went missing, the jacket was not included in the property sent home but instead recycled through a supply depot on base. A few days after the Darden crew was reported missing in action, the airman went to the supply tent to see if any A-2s were available, and the sergeant handed him Lamar's, with his leather name tag still sewn on. He rejected it.

"No, I know that guy, and he's dead. I don't want to wear his jacket." Lamar never learned the final disposition of his beloved jacket.

The days began to blur as the unending routine continued. Yet there still were occasions for striking back at the enemy and for receiving good news. The Red Cross cigarettes—American brands—were the gold standard for smokers, and they were carefully hoarded for trading with certain guards. The penalties for both if caught would be swift and severe, but there were a few trusted guards who could be approached. The Allied officers, to ensure the safety of the Kriegies and the guards, allowed direct contact by just a few specified prisoners. Most of the guards at Stalag Luft I were either very old or extremely young, and few would be considered hard-core Nazi. For a few cigarettes, nearly anything could be obtained, and the enterprising American and British prisoners had obtained enough parts to construct a radio that would receive the BBC broadcasts of the progress of the war.

The radio was hidden inside a wall, and was activated when a wire loop was inserted into a couple of innocuous nail holes in the wall. The radio was a top-secret weapon in the prisoner's war against ignorance and misinformation, and its location and operation were closely guarded. To ensure that all in the camp received the latest and correct war news, the intrepid prisoners also became journalists. They had their own clandestine newspaper.

Each day during the BBC broadcast, details of war news were taken down in shorthand, then transcribed to small sheets of onionskin paper, one copy for each of the four compounds. The resulting "newspaper" was folded until it fit inside a wristwatch case, from which the movement had been removed, and a prisoner with duties in another compound carried it to someone there. In the event he were stopped, the hands of the watch were always set to the correct time. The news was read in a barracks, then passed along to the other buildings. The prisoners were careful never to publicly dispute the German propaganda broadcasts, nor to rearrange the battle lines on the large map of Europe that the Germans allowed the prisoners to have. That would have telegraphed that the Kriegies were getting accurate information from outside.

The days dragged on. Night came quickly during the winter that far north, and there was little to do once the sun set below the horizon. Lamar read books sent by the Red Cross, and he scribbled in his notebook. He dreamed of home, of wandering around the farm, of the carefree days of chores. He thought about his school days, of his classes at the university. Lamar and the others talked about home, and about food. About what they wanted to do when the war was over. About women. Cars. Sports.

There were stories, of course. Lots of stories, the kind that begin with "There I was, at twenty thousand feet, with Jerries all around me. . . ." Each man in the camp had his own tale of how he got there, and there was after a while a sameness about them that numbed the listeners to the individual experience. A few stood out—the tail gunner who rode down the aft section of his bomb-er without a parachute, the P-38 pilot who ripped open his leg on a counter-weight that projected above the horizontal stabilizer, the buddies who came down under a single canopy. But they all had stories, and newly arrived prison-ers were sometimes astounded to learn that no one wanted to listen to theirs. One young P-51 pilot, shot down on one of his first missions, thought he was regaling his barracks mates with his tale of bailing out of his burning fighter. He looked shocked when he was told to forget that—"We all have those stories, Mac, how do you think we got here?" Instead, they craved the latest news from home. What were the latest songs? What's the food like at home? Gasoline still rationed?

Winter slowly warmed into Spring, with a gradual lengthening of the days and slightly warmer temperatures. 27 March 1945, was much like any other day, but for Lamar it was his twenty-fourth birthday. He recorded the events of the day in his notebook:

I awoke about 07:45. The first thing I did was to hear Lt. Fogelberg declare that it was his birthday and that he was twenty years old. I hastened to inform him and the rest of the boys that it was also my birthday. We went to roll call at 08:15 and were informed that we would receive a quarter of an issue of Red Cross parcels, the first for one month. Later we received good war news. I considered this a sufficient birthday gift.[6]

The war was over for the Kriegies, at least the fighting part, but beyond the barbed wire the bloodshed and violence continued at a savage pace. The Germans had attempted a push-back in late December, in what came to be called the Battle of the Bulge, but they were finally smashed. Meanwhile, in the east the Russians were rolling inexorably toward Germany. The prisoners knew that it was only a matter of time before "Joe" (for Stalin) would push through and liberate the camp. Each day, the news from BBC was secretly circulated throughout the compounds. As the Kriegies turned out for calisthenics each morning, the cadence was changed from "One, two, three, four," to "One, two, come on Joe!" The German guards apparently never caught on to the subversive hidden meaning.

In mid-April, the POWs received the somber news of the death of Franklin Delano Roosevelt. FDR had been President for a majority of the time most of the young prisoners had been alive. The new commander-in-chief was a former senator from Missouri, but few had heard of him. Lamar reminded his barracks mates that he was from Missouri, and he had a dim view of Harry Truman. The Man from Independence had long been associated with Tom Pendergast, a political boss from Kansas City who was widely regarded as corrupt.

"I'm afraid we don't have much of a president, fellas." Lamar pronounced his assessment with a long face. He was later to change his mind completely.

Shortly after, it was evident that the Russians were within a few miles of the camp. There was worry that the Germans might decide to fight it out with Stalin's army, which would have been catastrophic for the prisoners. As April neared its end, it was still hard to determine what course the Germans would take. An antiaircraft artillery school south of the camp was a permanent facility with several large, red brick buildings. The school had trained antiaircraft gunners, and several times the prisoners had watched Luftwaffe planes fly low and slow over the area, apparently to give the gunners experience in tracking. Now, several large explosions were heard in the direction of the school complex, and the Krieges deduced that the Germans were destroying any equipment that might be helpful to the Russians.

Most of those involved in World War II recognized the magnitude of the experience, and thousands of books have been written by or about those involved. A fellow Kriegie, Lt. Morris J. Roy, had kept a journal since being shot down, with the intention of writing a book. He now began to solicit orders from his compatriots for the future edition. Obviously, no one had any money or a checkbook, but it was not unusual in those days for banks to honor any instrument that resembled a bank check. Lamar wrote out a check on a scrap of paper, payable on his bank in Dearborn, Missouri. It was honored, and a year after the war ended, Roy sent him a copy of *Behind Barbed Wire*. It remained one of Lamar's most prized possessions, and the author used it to gain a general impression of life in Stalag Luft I.

On the last day of April, they were advised to dig new trenches for latrines. Formerly, the latrines had been cleaned by Russian prisoners using an ancient "honey wagon," but apparently the senior Allied officers had reason to think that they would not be performing that loathsome task much longer. The next morning, Lamar and the other nine thousand Allied prisoners of war in Stalag Luft I awoke to find the Germans gone, the guard dogs dead, and Americans and British troops manning the towers. But now, the eyes of the guards were riveted outside the compound, not inside.

At other camps threatened by the proximity of Allied armies, Germans evacuated the compounds and forced prisoners to march in columns that were subject to air and artillery attack. The prisoners often were weakened and sick, and many died who might have lived had they stayed in the camps. The commandant of Stalag Luft I had called Col. Zemke to his office the previous night and announced that the entire camp would be evacuated the next day. Zemke refused, and said the prisoners would not cooperate. The prospect of controlling nine thousand recalcitrant prisoners, with the Germans facing harsh treatment and probably death if captured by the Russians, convinced the commandant to concede. A deal was struck: the Germans would leave late at night, but no prisoners were to be told. The guard dogs would all be killed, silently, and the Allied prisoners would be allowed to stay and be the sole responsibility of Col. Zemke. In the meantime, the Germans would head west as quickly as they could and try to surrender to American or British troops.

The harsh treatment of Germans—civilians as well as troops—by the Russians has been well documented. Certainly, one reason was retribution: millions of Russians and Slavs had been killed and brutalized by Germans after their invasion of Mother Russia. Operation Barbarossa, in June 1941, had caught Stalin by surprise, and the subsequent bloodletting on both sides came to be symbolized by the siege at Stalingrad. Now the Russians were paying the Germans back in spades, making little or no distinction between die-hard Nazis or those simply drafted, or even whether they were military or civilians. Little mercy had been shown in Russia; less would be given in Germany.

After the Germans slipped out of the prison camp, the German radio, which had been hooked to loudspeakers throughout the compounds, was quickly tuned to BBC, and the latest war news was broadcast across the camp. In

Lamar's barracks, the loudspeaker was in the hallway, and on this first day without German guards, men crowded into the long, wide hallway to listen to the program *Hit Parade.* The latest songs were played in a countdown to the most popular. Before the number two song was played, the program was interrupted by an Allied officer in camp who reported that the advance party of Russians was now at the Stalag gate. Lamar and his barracks mates cheered, but no one left the hallway. All were starved for American music.

The tune played, and the young American prisoners of war snapped their fingers, bobbed their heads, and swayed and juked to the music. Once more, the broadcast was interrupted to report that Hitler was dead. The men cheered loudly, but they still stayed glued to *Hit Parade.* Finally, the number one tune was played, and the irony was not lost on these men. The song? "Don't Fence Me In."

Chapter 17

30 April–20 June 1945
Purgatory

Lamar and the rest of the nine thousand prisoners of war at Stalag Luft I had been liberated by the Russians, but the meaning of freedom took a while to sink in. The routine of twice-daily roll-calls, of brutal consequences for small infractions, of deprivation and hunger, all took a while to shake off. When it did, there was a celebration that the former Kriegies would never forget.

An element of bedlam—here used in the exact original meaning of the London insane asylum—permeated the camp, as the not-quite-free prisoners began to celebrate their liberation. On 1 May 1945, the first day after the Russian army came through the gates to Stalag Luft I, Lamar was enjoying simply lounging around North Compound III. No guards, no mandatory roll calls, no fear. He reveled in the feeling of freedom.

Spring on the coast of the Baltic Sea is still chilly. There is sharpness to the air, a crystal quality that seems to transmit sounds with special clarity. Lamar heard, on this first day of freedom, a buzzing that grew in volume with each passing minute. He listened closely, but he was unable to identify it as anything he had heard before. It wasn't the sound of exploding ordnance, or the firing of guns, or the roar of the wind off the sea. These were all sounds that he now could easily identify. No, this was something else, something that had an organic quality to it, something that was alive, pulsating with blood and energy.

A Kriegie he recognized but whose name he did not recall rushed toward Lamar, his face glowing.

"They're tearing down the fences in the other compounds!" he screamed. In seconds, it seemed to Lamar, hundreds of ex-prisoners ran to the fences of the North Compound and in unison pushed and pulled on the hated wire and posts in a focused frenzy of determination and explosive giddiness. In his imprisonment, Lamar had never seen the Kriegies exert themselves in such a display of physical might; faces grew taut, hands gripped wooden posts and strands of wire, and without anyone calling cadence, they strained against the barrier that had enclosed them for months or years. The ten-foot-high fence began to sway; there followed a second wave of fury, and the entire ring of posts and wire fell in slow motion. Teutonic efficiency and precise engineering never really stood a chance against the pent-up sense of humiliation and outrage of the American and British ex-POWs. In a scene that might have resembled a football crowd toppling goalposts at the end of a championship game, the Kriegies pulled down the vile fences and the oppressive guard towers, cheering lustily as they fell. Colonel Zemke had hoped to keep the American and British former prisoners separated and safe from the Russians, of whom he was wary, but the Kriegies themselves thwarted his plan.

Later that day, Lamar walked down to the former Luftwaffe antiaircraft school, with its red brick buildings, and watched as German civilians carted away armloads of military gear. He poked around and came across a crowd, now dispersing, wearing heavy sheepskin-lined Luftwaffe flying boots that they had liberated from a storehouse. Warm and well made, the boots were a fine souvenir, but there were none left by the time the American lieutenant arrived. Later, Lamar traded his well-worn GI shoes to a German civilian for a fine pair of the flight boots.

The road out of the Stalag and the streets of the ancient town of Barth were a circus of frightened civilians, giddy American and British former POWs, Russian troops, and military vehicles. It was all too confusing, too noisy, too disorienting. Darkness was settling over the town and the compound, and Lamar decided to head back to camp. On this first day of quasi-freedom, he turned in early, nearly alone in the huge barracks. The next morning, he awoke to the sight of a large white goose hanging from the ceiling directly level with his third-tier bunk, and a net on the floor containing three or four large fish. The ex-Kriegies would not be hungry tonight. Lamar shook his head, rubbed his eyes, and looked around. The rest of the boys had dragged in at various times during the night, and brought with them an astounding variety of booty, wares, souvenirs, and provisions, piled on the floor in disarray and opulence. He swung down from the bunk and wandered outside to the compound. There, the scene resembled a movie set gone berserk.

An American ex-prisoner, obviously not thinking of the potential danger to himself, had found a full-dress German officer's uniform, and was strutting around in a caricature of a goose-stepping Nazi. Someone had found and liberated a German automobile. It was parked outside the barracks, and now it was being inspected by a crowd of admiring GIs. A pair of draft horses stood stoically, looking around with an air of bemusement. Several former Kriegies were energetically setting up a tent they had found, with the intent of moving out of the crowded barracks into the comparatively private quarters of canvas walls. Someone had discovered some flare pistols and cartridges; ribbons of red and green arched through the air, the still burning flares bouncing off the sides and roofs of the various barracks. Men chased each other through the compound, several singing horridly off-key renditions of popular tunes—"Don't Fence Me In" could be heard from several directions—and the clipped tones of a BBC announcer blared through the loudspeaker. It was a riot, it was dangerous, it was decidedly unmilitary, and it was completely delicious and contagious. The awareness that they were freed from their long nightmare of captivity had now sunk in, and the reaction that next morning took on the look of a combination of a county fair, the Fourth of July, and a Hedonist convention.

Col. Zemke and the other senior Allied officers let the celebrations continue for a while but they were worried about the safety of their men, so gradually a sense of decorum was reestablished. Drunken Russian soldiers were stumbling all around the area, and the order went out that no one was to leave the compound alone; only groups of ten would be authorized to leave the Stalag. But there is a long streak of independence in Americans, so they modified the order. They formed up in groups of ten to leave the camp, scattered when they hit town, and designated an area to form up again. The first ten men there trekked back to camp without regard to the original composition of the group. A couple of days later, Lamar left in the designated crowd of ten to explore the road that wended west out of Barth. Suddenly a Russian convoy appeared, headed east, back into Russia. Lamar and the others watched as a long line of captured German military equipment moved by; plodding behind all of them were horse-drawn farm wagons, loaded high with hay and driven by a single Russian soldier. On the seat beside almost every driver sat a woman, presumably Russian but possibly German, all with careworn faces and ragged clothes. The men watched the sad parade for several minutes, Lamar thinking that none of the Russians—Allies, ostensibly—looked friendly.

Then a lighter wagon came along, pulled by two well-cared-for horses and carrying four Russian soldiers, including two officers. The entire column had stopped, and this wagon was directly in front of the Americans.

One of the officers jumped down and walked over to the onlookers. "Americanski?" he asked.

The men nodded, unsure where this was going.

The young Russian officer spoke excellent English.

"We were losing the war until we received American supplies. After that, we were able to push back the Germans. Now, we would like to do something for you in return. What can we do?" His broad and friendly face looked at each of them without guile.

Lamar and the others were embarrassed and could think of nothing. Finally, one of them said he would like to see the Cossack dance.

"Oh, but that is a very, very strenuous dance, it takes a great deal. . . ." Just then, one of the other Russians, sitting in the driver's seat and apparently an enlisted man, grinned and pulled out his squeeze box, filling the air with musical notes. The protesting Russian officer smiled, and slowly he and another officer began the high-kicking, low-squatting dance. The appreciative Americans clapped in time as the tempo speeded up, and the two officers flung themselves into the time-honored dance. After a few minutes the column began to move again, ending the impromptu thank-you dance, and the Americans applauded the good spirits of the Russians.

The days dragged, with no word on when the ex-Kriegies would be transported to American lines. A couple of days after the Cossack dance, Lamar heard that the burgermeister of Barth had killed himself and his family, possibly out of fear of reprisals by the Russians or that he and his family would be sent off to a camp in Russia. That afternoon, Lamar was walking along a levee outside of the camp, north of the city. He saw a bundle of rags ahead, knots of clothing twisted in queer ways. As he drew closer, he realized that it was two adults, a man and a woman, lying in death beside a baby carriage. Both had been shot in the middle of their foreheads. In the carriage, a baby lay in death as well, a single, purple hole in its tiny forehead. On the ground nearby lay a large revolver.

Lamar stared in sad fascination at this family tragedy, trying to imagine the desolation and utter lack of hope that had led to it. He started to pick up the revolver, but looked once more at the face of the young woman lying in her final peace. He could not bring himself to touch the gun.

On another day, Lamar and Vincent Boothroyd, a P-38 fighter pilot who had been a barracks mate before "liberation," decided to walk into Barth, so they joined the required group of ten. Lamar had been intrigued by the red silk scarves that many of the former Kriegies had acquired in town, and thought he might pick one up. Boothroyd spoke and understood a bit of German, and the pair hoped to bargain for a few fresh eggs to add to their now much-improved diet. As they strolled through the streets, Lamar saw that most of the German population had displayed red scarves or small banners of red cloth from their homes, apparently as a sign of submission to the occupying Russian forces. Lamar and Boothroyd stopped several times as Lamar inspected some of the scarlet banners, but most were of very poor quality, fashioned from cheap cotton. Eventually, he found one that was bright, clean, and appeared to be of silk. He was pleased, and removed the thumbtacks that held it to the window frame of the German household. The pair walked on down the street as Lamar draped the scarf around his neck and knotted it in front, aviator-style.

They had not gone far when an angry—and very young—voice stopped them. Lamar and Boothroyd looked down to see a girl about five years old scolding them in a nonstop stream of indignant German. The girl was well dressed, clean, and stood with her hands on her hips while she continued to castigate them.

"What is it, Booth? What's she saying?" Lamar was amused but puzzled.

Boothroyd listened for another minute, then held up his finger for the girl to be still. She ignored him and continued to fire away in her verbal assault.

"She wants her red flag back. Says if it is not in her window, the Russians will do bad things to her and her family. You took her flag and she wants it back."

Lamar, embarrassed, untied the scarf and knelt in front of the tiny figure. He draped it around her neck and tied it loosely in front, a reiteration of his own sartorial style. With great dignity, the little girl turned to retrace her steps. "How can anyone say no to that?" Lamar asked. Boothroyd only grinned.

A bit later, they ran into a POW from the camp who told them he had been invited by a German family to move in with them, most likely with the idea that such a show of magnanimity would offer them some protection from the marauding Russians. Shortly after that, Lamar and Boothroyd began knocking on doors in an effort to find eggs, and at one house a pair of German women asked them to move in. The young fliers politely declined, but they did accept a couple of eggs offered by the women. At that point, they didn't feel particularly gallant toward anyone who was German.

During the period immediately following the liberation of Stalag Luft I, Lamar developed what can only be characterized as a nervous reaction to his months of combat and then imprisonment. He began to stutter, rather badly. Never before had he suffered this affliction, but it seemed to possess him as soon as he realized that the war was apparently truly over for him. The stress of flight training, the long and fearful combat missions, the solitary confinement and threats of the German interrogation officers, and the misery of life behind barbed wire had seemingly left him unfazed. But at the release of those pressures, the stress was manifested in his inability to speak quickly or smoothly.

Those who underwent combat stress or experienced the fearful conditions of prison camps exhibited a host of reactions, including nightmares, physical debilities, eating disorders, and psychological traumas. But Lamar never observed anyone else who suddenly began stuttering. The condition lasted about three weeks, and then stopped as suddenly as it started.[1]

In the meantime, Col. Zemke was growing weary of the constant excuses of the Russians for the delay in repatriating the ex-prisoners. Lamar later learned that the foot-dragging was the demand by the Russians for the return of a particular Russian general, who after being captured by the Germans had turned. He had organized other Russian prisoners into a unit that fought with the Germans. Stalin was outraged by this perfidy, and demanded that all Russians who had fought against the Motherland be handed over for suitable punishment.

The days dragged on, and the weariness of the ex-Kriegies was manifest. At one point, they raided the administrative offices of the former camp commander, and the personnel files they found were distributed around the camp. Lamar located his own file and kept it with him, a pink form with his photo—face and profile—pasted to the bottom of the page. It was rumored that an order directly from Hitler was discovered in the commandant's office that called for the execution of all Allied prisoners.

German forces had surrendered in successive waves as individual theater or army commanders capitulated—in Italy, in northern Germany, in the Netherlands and the Frisian Islands, in Berlin. Finally on 8 May the word came that the war in Europe was over: the German government under Admiral Karl Doenitz had surrendered unconditionally. Celebrations began in cities across Europe and the United States, and the ex-Kriegies at Barth joined in as well. But it was a subdued celebration. They were tired, irritable, and wanted nothing more than to go home.

On 12 May, B-17s of the U.S. 8th Air Force began flying into Barth to airlift the former prisoners to a repatriation center north of LeHavre. It was a tremendous effort, with hundreds of the heavy four-engine bombers, no longer needed for the long, costly air campaign against Germany, flying into the small field and departing with thirty of their friends and comrades. Since many of the British fliers had been imprisoned far longer than any of the Americans, Col. Zemke ordered that all the British ex-Kriegies would be flown out first.

Thousands of ex-prisoners, ragged, dirty, in tattered uniforms, lined the runways at Barth and cheered as the first of the heavy bombers landed. The pilots of most of the aircraft never shut off their engines. They taxied back along a parallel taxi-way and stopped with engines idling while a squad of thirty ex-POWs dashed out and climbed aboard. Within minutes the plane was airborne, and others pulled into position along the taxiway for boarding. All day, the ex-Kriegies watched and cheered as each plane arrived and flew another thirty men to freedom in a nonstop stream of incoming and departing bombers.

While sitting on a bench watching the planes, Lamar and a young 2nd lieutenant began a desultory conversation about food—food they had missed, food they looked forward to eating. The younger officer had been at the Stalag only a few weeks, but long enough to know the unspoken rules: don't tell your war story. Everyone here has one. Women, sports, food, those were the topics to shoot the breeze about with a fellow Kriegie. With mild curiosity, the two watched a pair of C-46 cargo planes land amidst the steady stream of bombers. They became infinitely more curious a few minutes later, when a Kriegie walked by and told the pair, excitedly, that there were American nurses aboard the two C-46s.

The young lieutenant grinned. "Hey, my sister's a flight nurse. Maybe I should go check!" Right, thought Lamar, but didn't want to argue. They strolled over to a tent near the flight line. The sheer size of the crowd of dirty, emaciated ex-POWs told them without asking that the nurses must be here. Sure enough, they made their way forward to see a definitely female head of hair bent over a table. The young woman moved slightly, and the lieutenant grinned.

"Hi, Sis."

Lamar witnessed one of the most unlikely meetings of the war. The young man had been reported missing after his plane had gone down in flames, and reports of witnesses stressed that no one could have survived. His sister, however, had not given up, and had searched everywhere she landed for news of her brother. Lamar caught sight of him as he was placed aboard the '46 for the flight out of Germany.[2]

The next day, 13 May, Lamar was in a group designated to board. The '17 landed, graceful with its wasp-waist and perky with its nose high because of a tail-wheel, and Lamar watched every detail of the landing and the taxi with professional interest. The pilot wheeled the big bird into position on the taxiway, and the Americans were directed to get aboard without delay—and to watch out for those still-turning props.

Lamar, knowing that many of the men in his group had been bomber pilots, figured that most of them would want to be in a part of the bomber where they could work their way forward and hang out near the cockpit. He decided against fighting the crush of men and opted instead to swing into the plexiglass-covered nose of the big bomber. He moved forward from the rear door where the others were rushing and moved toward the nose hatch. He reached for and turned the handle to the hatch through which the navigator and bombardier would normally pull themselves up into the aircraft. The whirling propellers of the two inboard engines were scant inches away, it seemed, but nothing really mattered except getting into that plane.

When he settled into the cramped nose position, he was alone. The familiar sights and smells of a spartan combat aircraft, with its exposed wires, hoses, lines, its marvelously complicated bombsight and instruments, its uncomfortable close quarters, its odor of high octane fuel and oil and old sweat, made him feel at home. But it was a new position. Lamar for the first time experienced the panoramic and heart-stopping view that thousands of very young men—wearing the wings of navigators and bombardiers—had experienced on countless takeoffs from bases around the world. Everything outside seemed near enough to touch, and there was no instrument panel or aircraft nose to obstruct his view—or lend the illusion of safety. The pilot taxied onto the runway, applied full power to all four engines, and the Flying Fortress began to move, slowly at first, then with terrifying speed. The tail rose, the pilot pulled back the yoke and the '17 lifted off. To Lamar, the trees at the end of the runway seemed frighteningly close. The nose position seemed very, very vulnerable to him now. He recalled being curled inside the ball turret of a B-24 during training, when Darden took the ship down to what seemed like inches over the Colorado plains. He now developed a new appreciation for the fliers in the noses of all those bombers.

Lamar watched with undiluted pleasure as the pilot took the ship over the center of the village of Barth and then over the now almost deserted prisoner of war camp at a very low altitude. He waited for the plane to climb to a cruising altitude of several thousand feet. He knew they would not fly above ten thousand feet, because there were no oxygen masks for the passengers, so he figured on six to eight thousand feet. It didn't happen.

Freed from the constraints of formation flying and exact times for forming up and attacking strategic targets, loosed from the fear of flak and fighters, the veteran combat pilots celebrated in flier fashion. On the long trip southwest across Germany to the French coast, they hedge-hopped, buzzing towns, skimming above fields, clipping the tops of trees. Lamar should have been frightened, probably should have been angry at this apparent disregard of his welfare. He wasn't. He was exhilarated, happy beyond all telling of it to be free from the Germans and the Russians both. He watched as the wrecked cities passed by underneath, many reduced to little more than piles of broken bricks. Bridges lay in shattered spans that no longer spanned, with rivers washing over them; highways were ribbons of concrete or macadam, with huge holes blasted out of them; rail lines were disrupted by bomb craters, their rails twisted into bizarre knots and stark, rusting sculptures of war art. But huge expanses of country appeared untouched by war, and many small towns displayed no apparent damage. The coming of Spring had hidden well the best efforts of man to decimate the land; green trees and green fields promised a new tomorrow. Lamar reflected on his own missions, and thought of his family back in Faucett. He thought back over his training days, his time at the university, his capture and imprisonment. The flight over the now-vanquished Germany, away from his months of captivity, away from the terrors of combat flying, was the most memorable flight of his life. Lamar would never forget it.[3]

At Reims, for what seemed like hours, they waited in the B-17, not allowed to disembark. Finally, trucks arrived and they were herded into the backs. They were too late for dinner, they were informed, so there would be no food for them that night. The exhausted and hungry soldiers were driven to a large tent camp, where Lamar and the others found empty cots and fell into them, ignoring their gnawing stomachs and tired limbs, thankful just to be out of Germany.

The tent camp was to be a temporary staging area for their eventual return to the U.S., home, family, and peace. It was only one of several hoops the now EX-POW's had to jump through.

The next morning, Lamar and his fellow ex-POWs awoke and found their way to the mess tent, where they enjoyed a GI breakfast of eggs and pancakes. It was a little bit of heaven for men long used to rutabaga soup. After eating, Lamar carried his mess kit to wash it, in the time-honored tradition of the army, looking for the familiar three barrels of water. Unable to find them, he stopped a sergeant walking by. "Let the hired help do that," the noncom replied, pointing to a large pile of dirty mess kits. Beside the pile knelt two German prisoners-of-war, scrubbing each one clean. Lamar grinned, and tossed his kit onto the small mountain.

As Lamar walked about the tent city, wondering what would happen next, an Army truck pulled up, the back loaded with former Kriegies.

"Want a shower?" The friendly corporal behind the wheel jerked his thumb for Lamar to climb aboard. After a long drive, they arrived at another facility, with rows of outdoor showers. The filthy, lice-ridden ex-prisoners were instructed to throw their old clothing onto a large mound of tattered rags; they would be issued new uniform items. Lamar kept a few items from his pockets, including his German ID tags, and tossed the flight suit he had worn for six months onto the pile. After the shower, the men were issued new underwear and one set of enlisted men's shirt, trousers, and socks. When they returned to the tent camp, the cargo plane that was to transport them to Camp Lucky Strike had departed. A transient C-47 pilot agreed to take Lamar and the others to LeHarve, where they would grab a truck to their next stopover.

Now imprisonment was to start over, the result of someone not thinking this through very well. From the initial camp at LeHavre, they were to be transported to RAMP camp—army-speak for Repatriated Allied Military Personnel—which was in some respects a replica of a Stalag but without the comfort of permanent housing. Thousands of Allied soldiers, just released from months or years of captivity, were incarcerated—the term is harsh, but appropriate—in this makeshift camp. The only things missing were barbed wire and guard towers.

Camp Lucky Strike was an ex-Kriegie's nightmare. Twenty-thousand men were crammed together in tents. In contrast to the Stalag, they were fed well. That is, the food was good, but on doctor's orders there were no seconds of any food item for fear the men would become ill after so long on a slim diet. After eating, there was absolutely nothing to do. The former Kriegies could only walk around the area between the tents or lie on an army cot to pass the time. There was no entertainment—no sports equipment, no books, no movies, no classes, no tours. If they had any money, there was no place to spend it. It was Kriegieland boredom all over again.

The war was over in Europe; England and France were now free of the menace of the Third Reich, but it appeared that no provisions had been made for the thousands upon thousands of liberated prisoners of war beyond minimal shelter, food, and clean clothes. Lamar and several of his new friends inquired about passes to go to Paris, or anywhere outside the compound of Camp Lucky Strike. The answer: wait until you are processed so you will have proper new uniforms and some money to spend.

After what seemed like an eternity, Lamar was processed, an event that took less than a half day. With a new uniform and some back pay, he immediately applied for a pass. The reply: we can issue only 180 three-day passes each day, for that was all the rooms that had been secured in Paris. Lamar did the math and thought it could be months before his turn would come. He was very, very discouraged. For several days, he sat on his cot, along with his tent mates, and tried to pass the time by swapping stories. The insipid entertainment slowly ground to a quiet halt.

One of his friends had had a French girlfriend before he was shot down, and he suggested to Lamar that they go see the officer responsible for issuing passes. Maybe a story of true love might sway the cold hearts of the military bureaucracy. Lamar doubted it, but even a trip to the camp administration shack was something to do, so he tagged along. The other pilot went into an inner office in the small wooden building, the only semipermanent structure in the entire camp, while Lamar waited beside a desk in the outer office. While looking around, he noticed a thick pile of pass forms neatly bundled and bound with copper wire.

When his friend emerged from the office of the major, he looked downcast. They stepped outside.

"Get your pass?"

"Naw. Not a chance. Wanted me to wait and take a leave. I don't need a week's leave, just a 3-day pass. That's all it'll take to figure out if my girl is still around."

Lamar reached into his tunic pocket and handed his buddy two pass forms. He still had twenty-five or thirty that had somehow slipped out of the wire binding and found their way into his pocket.

Armed with the passes, Lamar and an old friend from St. Joseph headed out of Camp Lucky Strike and got a ride from an army truck driver who advised them where to go in Paris to find the hotel for military personnel, and a few tips on what to see. The driver was going only as far as Versailles, and there Lamar and his friend boarded a train for Paris. The entire car they boarded, it seemed, was filled with ex-Kriegies. As it turned out, none had passes, but Lamar soon rectified that oversight. The lieutenants, captains, and majors all knew the need for a properly signed official pass, so they dutifully filled out the forms, then handed them to the man on their right to sign the line authorizing their excursion.

When they arrived at the designated hotel in Paris, it was full. A Red Cross matron directed them to a nearby hotel for enlisted crew.

"I don't understand why we're full, and there are so many more of you." Lamar and his friend left hurriedly and checked into the enlisted hotel. There they were given a brochure from the Seine Section, U.S. Army: "United States Army Paris Guide: For Leave Troops." It contained useful information on sights to see, how to use the subway, and a warning not to visit houses of prostitution. It also contained helpful hints regarding Military Police: "The Military Police in the Paris area are here to help you. . . . They know your problems. When in doubt, ask the Military Police." Lamar and his friend decided against such advice, well-intentioned as it might be.[4]

They headed out to tour the City of Light. It was unlike anything either of them had seen before: the narrow streets of the Latin Quartier, the soaring grandness of the cathedral of Notre Dame, the Hotel des Invalides and Napoleon's Tomb. They had heard of the Folies Bergiere, but when they finally found the place the last show was well under way. They headed back to the hotel. They would plan to get up early the next day to see the Champs Elysees, the Arc de Triomphe, and the Eiffel Tower.

That evening as they sauntered along the sidewalk, a couple of French girls kept looking back at them. Finally they stopped, and in schoolgirl English told them they were not the sort of girls soldiers were looking for, so please stop following them. The pair finally convinced the girls that they had merely been heading in the same direction at the same time. More conversation followed, and the girls were finally convinced that Lamar and his friend were not just on the prowl; they agreed to show them some of the sights of Paris the next day. Much to Lamar's surprise, the two young women did arrive as planned, and they proved to be witty, intelligent, and sensitive tour guides. Over the next two days, they saw everything a tourist might wish. At one point after the airmen had paid for lunch, one of the women turned to the waiter and angrily demanded that he give Lamar the correct change. "Some of these people cannot be trusted," the girl explained.

Later that day, they were outside an opera house in the Trocadaro. Neither Lamar nor his friend had been to an opera and wanted to experience this bit of culture. *Non,* it was very expensive, both girls demurred. For a couple of American fliers, the price of admission was ridiculously small, but for the two poor college students it seemed outrageous. They went in, the four of them, and Lamar enjoyed the spectacle without being able to understand a word. The girls whispered what was happening. After, they signed the program for Lamar: Annick Pommeret and Marylene Le Mercier.

Lamar and his buddy returned to Camp Lucky Strike to find that no one had missed them. In fact, hundreds, perhaps thousands, of ex-Kriegies, fed up with the routine and apparent lack of preparation for them, had simply left the camp and hitchhiked to Paris, to London, to all points of the compass to find their old units, to anywhere outside of the camp. So many had gone missing that *Stars and Stripes,* the military newspaper, began running notices in large type:

> Notice to all RAMP personnel. Please return to Camp Lucky Strike. Transportation is now available to the States.

The wording struck Lamar. Never had he seen military communications use the word *please.* Perhaps someone realized a mistake had been made in the processing of the ex-prisoners of war.

Near the middle of June 1945, Lamar finally received word that he was to board a Liberty ship at LeHavre for the trip home. There was a final thumbing of noses by the disgruntled ex-Kriegies. As they stood on a ramp to board the ship, a Red Cross truck pulled up. Two young women emerged from the cab, lowered the sides of the truck bed, and began serving coffee and doughnuts. Lamar had been accustomed to seeing the girls and the truck after every mission, but these were the first he had seen since getting shot down. The entire formation of men turned around and headed for the truck. A frazzled major, supervising the orderly boarding, began shouting for the men to return to the line.

"Hell, Major. We got to have our coffee and doughnuts!" They queued up for the treats, took their time consuming them, and finally returned to board the ship. The major finally joined them, seeing the futility of resistance. To Lamar, it signaled that the men were losing their patience with the Army's way of doing things. They would fly dangerous missions when scheduled. They would endure, honorably and quietly, the rigors and terrors of being captured and imprisoned. They would wear the uniform correctly, and salute superior officers. But they'd be damned if anyone was going to order them to forego coffee and doughnuts, served by fresh-faced young Red Cross girls. Some things are simply not to be tolerated.

Several years after the war, Lamar met a former lieutenant colonel who said he had been on a committee charged with planning for the handling of the ex-POWs after they were liberated. He told Lamar that a resort area in France had been selected for the ex-prisoners to relax and recuperate while awaiting transportation back to the States, but it had been taken over instead by officers from headquarters. "I'm sorry," he said. "We had little time left and did the best we could after that."[5]

Chapter 18

Home at Last

Lt. Lee Lamar, twenty-four years old, bomber pilot and ex-POW, arrived at Hampton Roads, Virginia, on 20 June 1945. He left for Camp Sheridan, near Chicago, the next morning, where he would be processed and then given leave. He planned to visit his sister Mildred and her husband before heading home to Faucett.

We speak today of the "Greatest Generation," and we stand before them in awe. But don't think that for the returning GIs it was all parades and kisses. Those might come later, for many, but often the soldiers came up sharply against indifference, venality, or poor planning. On his first day back in the States, Lamar decided on a haircut to celebrate his return. A brief fad at the time was for a barber, after trimming a customer's locks, to light a strip of newspaper and singe the man's hair—for an extra seventy-five cents. Lee didn't care about such self-indulgence, and declined the service. The barber, however, after clipping Lee's blond hair, lit a strip of newspaper and before the young pilot could object had quickly passed it back and forth over the top of his head. He then insisted on the additional six bits.

That experience left a bitter taste in the young lieutenant's mouth, but he was eager to board the train for Camp Sheridan the next day and put it behind him. The two-day trip aboard the crowded train was another sour experience, however. It was packed, and the weather was hot; there was only a minimal amount of poorly prepared food. Lee had to sleep in the aisle in a sleeping bag he acquired at Camp Henry.

At Camp Sheridan, the men, all ex-prisoners of war, were processed quickly. There were more unpleasant surprises. Repeatedly during his tour of combat, he and his fellow fliers had been told, by a variety of authorities, that in the event of being shot down and captured, all of their pay and allowances would continue until they were liberated. When Lee received his back pay, it did not include his flight allowance, which was fifty percent of his monthly rate. When he inquired about it, he was told, "You weren't flying, so you don't get flight pay." Years later, however, when talking to other ex-POWs who had been fliers, they all said that they had gotten flight pay for the time they were imprisoned. Apparently it depended on the interpretation of the pay officer where the men were processed.

(However, this wasn't a case of sloppy army record-keeping. Two years later, while a student at the University of Missouri, Lee received a letter from the Department of the Army: he had not been billed $6.10 in 1944 for his GI insurance. Please remit the amount due. Not all the record-keeping was so soulless. Lamar learned that Casa Mañana, the *Bottoms Up* officers' tufa-stone house, had been sold to a new crew for $200; subsequently, $50 was forwarded to the next-of-kin of each officer by Maj. Anderson, the executive officer, as directed by Col. John Price.)

At Camp Sheridan, Lee was given a sixty-day leave, with orders to report to Miami, Florida, no later than August 28 for reassignment. The war with Japan was still raging, and he assumed that after his leave he would be trained on B-29s for another tour, this time in the Pacific.

He phoned his sister Mildred in Chicago, but got no answer. After calling his home in Faucett, he learned that Mildred and her husband Norman were there on an extended visit. Lee took a train to Kansas City and walked to the Greyhound bus station where he hoped to catch an early bus to Faucett. He was too late and would have to wait several hours for the next one. He called his sister-in-law, Lovella. Brother Dick, who owned a service garage, was not home, he learned.

"That's okay. I'll stay here at the station and catch the next bus to Faucett." Lamar checked his small bit of luggage in a locker at the station and headed out to explore Kansas City on foot. In the meantime, his brother had returned home shortly after Lee's call; he and Lovella immediately headed to the bus station in Kansas City to pick up the young soldier home from the wars.

They got to the bus station, but couldn't find Lee. Dick had gone outside to see if he could find him, and returned, downcast at his failure. Lee, walking behind him, had not recognized his brother from that angle. Lovella saw the two of them and wondered what had happened between them to cause such dark looks. When the three realized what had happened, Lee's first emotional reunion occurred in the bus station.

The second took place about 10:30 that morning. After his phone call to Thelma, word had spread quickly that Lee was coming home, and neighbors and family had gathered at Urvie and Nannie Mae Lamar's place to rejoice and welcome him back from his long ordeal. His mother had fried a chicken, and there was an abundance of fresh milk and mounds of garden vegetables. After a few bites and a half-glass of milk, Lee could eat no more.

"Can't eat another bite, I'm afraid," he said in apology. His mother looked at his gaunt frame, and shook her head in sorrow.

"I understand, son. Your stomach has shrunk."

Lee spent the next two months with his family. There were hugs, tears, and laughter each time a friend, neighbor, or relative met up with the young man, who still wore his khaki uniform much of the time.

Lee had been given a card while in Camp Patrick Henry about the process of claiming his personal effects, if next-of-kin had not already done so. As it turned out, the national Personal Effects Bureau was in Kansas City, at 18th and Hardesty. One afternoon he jumped in the family car to go into the city to get his gear, if indeed anything had been sent. He used the gasoline ration cards he had been given at Camp Sheridan, and filled up at his brother's garage. His brother refused to take the coupons. "I never take the coupons from servicemen. You keep them for later."

He drove into Kansas City, where a pretty young woman helped him fill out the paperwork to claim his personal effects. In five minutes, a box, weighing 180 pounds, was wheeled out onto a dock and loaded into the car. He was surprised at the size. It turned out that the flight crews had taken only the basics they would need when they flew to the war zone; the rest was placed on a ship to be delivered later. Lee was shot down before the bulk of his gear arrived in Italy. He had heard many stories about the gear of fliers who were shot down being divided among squadron mates, but that was not the case here. Virtually everything had been carefully packed and sent back to the States—except for his leather flight jacket, of course.[1]

A thrill for Lamar during this leave was taking his grandmother for her first airplane ride. He rented a small Aeronca at a grass field near St. Joseph; the elderly woman loved it. When he set it down, his sister Thelma was waiting for a flight. Following that, his mother was waiting, and, for Lee, the greatest shock of all: his father, who had been so against Lee's flying, was patiently awaiting his only ride in an airplane.

At some point during his leave, he learned that a cousin, Maurice Lamar, had also been a POW, captured during the Battle of the Bulge. He was in the Army hospital at Rosecrans Field in St. Joe, and Lamar went to visit him. Maurice was soon shipped to another hospital, and he suffered medical problems associated with his captivity the rest of his life.

During that leave, and in the years that followed, no one ever asked him about his experiences. But many years later, when his sister lay dying, she looked up at Lee and asked him about his time in the war. "Lee, you've never said a word about it." A much older Lee Lamar looked at her tenderly, and said "No one ever asked. I assumed no one wanted to hear about it." He was stunned by her reply:

"Lee, we were told by people from the army never to ask about it. They said you and the rest of the boys just needed to get on with your lives, and talking about it would be bad for you."

Lee went on to finish a degree in engineering at the University of Missouri. He married Bonnie in 1950, had a daughter, Kathy, and lived a long, healthy, prosperous life. But the only reunion he had with any of his crew after liberation was one he initiated. While still on his sixty-day rest and recuperation leave, a hurricane struck Florida, and he received a notice that his leave was extended to September 27. His sister and brother-in-law were going to drive back to Chicago, and Lee opted to go with them. They arrived in downtown Windy City just as news of the surrender of Japan was announced, and they witnessed the wall-to-wall crush of deliriously happy Americans as they poured into the streets to celebrate. The next morning, Norman awakened Lee with the news that the President had lifted gas rationing.

"We have a full tank of gas. Where do you want to go?"

Lee had learned that Don Reynolds, his bombardier and best friend from his crew, was at Truax Army Air Base near Madison, Wisconsin. He wanted to see him.

When they arrived at the base later that day, Lee Lamar and Don Reynolds held their private reunion, leaning over the hood of Norman's car while a small crowd of soldiers stood by, curious to hear their stories. Reynolds told Lamar of seeing him and Darden being driven away in a German car near Vodnjan, and of his eventual discovery by Partisans. There were many close encounters with German troops, many cold and sleepless nights, almost no food. Many of the Partisans who were part of the rescue party were killed.

Lee also learned that Hurston Webb, their engineer who had been so insistent on changing his boots while the bomber was plunging earthward, had bailed out safely but his parachute was hung up in a tree. When Partisans found him, they set about cutting the shrouds that held him to the ensnared canopy. The result was that Webb fell several feet, breaking his ankle. The Partisans had no means of caring for him; after several days, Webb's ankle was turning black, and the decision was made that Webb would be left to be captured by the Germans, who it was hoped would provide him medical attention. He did not get to use those boots at all. Webb was captured, hospitalized, and survived the war.

That impromptu reunion, initiated by Lee, was his only meeting of any of the crew of *Bottoms Up* during the war. For many years, Lee wondered what happened to the rest.

"The best thing the Army could have done for us, and all the other POWs, was to arrange a meeting of the crew," he said many years later. "We needed to be able to see each other again, to tell our stories, to reassure ourselves about the others.

"But I guess there wasn't time for that. There was still a war on."[2]

It would be more than forty years before Lamar learned the stories of all of his crew. It would be more than sixty before he would once more meet with *Bottoms Up.*

Chapter 19

Olathe, Kansas
2006

In the summer of 2006, I was preparing to teach a new course at my university on the history and literature of World War II in the air. My nephew, Kevin Brown, phoned to suggest that we attend an air show at New Century Airport in Olathe, Kansas, the former Olathe Naval Air Station. It was an event sponsored by the Heart of America Wing of the Commemorative Air Force, and I thought perhaps it would be a good opportunity to meet some veterans of the air war of World War II. I was not disappointed.

Colorful wartime aircraft, lovingly restored to original condition, were lined up on the ramp, some in gleaming polished aluminum, others in olive drab, all sporting the stars and bars insignia denoting military aircraft. Kevin, my son Haakon, grandson Chase, and I strolled among the trainers, bombers, fighters and transports, taking pictures and watching the start-up of some of those wonderful round engines. But I kept a weather eye open for signs of veterans who might have flown these birds. Some speakers would add a lot to a college class filled mostly with students for whom the Second World War is history as ancient as the American Revolution.

Then, inside the CAF hangar out of the blazing Kansas sun, I saw a row of seven or eight—the makeup of the group tended to shift—veterans sitting behind a table covered with photographs, aircraft models, and a pile of books which they were autographing for a crowd of visitors. I'm a pilot and flight instructor, have been for years. I own and fly a restored 1942 Army liaison plane. Yet all of the hardware, all of the sounds of engines starting, of planes taxiing and taking off and landing, all of that seemed unimportant when I saw the veterans telling their stories. I bought a copy of *The Heart and Soul of America: Experiences and Antics of World War II Flyers,* by Harold E. Davis. Davis is a member of the CAF, a retired educator, and a Navy veteran who had set out to record the stories of area military flyers. Many of the men behind the table were included in the book. I stood in line to get their autographs and to chat them up a bit.

Dan Fedynich was a B-17 ball turret gunner in the 8th Air Force. He flew thirty-three round trips from England to Europe, mostly Germany, with the 613th bomb squadron, 401st bomb group. He was eighteen years old when he finished his tour. His original leather jacket displayed a painted Flying Fortress on the back, along with two German crosses, the meaning of which I immediately knew. Yes, he would be happy to talk to my class. Bob Zulauf flew seventy missions as pilot of a B-25 out of Corsica and Italy; he had been there at the same time as Joseph Heller, author of *Catch-22*. Zulauf was wearing his original leather flight jacket, decorated with a fading leather squadron patch. He, too, was very gracious in agreeing to speak to my class. As it turned out, he had been a student at my school—Park University—when he was called into service in 1943.

Then there was Lee Lamar, a B-24 pilot and former POW. I was fascinated by his deep voice, his blue eyes that peered over the top of his glasses, and by his stories. So fascinated I failed to get his autograph.

I tracked down Davis, author of the book who was standing nearby, and asked about joining the CAF. He immediately hooked me up with someone who provided me with the necessary forms to complete, and I attended my first meeting in September. At that meeting, Lee stood up and announced, in his sonorous, slow voice, that he had received a strange email. Someone claiming to be an archaeologist in Croatia had found what he believed might be Lee's bomber. There was a buzz of responses from the assembled CAF members. Lee said he was taking it slow, trying to determine if he were being scammed, and whether the correspondent was legitimate. He would keep us advised.

My brain began to whirl. I approached him following the meeting, re-introduced myself, and asked if he were thinking about a trip back to the site of his bomber's crash.

He paused, frowning in thought. "I don't really know. I think maybe so, but we don't even know if this is the right one. Don't know if this fella is who he says he is."

He did agree to speak to my class, and he gave me his phone number. At the next CAF meeting, he said that the archaeologist, Luka Bekic, was legitimate, but there were some questions about whether the bomber he found was *Bottoms Up*. Many planes had been downed over what had been Yugoslavia, in the region now known as Croatia. But it was easy to tell that Lee was becoming a bit excited about the possible discovery of a bomber in which he had flown wartime missions and in which he nearly lost his life.

In the meantime, my semester had started and I was deep into the life of academia once more: teaching, committee assignments, advising students, grading papers. Easily my favorite class was the Lit of the Air War, and already some veterans had graciously shared their stories with my students. Bob Zulauf was the first, and as he parked his gray Toyota outside my classroom building, he paused and looked it over. It's an old stone affair, built in 1916, and it had been a dormitory before being converted to classrooms.

"Yes, this was my old dorm," Bob said to me as we walked slowly into Copley Hall. "My room was on the second floor." Bob had met his wife at Park, then left school his sophomore year to enter the Aviation Cadet program. When he returned from the war, he enrolled at the University of Missouri and received a degree in journalism. In the years until his retirement he had worked for several advertising agencies. My students were fascinated by his stories about Park, and then he transitioned to his short career flying medium bombers. I looked around the room as he spoke. All eyes were on him, transfixed. A good idea, this, to bring in veterans to speak.

Lee came to my classroom in October. By then, he had had a series of email communications with Bekic, the Croatian archaeologist, and was increasingly convinced the wreckage discovered near the village of Krvavici was *Bottoms Up*. My students were fascinated with his story, and I could see they were now making the connection between history in a book and real experiences of men, now old, who had been young when called to arms in the most destructive war ever fought. He concluded his story with the email from Bekic. Once more, they were all ears.

The next day, I went to our Office of International Studies, where I met with Dr. Olga Ganzen, executive director of the center, and her assistant, Angie Markley-Peterson, and presented Lee's story to them. The university had sponsored several classes abroad, and I pitched this as an opportunity to take students into the past as well as a different culture. We could assign each student a task for research, and also take along video cameras from the university's communications department and film the event.

Olga looked at me and grinned. She and Angie both asked numerous questions—how unusual is it for a veteran to visit the wreckage of his wartime plane, exactly what would students do on the trip, what would we do with the film—and then Olga said she thought it was a great learning opportunity. We would probably be able to send eight students on full scholarships. What about Lee? I asked. Of course, the university would pay his way and expenses as well. Olga wanted a formal proposal for the project, and I promised her one in the next couple of days.

I left the office feeling exhilarated. That night I called Lee and told him of the plan; he hesitated, and finally revealed his reluctance.

"It all sounds pretty good, but some time ago I promised Ron Wright that the two of us would go if anything like this should ever happen. I wouldn't want to break my word to Ron."

Dr. Ronald Wright was another member of the CAF, a pilot, a retired Army Reserve colonel, and a dentist in Overland Park, Kansas. A few years previously, Ron and Lee had been at a meeting in the Midland, Texas, headquarters of the CAF. Sitting around one night, talking about World War II and Lee's experiences, Ron posed the question: "Have you ever been tempted to go back to find your bomber, or the remains of it?" Lee had said he didn't think there was a chance of finding it, and that after all the intervening years it doubtless had been hauled away for scrap.

"Well, you know, strange things happen," Ron said. "I promise you this: if you ever want to go back to look for it, I will go with you and we'll find it together."

That posed a major problem for my carefully prepared plan, of course. I called Ron that night.

"This is no problem at all," Ron said. "Set your plan in motion, and—if it is okay with you and the university—I will plan on going along. My wife and I will pay our own way, of course."

Back on the phone to Lee. "Okay, if that works for Ron, then yes. Let's go."

In the months until we departed, there was a great deal of work to accomplish: logistics of the trip itself; funding by the university; competition for the scholarships; coordination with Luka Bekic in Croatia; research about the air campaign in Italy; details of Lee's own military service. And there were questions that deserved answers: how did we know this was *Bottoms Up*? How exactly had the wreckage been discovered? Who had helped Reynolds and other crew members escape? And what had happened to the rest of Lee's crew after bailing out of their stricken bomber?

As it turned out, Lee himself had spent years trying to learn the answer to the last question.

Chapter 20

The Crew
Their Stories

For several decades after Lee Lamar's impromptu car-hood reunion with bombardier Don Reynolds, the pilot had often thought of the rest of his crew, the men who were little older than boys with whom he had trained and faced death. What had become of them? How many were still alive? Exactly who had escaped, who had been captured? What were their stories after leaping from their crippled bird? But there was no mechanism for answering those abiding queries.

Military records, which might have been helpful in such a hunt, were closed to all but the veteran or certain specified surviving family members. There was of course no Internet, no accessible national database, no clearinghouse for locating old comrades. Still, as the years went by, Lamar—and doubtless hundreds of thousands of other former soldiers, sailors, and marines—checked phone books in towns where they traveled, made lots of calls to wrong individuals, wrote to the historians of their combat units. Sometimes such efforts bore fruit; often, they were left with nothing for their pains.

Lee knew firsthand of the fate of the pilot, navigator, and bombardier. He had, of course, been captured with Randall Darden, imprisoned with Mike Craig, and reunited with Don Reynolds.

Over the span of four decades, Lee eventually was able to make contract with all of his former crew. Despite having a list of their addresses at the time they had entered the service, it was not easy because many of them had moved, gone off to college, taken jobs elsewhere, and in the case of one, had remained in the Air Force and died in mysterious circumstances.

Darden, the pilot from Texas, was captured with Lee and spent the remainder of the war in Stalag Luft I. He remained in the service for a year or so after the war. He divorced his wife, remarried, and moved to Bakersfield, California, where he became a cattle trader. In the 1980s, he died of a heart attack.

Mike Craig, the young navigator from Nashville, was also imprisoned with Lamar and Darden. After the war, he returned to Tennessee, completed college, and operated a neon sign business for many years. In the 1990s, a relative wrote a short account of his wartime exploits. He recounts being helped by a local resident, who allowed him to spend the night in his house, and he was captured the next morning when he left.[1] Lamar relates that Craig began working his way toward the crashed bomber immediately, and was captured very quickly the first day by a German soldier who shouted "Halt, Achtung!" In any event, Craig suffered the deprivations of a prisoner of war, and in 1950 developed multiple sclerosis, which eventually robbed him of the ability to walk. At the time of this writing, he still lives in Nashville. Talking is difficult for him.

Additional details of Reynolds's escape with the aid of the Partisans revealed just how vicious the irregular war was in Yugoslavia. Reynolds had been found by Partisans the second day after bailing out, and he was reunited with Hurston Webb, who had broken his ankle. Webb eventually was left for the Germans to find in order to get him medical attention. For the next two months, Reynolds and several other American fliers from other downed aircraft were protected by the Partisans as they worked their way south to a seaport town.[2]

The odyssey was incredibly dangerous and challenging. On one occasion, Reynolds told Lamar, he had lived on two turnips for several days. The nights became bitterly cold, and the Partisans had little warm clothing to spare. They were nearly caught once by German soldiers, and the entire band began running across a field with the Germans shooting at them. Reynolds saw one of the Partisans drop a blanket. The bombardier had nearly frozen the night before, and despite the bullets kicking up dirt around him, Reynolds turned back to recover the blanket for himself. Later, the band, which had grown as they picked up more fliers and more Partisans, had been surrounded on a hilltop. The Partisan leader sent out a man to work his way out of the encirclement and seek help. The sound of machine guns firing told them he had not made it. The commander sent another man, with the same result. This continued, and no man refused to go. Eventually, they made their way off the hilltop, but several Partisans had been killed. In February, Reynolds was taken at night by boat to Bari, Italy, and he eventually was returned to the 460th BG in Spinazzola. Shortly after his arrival, Col. John Price pinned the Air Medal on his chest in a base ceremony.[3]

After the war, Reynolds became a rural mail carrier in Wisconsin. Few of the recipients of his deliveries probably ever had a clue about his horrendous wartime experiences. He eventually divorced his first wife, remarried, and moved to Las Vegas after retiring from the Postal Service. He died of cancer in the 1970s.

Hurston Webb, the flight engineer and top turret gunner who broke his ankle and eventually was left for the Germans, spent the remainder of the war as a POW. He did receive adequate medical attention and his leg, which had begun to turn black and possibly gangrenous, was saved. He returned to his home in West Virginia. Lamar spoke to his widow a short time after he died of cancer, and she said her husband had had nightmares all of his life after leaving the service, frequently shouting out in the night, "We're going down! We're going down!" Such was the profound impact of that traumatic event that his widow said they were some of the last words he spoke on the night he died.[4]

One of the first men out of the Liberator that fateful day in November 1944 was John Nordback, the nose gunner from North Dakota. He had managed to link up with Partisans and also returned to Italy after several months. In a chance encounter many years later, he and Swante Norlund had run into each other in a grocery store in Duluth, Minnesota, and had an impromptu reunion. In 2003, Lamar met with him in a nursing home in Rice Lake, Wisconsin, but by then Nordback had suffered a stroke and had a difficult time speaking.[5]

Bernie Sturtz, the tail gunner who had borrowed twenty dollars from Lee so he could take his girl out to dinner while they were in Combat Crew Training in Pueblo, and who had witnessed the horrifying midair collision of two Liberators over the Adriatic, returned to his home in Pennsylvania after the war. Sturtz was one of the three gunners who had not heard the signal to bail out and were working to release the ball turret to lighten the ship when Lamar burst into the waist compartment of the bomber. He had struck his mouth on the lip of the photo hatch as he bailed out and lost his dog tags, and it was he about whom the Germans quizzed Lamar and Darden. He too had linked up with Partisans and eventually made his way back to Italy. Sturtz and Lamar remained in close contact after the war—Sturtz driving to Missouri with his wife to attend Lamar's wedding in 1950. Sturz died 13 December 2007.

Little Henry Alder, the ball turret gunner who had teased Lamar in the equipment room before a flight and caused the co-pilot to bump into Lt. Gen. Nathan Twining, was another of the three tardy gunners. After his quick exit, he landed safely and managed to locate Sturtz as they made their way through Yugoslavia over the course of several months. The two returned to the States together, but Alder remained in the service. In 1950, his mother, still in Sneedville, Tennessee, received a letter from the U.S. Military expressing deepest condolences over the loss of her son, whom they said had apparently been killed in the crash of a transport flight out of the Azores. The letter indicated that the plane on which Alder was a crewman had simply vanished over the Atlantic without a trouble call. However, when Alder's family attempted to obtain more information, they were rebuffed, and they sought help from their congressman and senator. Those officials were advised that the case was "Highly Classified" and were to cease their queries.

Lamar has concluded that Alder probably was aboard one of the intelligence-gathering aircraft that frequently penetrated Soviet airspace. Several of these planes were shot down, with neither the American nor Soviet governments officially acknowledging the incidents at the time. In 1950, the planes most commonly used for this aerial spying were the B-29 Super Fortress, or its beefed-up cousin, the B-50.

Mario Briganti, who flew with the Darden crew for only one mission—its last—had stood in for the ailing Joe Betine. Briganti was already a seasoned combat veteran, who had bailed out of his bomber while flying with the 8th Air Force out of England. He had been transferred to the 15th Air Force in Italy. Such are the fates of war that on his first combat mission in Italy, he was shot down again.

Briganti was also in the waist of *Bottoms Up*, and he too bailed out safely and made contact with the Partisan irregulars. After a harrowing several weeks, he was able to return to Italy. The military authorities apparently decided he had used up his allotment of luck, and despite the fact that he was unwounded, sent him home to the States. At the time of this writing, Briganti still lives in Connecticut. Lamar and Briganti have spoken on the phone a few times, but they have not seen each other since the day they jumped out of *Bottoms Up*.

Perhaps the most poignant story of the *Bottoms Up* crew is that of Joseph Betine, whom Briganti replaced for the 18 November mission because the assistant engineer and gunner had a cold that day. Flight crewmen were always grounded for this seemingly minor affliction because rapid changes of air pressure as an aircraft climbed or descended could severely and permanently damage their hearing if the eustachian tubes were blocked.

Betine waited for the return of his bomber and crew, but the only news he received were the reports of other aircraft whose crews had last seen *Bottoms Up* badly damaged and going down. Nine men with whom he had trained, flown dangerous missions, broken bread, drank and laughed and shared unspeakable sights, survived enemy fire and the lethal combination of bombs and high octane fuel on overloaded takeoffs—these nine men and the unknown (to him) gunner who had replaced him for a single mission, were gone. It was a shattering blow, one that left him feeling alone and bearing a tremendous burden of guilt for not being with them.

Four days later, on 22 November 1944, he was assigned as a replacement gunner aboard the David Gross crew. That bomber was shot down on its mission over Salzburg, and the entire crew was captured; Betine was sent to a different Stalag than the Darden crew. He never learned that his original crew had all jumped from the bomber safely.

Betine stayed in the Air Force after the war, retiring after thirty years. In those three decades, he had been unable to learn anything further about his former crewmates. In 1990, Lamar located the address for Betine in Panama

City, Florida, and sent a letter inquiring whether he was the same man who had been a gunner on the Darden crew out of Italy.

A few days later, the phone rang in Lamar's Overland Park, Kansas, home. Bonnie answered the phone. It was Mrs. Betine. Joe, she said, was very emotional at that moment but wanted to speak to Lamar. A few minutes later, Joe Betine got on the line.

"Lee, I thought all you fellows were dead. I did not find any of you in the POW camp. I was in the Air Force for thirty years and never ran into any of you." Lamar assured him that the entire crew had survived the mission and the war, although several had since passed. Lamar advised Betine that Bernie Sturtz was now living in Tavares, Florida, and perhaps they should get together.

Three weeks later, Lamar received another call from Mrs. Betine. Joe had left to visit Bernie Sturtz, and she wanted Lamar to know more of Betine's story.

"Joe is a different person since he learned that all of the crew survived. All these years he has thought he was the only survivor on that crew and he has kept that bottled up inside. He would not talk about World War II. He would never tell his son what he did in that war, and he could not watch a war movie on television.

"But since he has talked with you and learned that everyone survived, he has come out of his shell. He has talked to his son and told him what he did. His son is so thankful. Joe and his boy can now watch a war movie."

Betine's wife also revealed that it nearly had not happened. Lamar sent his letter to Betine with the return address of Lee Lamar, Consulting Engineer, and she had nearly discarded it, thinking it a solicitation letter. But she opened it, quickly realized what it was, and when Joe returned from the fishing trip he was on at the time, she told him he needed to finish washing the boat and get inside. There was something he needed to see, something that would knock his socks off. "Did I win the lottery or something?" Betine had offhandedly asked.

The letter was better than winning the lottery, Mrs. Betine said. "When he came in, I showed him the letter and he sat down and bawled like a baby."

Only a short time later, Betine developed a fast-growing, aggressive cancer and died. Lamar was always pleased to have made contact with him in time for him to know the truth. He only wished he had been able to make the contact many years sooner, thus shortening the time Joe had to live with that added burden.

In several conversations I have had with Lamar over the past three years, the veteran combat flier has sounded a single theme:

"The worst thing the military did to us, the POWs and the evadees, was not to make an effort to get us together after we were shipped home. Often decades went by before we were able to learn what had happened to others on the crew.

"We had become like brothers, and then we weren't able to talk to each other again, to tell our stories, to hear what had happened to each other. That was a terrible disservice to all of us. It would have been healing for us if we just could see each other one more time."

He usually paused at this point, and his eyes teared up. "How many were like Joe Betine, but died before they ever learned the truth?" Another pause. "But there was a war on, and the government had other priorities. It surely would have been a monumental task, probably impossible. And I think they learned something from that mistake. I guess they did the best they could with what they believed at the time."

Chapter 21

Short Focused

In the months leading up to our trip—grandly dubbed our "expedition"—we had largely focused on the story of Lee Lamar, expanded it to include the others in his crew, and then had gone beyond that to the air campaign in Italy. Each week during the summer of 2007 until we departed for Croatia (by way of Venice), the eight students selected for the class met with invited speakers such as Dr. Judy Vogelsang, the honorary Croatian Consul in Kansas City, and of course, Lee himself.[1] I assigned more tasks to the scholars, and Angie Markley Peterson, now very pregnant and looking uncomfortable, provided briefings of the area and detailed the university's expectations for the students who were traveling on scholarship.

Dr. Olga Ganzen, of the International Education office of our university, had contacted the local Public Broadcasting Station affiliate in Kansas City, and they had expressed interest in the project. Brian Burnes of *The Kansas City Star,* one of their premier feature writers, had contacted me about doing a story when we returned, and he asked me to stay in contact by email while we were overseas.

But there were complications. Our proposed partnership with the local public television station had looked promising, and a two-person film crew had been selected. The idea was that the university would pay all their expenses for the trip, and they would produce a documentary film to air locally, with possible national distribution. However, the station—like all arts projects, it seems—was also in a bit of a money bind. We met in June with Victor Hogstrom, then CEO of the station, as well as the film crew. The bottom line was the bottom line: the station needed production money up front before they could sign any sort of agreement. The university had already spent a great deal on the project, and had some major building projects coming up. No dice.

I remembered that an old friend and mentor, the poet Dan Jaffe, had recently moved back into the area, and that his daughter and her husband had their own film production company. I contacted Anna Jaffe and Mike Horine of Curious Eye Productions in Parkville. We arranged to meet soon to talk about their possible participation.

Meanwhile, out of curiosity, I did some research to learn how many B-24s were still flying out of the eighteen thousand built during the war. I was astounded to learn there were only a handful still airworthy around the globe, and the Collings Foundation, in Stow, Massachusetts, had the last flying B-24J, the model flown by Lamar and his crew. It was one of the last variants of the Liberator, with a large rotating nose turret among other readily identifiable features.

The Collings Foundation owns a number of World War II aircraft—everyone in the know calls them Warbirds—and flies them around the country during the summer to keep alive the memory of that heroic and tragic time. Out of curiosity, I called the foundation to see if *Witchcraft,* their Liberator, would be anywhere near Kansas City that summer of 2007. How cool would it be for Lee to be able to get inside a Liberator again? I spoke with Hunter Chaney, their director of marketing, about Lee's wartime experience and the upcoming trip back to the crash site. He was very interested, and yes, *Witchcraft,* together with the foundation's B-17, would be flying into Kansas City Wheeler Downtown Airport in the first week of July.

I was excited. As far as I knew, Lee had not been back in a B-24 since he bailed out nearly sixty-three years earlier. I could imagine the memories that would come flooding back if he were able to sit in the right seat of the Collings Foundation Liberator. Later that afternoon, I met with Anna and Mike, and their enthusiasm for the project was palpable. They would gladly accompany the group back to Italy and Croatia, film the experience, and then help find the funds to produce the film for distribution. The university would pay their expenses, and they wanted no money up front. A meeting with Dr. Ganzen was arranged, and we had our film crew. Could things get any better, I wondered?

The answer came the next day. Hunter Chaney called. If we—Lee, our cameraman, and I—could somehow get to Fort Collins, Colorado, on July 5, we could fly in the Liberator back to Kansas City. An amazing and generous offer, I told Hunter. I'll call you back, but I think this can work.

First call was to Olga. She didn't blink. Get me numbers for your flight to Denver, the cost of a rental car to Fort Collins, and a night's stay there. We'll make the arrangements. Stand by, I advised. Haven't called Lee yet. But first, I contacted Mike Horine. Mike is a calm, laid-back perfectionist, if such a creature exists. He was a news cameraman for more than twenty-five years, and after meeting Anna while they were both enrolled in a graduate degree program at Kansas State University, they decided to marry and launch their own film company. They learned it was hard work, and sometimes the jobs might be scarce, but they were talented and wanted the creative freedom to be on their own.

Horine jumped at the opportunity to film Lee inside the Liberator as it flew into Kansas City. "Tell me where to be, and when. Let's do it!"

I wasn't sure why I hesitated to call Lee first. I didn't want to dangle an opportunity and then snatch it away; it had to be set in concrete before I alerted Lee. That afternoon I reached him.

"Lee, how would you like to fly in a B-24 in a couple of days?" There was a pause. I pushed ahead, telling him about the offer of the Collings Foundation, and what we would have to do. All his expenses paid, of course.

I think it would be possible to get Lee excited, but this wasn't the time.

"Well, I guess I could do that," he said in his distinctive slow, deep bass, the sonorous voice of a natural storyteller. "Tell me what I need to do."

At Fort Collins, we walked up to the olive-drab Liberator after being cleared to the ramp. It has been lovingly restored, and the names of many contributors are painted along the fuselage, along with the nose-art names of dozens of World War II B-24s. Lee scanned the names of the planes. He pointed to one.

"That's the plane I got shot down in, right there." He stared at the letters forming the name *Bottoms Up* for a long minute, tracing the letters with his fingertip. It may or may not have been the same aircraft memorialized on the side of the Liberator. There were tens of thousands of aircraft produced and flown into combat, far more planes than popular or imaginative names available, and it is not uncommon to see the same nickname in photographs of different aircraft. Still, it felt right, and it set a good tone for our flight back to Kansas City.

The noise of a B-24 starting each of its four mighty engines is something that must be heard to be appreciated. I had watched Warbirds of various stripes—P-51 Mustang and P-47 Thunderbolt fighters, B-25 Mitchell medium bombers, B-17 Flying Forts, as they were started at various airshows. Each fires up with an impressive, guttural whine that quickly turns to a deep, throaty growl, accompanied by much popping and snapping, and they emit huge clouds of bluish-white smoke as the power plants finally settle into a continuous, throbbing roar. It is immensely impressive to watch the precise ritual for start-up—repeated for each engine on a multi-engine aircraft—and to sense the power unleashed through such mechanical contrivances. I have started the R-985 Wasp Junior radial engines on a SNJ-5, the Navy version of a Twin Beech or C-45, and felt the power transmitted through the airframe and the throttles as I made the take off.

But to be a passenger in a B-24, sitting on the metal floor of the waist compartment belted to a bulkhead, was a never-to-be-forgotten experience. I imagined how those crewmen in the wartime bombers must have felt on each takeoff, as they sensed right up through their tailbones the quivering, vibrating power of nearly five thousand horses begin to send them down the runway, agonizingly slowly at first, then faster, louder perhaps, until the rattling and thumping of the tires is suddenly gone and you sense the wind under the wings and know you are airborne. Will it climb? Will the four engines keep working together to get you through this dangerous phase of not-quite-flight, no-longer-on-the-runway? You hear the clump of the main gear raise into the wells, and you begin to relax.

The gunner's side windows in *Witchcraft* had been left open and the warm July air flowed in. After a while, the crew let us know that we could unbuckle and walk around through the aircraft. Before boarding, the crew chief had briefed us on moving from the front to the rear of the aircraft, through the bomb bays which were hung with dummy bombs. "The catwalk is narrow, but you must stay on it. The doors are flimsy. If you should step on them, I can't help you. No one can."

I didn't need more warning, and I knew just a bit about the catwalk from hearing Lee's story. I was very—very—careful as I wandered through the Liberator while it plowed through the sky over Kansas at about five thousand feet. Once more I was struck by the starkness of the completely restored old bomber: no insulation, just the green back of the aluminum skin, thin enough to stick a screwdriver through, festooned with wires, electrical lines, hydraulic tubing, placarded with warning signs and studded with switches and monitors every where you looked. Decommissioned .50-caliber Browning machine guns were installed in the side ports, the tail gunner position, the nose turret, the top blister, and the ball turret, adding a sobering reminder of the reason for the existence of this old flying machine—and the cold hard reality that other aircraft would have been trying to shoot it down. Long belts of inert .50-caliber brass shells snaked from boxes to the various gun stations, each shell nearly the length of my hand. There were connections for oxygen to each crew station, as well as couplings for the electrically heated flight suits and outlets for communications. I worked my way forward, to where Lee was sitting at the flight engineer's station behind the cockpit, and I could glimpse past the pilots the row upon row of old, black-faced dials and gauges—now often called "steam gauges" in the age of glass cockpits—and the banks of switches and the pedestal of controls. I grinned at Lee.

In the dim light of the bomber's interior, I saw Lee sixty-odd years before. He was transformed by the place, the lighting, and his clothing. For several years, a group of old fliers and CAF members had met weekly for breakfasts at the Old 56 Highway restaurant in Olathe, and shortly after I joined they were kind enough to invite me. It was the sort of weekly court where the first liar never stands a chance (never try to out-story a pilot). But when Lee began a story, usually as a result of a question from one of the others, everyone listened. Several of those gathered wore leather flight jackets at every opportunity—I confess to being one of them—and Lee was asked about his original A-2. He told the story of having left it on base for his last mission, of its being reissued, and of meeting up with a POW who reported he had turned down the offer of the jacket when he recognized Lee's nametag still sewn to the left chest.

Ron Wright and John O'Neal, a retired Army Reserve colonel, vice-president of DST Systems, and a CAF member, asked me about pooling in to buy Lee a new A-2. Within a few weeks we were able to give him a brown horsehide A-2, with his nametag and a 460th BG patch sewn on. He beamed, tried it on, and his wife Bonnie said he wore it every day for weeks.[2]

Now, in the Liberator over Kansas, he wore his flight jacket and a reproduction of a "crusher" pilot's service hat, loaned to him by Wright. He looked the part of the fearless aviator.

Then, a huge surprise. The aircraft commander, Jim Goolsby, came back from the cockpit, leaned down and shouted into Lee's ear. Lee looked up with a surprised expression, then he slowly grinned. He climbed up into the cockpit, worked his way into the left seat, and pulled the headset over his crusher cap. Buckled in, he looked at the co-pilot, Carl Reise, and nodded. The right-seater raised both hands. Lee was at the controls of the Liberator.

For the next forty-five minutes, Lee Lamar flew *Witchcraft* over the flat fields of western Kansas, occasionally making small adjustments in his course, making a tentative turn, testing the rudders. I watched from the cockpit door, in awe of being able to fly one final B-24 mission with this man I had come to know and love. He was absolutely in his element.

We were approaching Kansas City, and at last it was time for Lee to vacate the pilot's chair. He climbed down out of the cockpit, and I shouted in his ear: "How was the flak over Kansas?" A grin of pure delight split his face. "Light, Inaccurate," he growled, and laughed happily.

When we landed in Kansas City, Lee and I took our time disembarking. It had been an emotional and heady flight, and we were not quite ready to give it up. We walked slowly around the interior of the aircraft, Lee pointing out where the various members of his crew had been stationed, and we inspected the bolts that held the ball-turret to an anchor plate inside the aircraft. These were the bolts that Alder, Briganti, and Sturtz were trying to remove to lighten *Bottoms Up* and did not hear the bail-out alarm.

Finally, we stepped down into the open bomb bay and ducked out onto the tarmac, looking back once more at the slab-sided bomber as we left her. Then we turned to the terminal and stopped dead in our tracks. Several hundred onlookers, it seemed to us, had lined the chain-link fence to watch the old bomber arrive, and several news stations were on hand to interview Lee. They had been alerted by the Collings Foundation, which realized the value of this unique opportunity for Lee and for them. A ragged cheer went up from the crowd when they saw Lee in his flight jacket and crusher, and he stopped. I only then realized just how emotional this flight had been for this quiet, taciturn old warrior. "My gosh, what's all that?" He looked at me in bewilderment.

"Lee, I think they're here to see you, as well as the plane." His eyes watered, and a quiet sob escaped.

"Lee, let's turn back and look at this old bird again. Can't have you meeting your public crying like a baby." For a couple of minutes, we stood with our backs to the crowd, and Lee regained his normally stoic composure.

Interviews by the electronic news media were quickly arranged, and then he was interviewed by a young female reporter from *The Kansas City Star*. This was done in the relative quiet and cool of the old terminal building. Several of my students had come down to watch the landing, and I met with them briefly in a corner of the terminal. After a few minutes I wandered back over to Lee, since I had been approached from someone from the Collings Foundation who requested that Lee go back out to the parked Liberator and tell a few stories to the crowd that was now gathered around her.

I was able to witness the most practical side of Lee Lamar, the side of the engineer, the part that deals with measurements and precision and absolutes. The young reporter was wrapping up her interview, looking up at the tall old bomber pilot in his period togs. She had one last question.

"So, how did you feel when you were able to fly that bomber for—what? The first time since you were shot down in 1944?" She smiled up at him, perky and expectant.

Lee turned to me with a look of disbelief. Slowly he turned back to the reporter, standing with her notebook and pen.

"Young lady," he began in a stern, firm voice. "That just may be the dumbest question I've ever been asked. Do you have any more questions for me that aren't dumb?" I was squirming a bit, but this was Lee's interview.

An awkward silence followed, probably only a few seconds but it seemed like minutes. Finally, the reporter worked up a smile. "I'm guessing you felt pretty good about it?"

"That'll work."

As we walked out to the flight line to return to *Witchcraft* and a waiting, curious crowd, Lee turned his head to me and growled. "Wasn't that about the dumbest question you ever heard? Heck, ask me how high. Ask me how fast. Ask me how far. Those have answers. But 'how did I feel?' That's not a question a man can answer."

I was beginning to know, however, a little something of how this man did feel about this whole return to his past. I would learn more.

Chapter 22

The Real Work

During that hectic spring and summer of 2007 leading up to the trip of a life-time for many of us, it seemed that there were a thousand details to be covered and a constellation of issues to be resolved. I made some changes in the list of scholarship students when the research skills and dedication of some became an issue, and we all continued to grind away at making Lee Lamar's return to his past—and the bones of *Bottoms Up*—a success.

But our viewpoint was of course skewed toward what we knew and what was happening from the American end of this international story. But in truth, much of the really important work was being done in Croatia by Luka Bekic and his colleagues at the Conservation Institute. While we were busy with re-searching the air campaign in Italy and Lee's own personal saga, Bekic had been painstakingly seeking answers to questions that continued to nag him.

All of this remarkable story might never have happened if key elements of persistence, curiosity, and luck had not all fallen into place. Bekic's first email to Lee might easily have been deleted by anyone accustomed to scams on the internet from overseas sources. Lee, at 85, could also be excused for not being tech-savvy or for being computer-phobic. But he was, in fact, extremely adept at computers and understood the Internet. He assembled his first computer years before, and his engineer's brain had been fascinated by the promise of the computer age. So, on Sunday, 17 September 2006, Lee and Bonnie's fifty-sixth wedding anniversary, he had opened his email to find a message with the sub-ject heading "B24 Airplane Crash Istria." He clicked on the message:

> Dear mister Lee Lamar,
> my name is Luka Bekic, I am an archaeologist at Croatian conservation insti-tute in Croatia.
> Excavating a roman villa, we have accidentally found an airplane crash site nearby, in a remote location near village Krvavici, Pula, Istra, Croatia. We recov-

ered more than 3000 various parts of airplane and equipment. Investigating the finds, right now we know:

A silver (aluminum) B24 with blue markings (probably US star) crashed northeast of Pula, near village Krvavici, Marcana (then Italy and Yugoslavia, now Croatia).

Allegedly plane was hit by flak near Pula flying from mission in north Italy, at end of '44. Some of the crew, about 5 of them, bailed out over village Filipana, and their whereabouts is not known. Two parachuted near crashsite itself, one was immediately taken prisoner by Wehrmacht, other was saved by partisans.

Bekic detailed the eyewitness accounts of surviving villagers, and went on to add that he had found Lee's story, placed on the Internet by the Nieman Elementary School of the Shawnee Mission School District. The details seemed to match. Lee and several other veterans had been interviewed by students of a special school group several years earlier, and the teacher and students had created a website of Lee's wartime experiences.

"Browsing through the internet we have read stories about your crash in Istria in 1944. Many things point out that our plane might have been Yours!" Attached to that first email were photos of many of the recovered aircraft parts.

The email was an adrenaline shot for the old warhorse. Lee responded the next day:

Dear Mister Luka Bekic, Thank you very much for your message. It is quite exciting for me. I believe you may possibly have found the aircraft crash remains belonging to our World War II B-24. I have not, however, been able to identify any thing on the picture you enclosed, except that it obviously is an American aircraft.

Lee went on to detail his recollections from that last mission, recognizing the aid provided by courageous locals to several crewmembers.

"Some had hardly landed in their parachutes before friendly people grabbed them up and hid them from the Wehrmacht."

He included his last view of *Bottoms Up*:

My last visual image of the aircraft was, as I remember after many years, about a second before I landed. At that time the aircraft was just clipping the tops of some trees along the south edge of an open field. I did not see the aircraft crash, but as I picked myself up, I saw the smoke beginning to boil up from the crash site. At the time of my last observance, the aircraft nose was pointed straight ahead and not downward. Thus, I have believed that as it crashed the remains were probably scattered across a large area. I have not believed the aircraft hit the ground at a steep angle such as to bury itself in a deep hole.

Lee included in his first response to Bekic a reference to his parachute, which would become such an important element in his return to Croatia:

> I remember burying a perfectly good parachute under a pile of leaves near a stone wall. The Wehrmacht officer that took us into captivity tried to get me to tell him what I did with it. I pretended I could not understand him. As far as I know what remains of the parachute is still buried there. If I ever get to come back to that area, I believe I might be able to find the remains should they still be there.

As excited as Lee was to hear from Luka Bekic, his response to the Croatian archaeologist generated an equal amount of excitement there. On 18 September, Lee received a second email from Croatia, one that revealed both euphoria and scientific skepticism.

> Dear mr. Lamar,
> Thank you so much for answering my mail. I have read it a few times, just like your interviews I have found on the net. My colleagues also know the story, they also are excited that we managed to contact you, it was the news of the day here! Your story about the crash is very important for us, because we think this could be your plane! But we are not sure, and have a lot of investigating to do before we can conclude this story. You know, we are scientists, and we want to be 100% sure in our theory.

Bekic then detailed a series of events that matched the stories of Lee and the villagers who had witnessed the shoot-down, including the flight path of the doomed aircraft, the approximate date, the number of parachutes seen, and the flat angle of the aircraft when it hit. But there were disturbing differences, the most notable being the color of the aircraft: "Duane L. 'Sparky' and Betty Bohnstedt, historians of your 460th BG, tell me your plane was named 'Bottoms Up' and that it was olive drab in color, and not natural metal finish (silver) as we think our plane was."

But the human contact between Lee and Luka had obviously excited the archaeologist, and the desire for the crash site to be the remains of Lee's bomber was evident in Luka's postscript to his second email: "PS If it turns out not to be your plane, it doesn't matter. Right now we have to identify this plane, find its crew, and write the story about it. But I promise we shall look for, and find your plane anyway."

How could it be proven that the truck-load of crushed, broken, and twisted aluminum, smashed machine-gun bullets, and shards of plexiglass were in fact those of Lee's doomed aircraft? It would be a relatively simple matter if the engines or machine guns could be found, since they had serial numbers tagged to a particular aircraft. But the guns, engines, and other major components of the crashed bomber had been hauled away by German troops during their three-day occupation of the site. It was evident that Luka very badly wanted the remains of the aircraft he had unearthed to be Lee's bomber, but he was not willing to let his hopes drive his inquiry. The truth would be his guide.

Early in his search for information, Bekic had posted on a website photographs of the crash site, including several of him and his team using metal detectors to locate more parts in the overgrown fields. He had done this in hopes that someone would know something of this crash site. Clearly visible in the outside photos are the stone walls that surround the fields across the entire Istrian Peninsula. The inside photographs reveal thousands of pieces of mangled wreckage laid out in rows on tables; these include dozens of rounds of caliber-50 machine-gun bullets, some of the few easily recognizable relics of the crash. Also displayed are numerous small switches and other components, most with visible English markings, as well as a twisted and smashed wristwatch case with English imprinting, half an oxygen tank (it had been sawn in two by a local farmer to use as a milk pail), and a large, corrugated aluminum door, peppered with small holes and some longer rips. Lee positively identified this door as unique to Liberator bomb bay doors.

But the color of the bare aluminum parts, including the door, continued to be an obstacle to positively identifying the crash site as that of *Bottoms Up*. As replacements, the Darden crew usually flew one of the older aircraft, which were still covered with the olive drab colored camouflage paint and not the shiny new unpainted aircraft. They had been flying *Bottoms Up* for several missions. It was one of the original aircraft in the squadron, and it still bore the olive-drab coat of paint that was applied to the earlier combat aircraft in an effort to make them less visible to enemy aircraft flying above them. The problem was obvious: the bomb bay door and other bits and pieces from the crash site lacked any evidence of being painted. They all appeared to have been bare aluminum, which would indicate a newer aircraft.

This was a conundrum. Could it be that all of this excitement and anticipation were for nothing?

Lee was insistent that *Bottoms Up* had been painted OD, and it seemed logical that it should be. His record keeping and memory both had been phenomenal regarding these events in his life. But a painting of the downing of Lee's bomber, done for him by a fellow POW in April 1945, was problematic. Frank Hokr, a prisoner at Stalag Luft I, had painted in watercolor a small, rather lurid, rendition of *Bottoms Up* over Pula, bracketed by black puffs of flak while a few red explosions punctuate the sky around her. It is a detailed painting, clearly showing the left two propellers feathered, and the yellow-and-OD tail markings of the 460th Bomb Group. *Bottoms Up* is printed in red across the nose of the doomed bomber. Lee paid Hokr the extravagant price of half a chocolate bar for the artwork.

In the painting, this aircraft is depicted as silver. I questioned Lee, not wanting to doubt his memory or suggest that he was wrong.

"No, that's true, the painting is of a silver '24. But he was just going by my description of the events, and I guess I hadn't stressed the color," he told me. Photos in the *460th Bomb Group History*, by Sparky and Betty Bohnstedt, confirmed Lee's insistence. We discovered on page eighty-three a small photo showing Col. Babb standing by the front of a Liberator; nose art of the upturned blonde with the name *Bottoms Up* in quotation marks is clearly visible. The plane is very obviously painted a dull, dark color.

So now we were back to the same seemingly intractable problem. Lee's plane was definitely OD. The crash fragments appeared to be absent any indication of the wartime brownish green paint. But obviously, Lee knew the configuration of his bomber far better than anyone, and he set out to solve the puzzle. In the meantime, Luka had continued to dig into the mystery from his end. There were some false leads, it turned out. On 21 September, he wrote about the frustrations of determining even the number of bombers that might have been shot down in the area.

The nose art of World War II bombers has become iconic to that conflict. Thousands of photos exist that show, mostly in black and white, young men in flying togs standing or kneeling in front of their aircraft, usually with their "mascot" fully displayed behind them on the nose of the plane. Quite often, the plane is referred to in unofficial unit histories by the nickname bestowed by the bomber's original crew. However, official reports such as MACRs (Missing Air Crew Reports) usually referred to the aircraft serial number, normally displayed in yellow or black letters on the tail. Further complicating the issue of identifying a particular aircraft was the Bomb Group practice of referencing the aircraft by its battle call sign, normally a letter painted on the fuselage in the colors of a particular squadron. This confusing array of varying identifiers tripped up Luka.

Sparky Bohnstedt earlier had responded to an email query by Luka about Lee's aircraft. It was built by Ford at Willow Run and assigned the Army serial number 42–51926. Its call letter was J, nickname was *Bottoms Up*. Lost on 18 November 1944 on a mission to Udine; the copilot believed it crashed near Pula, Bohnstedt wrote. Then, on a website devoted to B-24 crash sites around the globe, Luka had discovered what appeared to be a *second* Liberator that crashed in the same area on the same day, an aircraft referred to as Blue J. A search on the internet had revealed a number of B-24s bearing the name *Bottoms Up,* and nearly as many with the nickname *Blue J.* Here was a problem, and Luka immediately emailed Lee with photos of the various bombers he found to try to clarify what was becoming a confusing number of aircraft falling from the sky around Pula.

Lee responded with an insider's depth of knowledge:

> All American military aircraft had the bar and star emblem on each side of the rear fuselage, as well as on the top of the left wing and the bottom of the right wing. Markings that indicated the bomb group and the wing they belonged to were marked in various ways on the vertical stabilizers and the top of the horizontal stabilizers. Various aircraft in the bomb squadron were given letters of the alphabet from A to Z to identify them from each other. These were referred to as Battle Call Letters. The letters were painted on each side of the fuselage to the rear of the bar and star painting. The letters were repeated in different bomb squadrons within the bomb group, but they were given a different color. In our bomb group, the 760th letters were in blue. The 761st color was red, the 762nd was white and the 763rd was yellow. The *Bottoms Up* battle call was Blue J for Jig. These same letters of the alphabet and colors were repeated in other bomb groups and bomb wings. Thus, the picture you show of another Blue J is understandable. I am sure if you look at the markings on the vertical stabilizers, you would find completely different markings than on our Blue J, which was our own *Bottoms Up*.[1]

Luka emailed back that he was embarrassed by his mistake, but Lee quickly assured him that such arcane, specific information could hardly be known outside a small group of hard-core specialists in World War II aviation or veteran fliers from that conflict. That still left the question of the color of the aircraft discovered by Luka.

Lee had been carefully looking over the photographs of the salvaged bits and pieces of the crashed plane that Luka had posted, including the photos of the half oxygen tank. There was something strange about the tank, it seemed to him. Then it struck him: the tank half, now used to water a Croatian farmer's cows, was silver. It shouldn't have been. Lee wrote Luka on 24 September:

> I have looked at the pictures on the web site. . . . It seems to me that in all the B-24's that I have been in, these oxygen tanks were painted in a yellowish green color. I have often assumed that this was for anti-corrosion purposes. I also seem to think that the rest of the interior aluminum was painted in a similar manner. Could it be that in the environment that this metal has been in almost 62 years that the paint has simply deteriorated away? Could the olive drab paint on the outside have similarly deteriorated away? Considering that all the aluminum surface area of all the sheet aluminum that went into the manufacturing of the entire aircraft would be such that the outside part painted olive drab would be a small percentage. Then, considering that while you have over 3000 pieces of metal, only a small part is of aluminum itself. Could it be that your sample of the

aluminum could be so small you did not find any outside pieces painted olive drab color? It seems to be something to consider.

Luka was willing to consider the possibility, but as a scientist was not yet convinced. He wrote back:

> A large number of "our" parts, found in the field are in fact "corroded" and sure enough, they could have been olive. But there are enough aluminum parts that are not corroded and have writings in various colors on silver surface. I found black and red letters that I think are written in factory. Those letters are nicely printed, with quality color, and are rarely fading.

Lee persisted. Looking at the photographs for what must have been the hundredth time, he noticed what appeared to be greenish overspray on some of the red letters on a few of the pieces of aluminum that formerly had been a Liberator. He emailed Luka with his observation.

In the meantime, Luka had been talking to a couple of local experts on World War II aircraft crashes. In particular, he wanted to know about paint, paint schemes, and the durability of camouflage paint. What he learned did not completely sway him, but it caused him to doubt his original assessment. On 28 January 2007 he wrote:

> Now I am not certain what to think. One expert told me green camouflage color was painted by the army, not at the factory. Therefore they used some paint which lasted only about 6 months, and then plane had to be painted again. I do not know if this is true.
>
> But, you had noticed green color over some red letters. Looking at that again, made me realize someone had overpainted red factory letters with green paint. It is evident that the green paint fell off the aluminum surface but the red letters worked as some sort of "primer" so green color did not fall off the letters itself. Note two parts in attachment again.

We were relieved. Lee now began to focus on the possibility of recovering some element of his parachute, which he had buried so hastily after bailing out. In fact, the possibility of finding his touchdown point and perhaps the metal clips and components of his backpack parachute assumed some aspects of a search for the Holy Grail.

At one point, having lunch with a producer from the public television station early in the process, the man leaned across the table and earnestly asked Lee: "Why is finding your parachute so important to you?"

Lee, sitting next to me, slowly turned to look at me, his face expressionless. I quickly turned away, trying to keep from smiling.

He turned back to the television producer, and in a slow, incredulous voice, asked: "Do you mean some reason besides the fact that it saved my life?" The man laughed self-consciously. "I guess you're right. That was a silly question." We quickly changed the subject.

Slowly, the rather formal correspondence between the pilot and the archaeologist had begun to sound more like emails between friends. The tone became familiar, yet as they exchanged information over many months, a deep respect for each other became evident. Both began to call the other by first name, and they exchanged personal information about their wives and families. Prior to our leaving for Croatia, Ron Wright, John O'Neal, and I decided to buy Luka a leather flight jacket, and Lee obliged us by writing Luka under the guise of trying to obtain a mental image. Lamar gave him all of his own measurements, and Luka responded. At 6'3", Luka was a very large man, but obviously very fit. He played baseball, rode motorcycles, and participated in a 1500s historical reenactment group. He was a combat veteran of the wars that followed the breakup of Yugoslavia.

Luka and Lee were forming long-distance bonds through the unlikely discovery of a long-lost bomber.

One can only imagine the video image left in the brain of someone who undergoes such a life-changing, traumatic event as having someone shoot holes in your aircraft until it is unflyable, forcing you to jump into the unsubstantial air with a parachute you are not sure will even work. For Lee, that image is burned indelibly into the deep recesses of his brain. He is able to relive, exactly, the sequence of events that led to his bailing out, and he is able to see the events that followed in great detail.

Luka sent a large-scale topographical map of the region in which the debris field of the air crash site is outlined and elevations, foliage, buildings, and roads clearly noted. Lee emailed me the copy Luka sent to him. The village of Krvavici was neatly defined, with each building represented; the roads and cart paths were marked, along with contour lines of the countryside with elevation figures. Later, Luka also sent a rather good aerial photograph of the area, in which he had drawn a red oval to indicate the debris field of the crashed bomber. Using the two, Lee attempted to match the depicted topography with the scenes in his memory.

He emailed Luka with some of his memories. Key among them was the fact that he had landed in a very rocky field; in fact, he had landed on a large, smooth rock that probably accounted for jarring his leg so badly. All around him was a kind of scrub oak vegetation, and stone walls that separated fields:

These two types of areas, as well as the stone walls are what I will be looking for when I get there. I want to find the landing site and the parachute burial site. There may be nothing left of the parachute, except possibly some galvanized metal rings and snaps. If I find the area, but we fail to find any parachute remains, I will be firmly satisfied that you have found our *Bottoms Up*. If we locate remaining pieces of the parachute, then I should be able to prove to any others that we found *Bottoms Up*. I hope to complete a sketch of these areas and mail it to you.

Lee requested additional aerial photos, if possible, but Luka responded that it would be problematic, and he was not sure that it would be legal to send aerial photos outside the country. The one he had sent had been taken to facilitate the construction of the gas pipeline that had resulted in his original archaeological exploration. But there was good news in his response, as well:

And one more thing. If you landed in rocky area, it must have been north or northeast of Pula, just as we thought. South and southeast of Pula areas are with lot of fertile land, and almost no rocky areas. The oak trees never grow more than 2–3 meters [*six to nine feet—author's note*] in height. It is typical for Istria oaks as they live in warm and dry climate. (It is why we even managed to find some patches of army uniforms in stone walls).

So the terrain features Lee remembered were another small bit of evidence that the crash site was that of *Bottoms Up*. We had invested a lot of time and hope in the belief that it was, but still there were some doubts, particularly in the mind of Luka Bekic. His skepticism drove us all, on both sides of the world, to keep searching for evidence that would seal the deal.

In the meantime, Lee, Ron Wright, and I poured over the topo map individually, communicating by email and telephone at frequent intervals. Since the map was only a portion of a much larger one, no legend accompanied it. Lines representing elevations, roads, and paths presented a confusing kaleidoscope, much like long strings dropped haphazardly on a floor. A particular kind of black line, with short intersecting marks, we at first thought designated paths. But then, it seemed to me that they instead marked boundaries.

In February, I emailed Lee:

Lee, this is quite a detailed map and I believe it can be very useful in determining the area in which you landed under canopy. I assume that the black lines with occasional short perpendicular marks are stone walls, and if they are the same walls that existed in '44 we might be able to nearly pinpoint the spot.

He responded:

I think your thoughts on the map are valid. I had just scanned the map lightly, and had realized it was quite detailed, but had not caught the fact that the stone walls might be shown. No legend was included since this was a copied portion of a larger map. Ron is printing the map for me since my colored printer is out of order. When I get a printed copy, I will look it over very carefully. I was sure it covered the area of my landing. (Incidentally, the term you used, "landed under canopy" was a new one on me. I guess I "soloed" during the first one of those type landings. Where have I been all my life not to have heard that term before?)

Luka confirmed that the zipper lines were in fact stone walls or fences. As it turned out, the walls were the same ones from 1944, and in fact had been in use for centuries. Little had changed in that part of the world since long before World War II. Lee spent many hours pouring over the topo, and finally he was able to use his engineering skills to establish a probable landing site for his 1944 parachute jump. In a long email to Luka in February 2007, he explained his method:

> On this map, I have found a number of features I remembered from November 18, 1944. Soon after this crash occurred and while still in custody of the German Luftwaffe, I estimated how long it took me to go from the aircraft to the ground. This turned out to be not more than seven seconds. With that in mind, today, I have used that seven second estimation in calculating how far I landed from the crashed aircraft.

Lee figured the aircraft was traveling about 200 mph when he jumped, the speed based on knowledge of the cruising speed of a Liberator, decreased for the loss of two engines, and increased for the downward pull of gravity as it descended. He applied his mathematical skills thus, using 1609 meters to equal one mile: 200 mph times 1609 (meters) equals 321,800 meters per hour, or 5363.3 meters per minute, or 89.17 meters per second. Multiplied by seven (seconds), Lee calculated that he landed 627.7 meters from the crash site. Next, minus a legend, he had to determine a scale on the map. Luka had said the debris field was 300 to 500 meters long, and using that as a guide, he was able to draw an arc from the crash site out 628 meters. Along the curve of that arc, he located an area that seemed to fit: a higher elevation where he landed, in conjunction with the stone walls in the configuration he recalled.

We were excited about the possibility that we might be able to locate his parachute after all these years.

"It was a perfectly good parachute, it saved my life, and I just didn't have the time to give it a good burial," he said to me one day. "I think I'd like to give it a proper burial, and I'd like for you to maybe say a few words over it." I felt honored beyond words at his request.

We were close to believing that this truly was the wreckage of *Bottoms Up*, and Luka was becoming more convinced. But, as a trained archaeologist, he still needed a bit more positive evidence.

Finally, in late February 2007, Lee received an email from Luka that was tagged "Great news from Croatia!" He opened it on a Saturday morning as he was preparing to leave for the monthly CAF meeting in Olathe, Kansas. He scanned it, and at the meeting which I attended, Lee stood up to read the email. I distinctly remember the moment.

"Well, it looks as if there is little doubt now that the wreckage in Croatia is my B-24," he told the assembled members. "I'll read you this email I got this morning, titled 'Good news from Croatia.'" He cleared his throat and began to read. The first part was about Luka's efforts to locate all World War II British and American aircraft crash sites in Istria, some fifteen in all. Then Luka mentioned a recent book he had discovered on the history of the area that included an article about World War II. The author, Herman Bursic, had been a Partisan working at Partisan Brigade Headquarters during the war.

Luka had located Bursic and visited with him for two hours. During the visit, he asked him about the crash of a bomber northeast of Pula: "He has positively identified a B-24 crash near Krvavici as a 18/11/1944 date!!!!"

Luka continued:

> He knows, because partisans went into action of rescuing your crew. He was not personally involved in this, but he knows them. He and the other partisans will never forget about this date and village of Krvavici, so he says, because they had a great loss that day.
>
> Commander Ivan Radosevic, a secretary of partisan committee for Pula got caught that day from same German search party that caught you! He was there in the woods, in partisan uniform, armed, with others trying to save your crew before Germans. But Germans eventually ran into him and taken him prisoner to Pula. From there he was taken to concentration camp in Germany. No one heard from him after, so they list him as killed.
>
> You have to know that German and Italian fascist troops did not recognize partisan troops as an regular army, then rather as terrorists, so captured partisans were usually tortured and killed with no trial.

Lee had not read the email carefully, and he was visibly upset when reading this portion of the communication from Luka. A great sob escaped him, and he looked up with tears in his blue eyes. "I never knew anyone had been killed trying to help us."

Luka's email concluded with his declaration that he was now 99 per cent positive of the identity of the airplane and its crew: "The feeling I have right now is a greatest reward for my work for more than a year, with help of many people, especially you, in resolving this matter."

He promised to continue working to discover more information, particularly about the wounded crewman (Webb), and to learn more about the Partisan efforts that resulted in several members of the crew evading and eventually working their way back to Italy.

With that, our work to make the trip to Croatia resumed with a buoyed sense of optimism and determination.

Chapter 23

Pula, Croatia
August 2007

We drove through the dark streets of Pula, winding past the first-century Roman amphitheater, up narrow, twisting roadways clearly not intended for automobiles, finally stopping before the Hotel Galija to unload tired travelers and their luggage. It was nearly midnight, and we were exhausted. But we were here!

The expedition had expanded, and it now included Lee and his wife Bonnie, his daughter Kathy and her husband, Kirt Hufstedler, their children Kraig, eighteen, and Katie, fourteen (the four *K*'s); our good friends Ron and Sharyl Wright; Mike Horine and Anna Jaffe, the husband-wife videographers who owned Curious Eye Productions; eight students from Park University; Angie Markley Peterson, from the university; and my wife Jeanette and I. The hotel staff was polite and efficient, quickly getting us checked into our rooms, and then arranging for a quick dinner of pizza. We were to learn that late dinners in Croatia were not unusual.

As we settled into our room, I couldn't sleep. My mind was filled with images of the last few weeks, and the hectic couple of days in Venice just before arriving in Croatia.

A multitude of last-minute details had finally been sorted out: some of the passports of the students had arrived at the very last minute; there had been questions regarding our being able to film in some places; some contract wording between the university and the film company. But finally on 3 August 2007, our entire crew had boarded a plane at Kansas City's International airport, bound first for Philadelphia, and finally, to Marco Polo airport north of Venice. We had taken a water bus to San Marco square, cruising past the landmarks of the old city that we had seen so often in photographs—the twin columns, the Basilica, the Campanella.

We spent two days in Venice, exploring the canals and *calle* (the narrow, twisting alleys that serve as streets in a city with no cars); walking up and over the many pedestrian bridges; feeding the pigeons in the piazza; exploring the Duke's palace; shopping in the dozens of tiny shops for jewelry, clothing, handbags; tasting authentic Italian food; and admiring the architecture and art of this low-lying city. Then we boarded a ferry for Rovinj, an ancient seaport town about thirty kilometers north of Pula across the Adriatic from Venice.

Lee had turned eighty-six in March, and in his words he was not a candidate to climb Mt. Everest. We all kept a close eye on him while in Venice, since walking was the only means of transportation, but he had been a trouper and had managed the long walk from the dock to our hotel in fine fashion.

On the ferry ride across the northern Adriatic, I watched him closely as we drew closer to Croatia, and when we spied the first low hint of land on the horizon, Lee rose from his seat and slowly walked forward to where he could have a better view. He was distinctive, wearing his leather flight jacket with the 460th Bomb Group patch, and a straw sun helmet with a 15th Air Force patch on the crown. Several Croatian youths on the ferry had been curious, and they were fascinated by the story when various members of our group spoke to them about what we were doing.

When the hydrofoil ferry docked at the old stone pier (I heard someone say the stones were Roman, but I have not been able to confirm that), we realized that there still might be problems ahead. Mike Horine had been doing an incredible job focusing his camera on Lee from the time we left Kansas City. Now, he wanted to film the moment of his arrival in Croatia, and stepped off the ferry to be able to do so. It wasn't to be. Several stern-faced customs officials detained him, threatening to seize his camera, while the entire troup disembarked. Mike was furious, but cognizant of his position: he did not want to end up arrested, sent back, or even detained. While the rest of us stood by our luggage on the pier, Mike finally was allowed to continue, but with the unmistakable warning that he was not to shoot any footage around the pier, the boats in the harbor, or the customs officials.

The sun was setting in glorious fashion as we stood there, with the clear waters of the Adriatic lapping against the stones and the ancient walls of the city awash in deep, chiaroscuric shadows and golden facets. At one point, Lee walked to the edge of the pier, and with his family around him watched the sun sink into the sea. It was a moving scene to realize the old warrior probably never had the opportunity to enjoy the beauty of this part of the world in his youth.

A few minutes later, as we began to move off the pier and walk through the narrow streets to where our bus was parked, Lee came over to me and started to say something, but in the emotion of returning to the place where his long nightmare of terror and captivity had started, he simply broke down, quietly sobbing for several minutes. The others had moved off the pier; it was only the two of us.

"I'm sorry," he finally said. "I'll try not to let that happen again."

I put my arm on his shoulder. "Lee, if you ever say you're sorry again, eighty-six or not, I'll knock you down." He grinned, and we headed off for the bus.

We were to meet Luka Bekic the next morning, and there was a certain amount of anxiety that accompanied this first meeting. Lee and Luka had established a close relationship through the mountains of emails that had passed between them, and each had sent pictures of themselves, shared details of their families, swapped biographies. But it is one thing to project a certain persona through the technology of the Internet; it is quite another thing to be the host to a large group from another culture for a week. Would Luka be the self-effacing, tenacious archaeologist we had come to know through his communications, or would he be vainglorious, rude, domineering, dismissive? After all, he was the professional who had discovered the wreckage and persisted in his inquiry. We rose early Monday, eating breakfast at the Hotel Galija while we waited. We sent the students across the street to an outdoor café, part of the hotel, and counted the minutes until Luka arrived at nine. I could sense the tension in Lee, as he became quieter than usual, and I knew how much depended on this first meeting.

At last, just a few minutes after nine, a taxi arrived and a tall, good-looking man with long, flowing, dark hair emerged, casually dressed in a blue tee shirt and khakis, sunglasses perched atop his mane. He strode up the steps, spied Lee immediately, and the two walked toward each other. A long, heartfelt hug—the phrase today is "man hug"—followed, and Lee exclaimed that he recognized him immediately. "And you're even taller than I had you in my mind."

Luka was cheerful, obviously moved by this first face-to-face meeting with the man whose story he had come to know so well, and he was gracious to a fault to the rest of us. But for the first several minutes, his attention was focused on Lee, and the two talked about the trip, their incredulity at actually meeting each other, and all the things two humans might say in such undreamed-of circumstances. This was followed by interviews with the press. Luka had notified them of Lee's expected arrival. We were to grow accustomed to such attention; it became a problem at one point the next day. But for now, we were simply happy to finally start this last stage of the long journey back into Lee's past.

About ten, we moved across the street so Luka could address the gathered students and others in the party, and it was clear that they were taken with this man; perhaps they had in mind Indiana Jones, or perhaps the women were simply taken with his good looks. In any event, he began telling, in very good English, the nearly two-year saga of the discovery of the wreckage of the B-24 and his long search for its story; everyone listened with rapt attention. We were soon joined by his wife, Iva, and his two young children, who sat at a table with some of the women from our group. Ron Wright gave Luka the A-2 flight jacket from him, John O'Neal, and me, and then Lee presented him with a metal model of a B-24J, painted exactly like *Bottoms Up,* down to the nose art.

After his presentation, Luka began talking with Lee, Ron, and me about World War II. Soon he began to speak of his own experiences as a young infantryman in the wars that followed the breakup of Yugoslavia in the early 1990s. He told of the lack of uniforms and arms, of little food and few medical supplies, and of the deaths of friends that still haunted him.

"I knew about war. So when I found this first piece of the bomber that day, I felt like a brother to the men who were on it. I had to find out what happened to them. Their story had to be told," he said to us. I looked over at his wife, who was staring at him in wonder. It was the first time, she told us later, that he had ever talked about his own war experiences.

We broke for lunch, and then left to follow Luka to the Croatian Air Force base 4.5 miles northwest of Pula. Once more, Luka had arranged an impressive greeting, an official review and reception by the fighter squadron commander, Maj. Stanko Hrzenjak, and his young pilots. He also had cleared us to bring the camera equipment on base, and to film anything that we were not expressly forbidden to shoot. The heat was oppressive that day, the sun glaring down on a tarmac outside the facilities of the fighter squadron, and there stood a line of pilots in their stifling fire-resistant flight suits. Luka also had arranged for a contingent of World War II Partisans to be present, including Herman Bursic, Tomo Ravnic, and Ivan Zenzerovic from the Istria branch of the Partisan Veterans Association. With Luka interpreting, Lee visited with them for several minutes.

Maj. Hrzenjak, the base commander, spoke English very well, and slowly he and Lee made their way down the line, Lee greeting each Partisan and pilot and airman with a firm handshake. In every case, the pilots, none of whom looked older than twenty-five, responded warmly and enthusiastically. The brotherhood of the air was evident. I felt sorry for the pilots, and wondered how long they had stood in the blazing heat until our arrival on the air-conditioned bus. The formal review was followed by a guided tour of the base facilities, including a stop at the flight simulator for a MIG fighter, the aircraft used by the Croatian Air Force. Lee was shown the mock-up of the cockpit, and then he was asked if he wished to try it out. Silly question.

Lee was soon buckled into the seat, while a young Croatian pilot who spoke flawless English—in fact, with a New York accent—explained the functions of the various instruments. It turned out he was, in fact, a graduate of the U.S. Air Force Academy, and had learned English from his roommate, a New Yorker.

We were asked not to use names of the military personnel. Maj. Hrzenjak stood on a raised platform behind the cockpit mock-up, and I joined him there. With a word to a young airman, who threw a couple of switches, a realistic depiction of the airbase and runway appeared on a giant screen ahead of the simulator. Lee started the jet fighter down the runway, and suddenly I knew exactly what he was going to do. On the flight over, he had shown me a book he was reading by famed aerobatic pilot Bob Hoover. The passage he wanted me to read was about an air show in Russia at which Hoover had taken off a Russian fighter, flipped it inverted as soon as he was off the runway, and proceeded to amaze the crowd with his routine.

Sure enough, as the screen displayed the runway streaming past, Lee pulled back the stick and the simulator appeared to rise from the earth. He quickly rolled the plane, and I heard the major's sudden sharp intake of breath. He said something in an urgent whisper to the young airman manning the projection controls, but I said "It's okay. He is just being a young pilot again. Everything will be fine."

For the next ten minutes, Lee rolled and looped and banked the MIG over the virtual Croatian countryside, clearly loving every minute of it. At last, he turned the fighter toward the airbase, a distant spot on the display, and it slowly enlarged as he approached. He set it up on final approach, keeping his airspeed above a stall, but suddenly the display switched off. The flight was over.

"You already crashed in Croatia once," the major said to Lee. "We won't let that happen a second time." Everyone laughed, with Lee's appreciative chuckle clearly identifiable.

Out to the flight line, where we were allowed to inspect a couple of MIGs flown by the squadron. The air force officers were very generous and courteous, allowing each of the students to climb into the cockpit while they explained the myriad of gauges, switches, and controls.

This was followed by a small reception with a gift exchange and short speeches. We left the air base with a warm feeling for the tiny fighter force and its fiercely proud pilots.

The next day, Tuesday, 7 August, we drove out to the small village of Jursici in which the Croatian Conservation Institute was housed in a former monastery. There, in a room crowded with news cameras and reporters, we saw the thousands of pieces of the old bomber laid out carefully in rows on tables. It was a sad but very impressive sight. The artifacts were permanently stored in the capital city of Zagreb, but Luka had arranged for them to be transported to this site for Lee's visit. It was another indication of how well he had planned things for Lee's return. There followed a series of interviews of Lee by the press, and it gave us an idea of the interest in Croatia of Lee's wartime experiences.

That afternoon, we drove to Krvavici, the ancient village that we remembered from the maps sent by Luka. We knew the crash site was very near, and so it was. Lee, Bonnie, and Luka climbed into Luka's four-wheel-drive pickup, and the rest of us walked along the rough road cleared for the planned natural gas pipeline, and at last, we came to an area of stone-fenced fields. Ahead, we could see a couple of trucks and a small gathering of people beside a line of trees on one side of the rugged path.

Luka was there, as were the ubiquitous newspeople. There were also several villagers, including Bepo Cetina, the farmer on whose land the bomber had fallen and who had witnessed the crash of the Liberator. As a child, he and his father had been working in a nearby field when they saw the bomber approaching. Lee shook his hand, and there followed an animated conversation with Luka interpreting. The wing of the bomber had clipped the top of the tree under which we were standing, Cetina told us, nearly shearing the wing and causing the bomber to spin ninety degrees in the second before it slammed into the earth. It tore itself to pieces as it skidded sideways across the field, going through a stone wall before erupting in a fireball. The image was clearly burned into the Croatian farmer's brain.

Lee listened to the story of the last seconds of the aircraft, then once more shook Cetina's hand. "I'm sure sorry about damaging your tree," he said. As Luka interpreted, laughter burst from the villagers.

Luka pulled a metal detector from the back of his truck, and we spread out over the field to search for additional parts. It didn't take long: a .50-caliber bullet, another piece of broken and twisted aluminum, a smashed machine-gun cartridge.

"You see, the Germans must have removed the guns, and they destroyed all of the ammunition by knocking the bullets out of the cases to prevent their use by Partisans," Luka explained. "All of the ammunition we have recovered has the same dent at the end, and all of the bullets have been separated from the cases." There was a story that teenagers had found one of the Browning machine guns—from Alder's ball turret?—and the villagers had hidden it, but now no one knew what had happened to it. There also had been the tale, Luka told us, of villagers finding a glove with a severed hand in it, but obviously that had not happened since none of the crew in *Bottoms Up* had suffered such a severe injury.

He pointed to a nearby stone wall. It had been repaired, he said, using some of the parts of the aircraft, and he had been able to recover some pieces of the bomber from it, as well as what he thought might have been parts of flying clothing, including possibly bits of a leather jacket. We spent a couple of hours at the site, recovering a few more artifacts from the field. Janice Gerke, one of my students, discovered a piece of the bomber lying virtually on top of the soil, and screamed in delight as she held it in her hand. It was a memento beyond price.

Standing on top of the stone wall, looking over the field that still held un-counted remnants of a war long ago and a chapter in the life of a man I had come to know so well, I was nearly overwhelmed by the realization that we had actually made this trip to this place. Ron Wright was also clearly moved by the moment.

At last it was time to move on, this time to another field owned by Bepo Cetina that was closer to the village of Krvavici. Here we discovered that the enterprising farmers had almost literally turned Lee's sword into plowshares. Cetina showed us a large section of corrugated aluminum, with a piano hinge running its length, that he used to cover his firewood. We had seen this piece in photos, and Lee immediately identified it as the bomb bay door to a B-24. As we inspected it, we ran our fingers over a scattering of small holes and gashes, wounds in the metal that Lee said were consistent with damage caused by flak. This was the largest extant piece of the downed bomber, and we all felt a certain awe at being able to see and touch the skin of the long-dead aircraft, and to probe with our fingers some of the wounds that had killed her.

Ron Wright and I briefly discussed offering to buy the bomb bay door and have it shipped back to the Commemorative Air Force hangar in Olathe. At length, we decided that it was exactly where it needed to be, doing what it was doing. A Biblical simplicity was evident in this quiet farmer's use of part of the fearsome bomber.

We had seen part of what we came for, and we were satisfied in our minds that Bepo Cetina's field was the graveyard of *Bottoms Up*. Now we needed to find the site where Lee actually landed in his parachute, and the intersecting stone walls where he had hurriedly buried it. We hiked back to where the bus was parked off the road through Krvavici, to look over the maps of the area on which Lee believed he had pinpointed the location. But things now became very tense.

While still in Kansas City Lee had insisted that at the parachute site, he needed a few minutes alone, accompanied only by Luka to guide him. He needed privacy as he came to terms with his past. We would not film that initial visit, but instead would come a few minutes later and interview him when he was composed.

A news crew from one of the largest television news organizations in Croatia, however, was waiting at the bus and they had not made such an agreement. They insisted that they would follow Lee as he searched for his landing site and parachute remains. As a former journalist, I understood their desire for a compelling story. As Lee's friend, and having given my word to respect his privacy at that moment, I was equally insistent that no journalist would film what surely would be a highly emotional event.

It turned into a classic stand off. While Lee and Luka inspected a map of the area that dated to 1800 (Luka said it was far more useful than the modern maps and aerial photographs he had tried to rely on), I continued to negotiate with the news crew. Hold off on the initial shot, I said, and we will reenact the moment when Lee is more composed.

"That would be a lie," the woman on-air journalist retorted. "We will not broadcast a story to all of Croatia and tell them it is the real thing if it is a lie. No, we will follow Mr. Lamar the first time."

"Well, I'm sorry you feel that way. It's the best we can offer. If you insist on intruding, we will pack up and go back to Pula and wait you out." As I said it, I knew it sounded melodramatic, but I was quite prepared to tell Lee and the rest of the party to board the bus.

For about two hours, we hoped to wait the news crew out, knowing they would have a deadline for getting on the air that night. They leaned against their vehicle, smoking and talking among themselves, and waited with us. I was growing upset, and knew it, but we had spent too much time and too much money to have this moment ruined for Lee.

Finally, we conferred with Luka. He understood our concern, but also obviously felt a little divided. He had, after all, alerted the media to the story of Lee's return. But he had no control over what they chose to do in this regard. If we left now and returned to Pula, the news people had vowed to return the next day as well. The tension was thick.

Anna Jaffe of our own film crew was adamant. "If we are to produce this film for distribution, it must be exclusive. If this part of Lee's story, the heart of it, is broadcast by the news, we no longer have exclusive rights, and I don't think it would be easy to market."

That did it for me. I talked to Lee and Luka explaining the issue, and we all decided to return to Pula. We might be able to return here in a day or two using a different route. We loaded up, and returned to our hotel to clean up and head out for dinner.

Dinners in both Italy and Croatia were proving to be all-evening affairs, served by courses, and as long as anyone continued to eat the food continued to be served. We were going in a group that evening to an outdoor restaurant, not far from the old Roman square. The flip side of the news coverage was displayed when a man walking by our tables spotted Lee, stopped, and excitedly asked if he were the American pilot he had seen on the television news earlier that day. Lee acknowledged it was he, and the man insisted on buying us all a glass of wine. Lee, who does not drink alcohol in any form, demurred. Ron Wright, sitting close to him, urged him to reconsider.

"If you refuse, you are going to hurt his feelings and appear to be very rude, Lee. We are in his country, and I hope you will rethink this, even if you just raise the glass to your lips." Lee thought about this, then agreed. The man disappeared into the restaurant and came out with an armful of bottles of wine which he joyfully passed among us. Everyone raised a glass to Lee, to Partisans, to victory in the war, and to friendship between our nations. Once more the Croatian man ducked into the bar and emerged with a guitar. Soon he was strumming and singing, people around were clapping, and Jackie Sloderbeck, one of my students, rose and walked over to Lee.

"Lee, I want to dance with a real American hero." Jackie held out her hand, but again Lee tried to beg off. "I'm not much of a dancer." At everyone's urging, he rose, and slowly the old war hero and the young college student swayed around the tables.

I left early, still feeling down about the run-in with the news crew, and concerned it would seriously damage our chances of finding Lee's landing spot and his parachute.

The next morning, the sun was bright in a brilliant blue sky, and I felt better. When we arrived at Krvavici with the bus there was no news crew, and we quickly headed out to the place Lee had determined was his landing spot based on Luka's topographical map and his earlier calculations. Temperatures were warmer today than at any time since our arrival, and we walked slowly, adjusting our gait to the pace of the slowest among us. The area was overgrown, with scrubby oaks and other vegetation that pulled at our clothing and tripped us as we walked. Luka, swinging a machete, walked ahead to clear a path. He did in fact look a bit like Indiana Jones. At last, we arrived at a point that Lee had marked on his map, and Luka looked expectantly at Lee.

He glanced around, trying to match the scene with the photo indelibly etched in his memory.

"I don't think it was nearly this overgrown," he said at last.

"No, it would have been much clearer," Luka agreed. "But many young people have left this area, and there is not much farming here now. You will have to try to picture everything without all of this brush."

We located an old stone wall, and Lee wanted to move along it to find an intersecting fence. But there was nothing, only more of the overgrowth.

"This isn't the place," he said, finally. His face revealed his disappointment.

"We have plenty of time. There are a couple of other places on the map you said might be the area, so if you are up to it we will go there now." Luka was still upbeat.

More walking. With students carrying film gear, Lee in his sun helmet, and Luka in the lead hacking at brush with his machete, we looked like an old-time safari. But despite our best efforts, again nothing looked familiar to Lee.

"It's okay. That was always a long shot anyway," he said. But I could tell he was disappointed. Finally, Luka announced that it was time to head back to Krvavici, where the villagers had set up a sumptuous lunch with everything prepared with produce raised there. Marcana district officials Zlatko Cetina and Marijan Kostesic had organized the fete, another indication of the respect they felt toward Lee.

We gathered on a paved courtyard and were seated at tables groaning under the weight of fruit, various meats, pastries, and wine. The prosciutto was paper-thin and delicious, the wine sweet and heady, but we were all just a bit down over the failure to locate Lee's entry point into Croatia. One of the farmers brought out the pail he used to feed his cows, made from half of one of the oxygen tanks from Lee's bomber. We all wanted to hold it and have our picture taken with the artifact. Local Partisans and witnesses to the crash spoke with Lee through Luka, while the rest of us drank too much wine and a local spirit that had a tremendous kick. It was here that Lee met Martin Divkovic, from Filipana, the very Partisan who had cut Hurston Webb from his parachute. Luka was a bit doubtful, but Lee questioned him and Divkovic detailed exactly how Webb had fallen, broken his ankle, and the subsequent infection and gangrene that set in. He was quite specific about where they had left Webb in the hope that Germans would find him and treat his wound. Luka was convinced.

While the party was in full swing, Luka tapped me on the shoulder. "Go out to the truck. There is another place to go, but not with whole party," he said quietly. I quickly put down my glass and walked around the house to Luka's truck, where I was joined by Mike Horine and Ron Wright. Lee got in front while the rest of us crawled over the tailgate into the covered bed. One of Luka's friends was already there. Leonardo Larusso was a Croatian Air Force pilot who had taken his annual leave to participate in the hunt, and who had befriended each of us while interpreting many of the local conversations. When Lee's son-in-law Kirt and grandson Kraig arrived, we drove only a short distance, then we got out and began walking once more.

What had once been a well-tended field was now overgrown, and it was impossible to see very far. But we soon came to a rock wall, and Luka turned left when we reached it. In a few steps, we were at an intersection with another wall. We climbed over, holding on to the small trees that grew beside it. Lee stepped up, and we helped him over the wall and down the other side. He slowly walked up to the right angle formed by the two stone walls, and looked around. The land sloped into a karst hole, and the other side rose gently to a small knoll, the top obscured by trees and scrubby bushes.

"Well, this certainly looks like the place," he said at last. Luka grinned. "I remember burying my 'chute, and walking down hill a few steps. The soil looked like home, and I bent down to scoop up a handful. It was rich and black, I remember clearly."

I walked down toward the karst hole, scooped up two handfuls of earth—rich and black—and held my hands out to Lee. He took a bit in his fingers, inspected it, letting the soil drizzle onto the leaves covering the ground.

"Yes, this is the place." He pointed to a spot near the wall. "Right there is where I dropped to my knees and asked the Lord for a little bit of help." By now, the memories had come flooding back, and they soon overwhelmed his ability to fight the tears. A quiet sob escaped from the old pilot. Ron Wright moved to hug him.

Luka introduced Ivan Cetina, who was twelve years old in 1944. His little seven-year-old brother had found Lee's 'chute at this spot partially hidden under sticks and leaves, a week after Lee had buried it. He didn't know what it was and ran home to get help from his older, wiser, and more experienced brother. Ivan helped him carry it home to the women of the family, who immediately started cutting it up for shirts and blouses for the entire family. Zlatko Cetina, the nephew of Ivan, lived on the property and said that he had at one time worn a blouse from that parachute.

"We knew they had found a parachute here, but we were not certain it was yours," Luka explained to Lee. "You were certain it was somewhere else, and I wanted to go to those places that you found on the map first. Who knows, maybe there were many parachutes here."

"Well, I am very glad to have found this spot, and I am very happy that the Germans did not get my parachute," Lee said to Luka and Ivan. "I thought maybe I might find parts of the buckles or hooks, even the D-ring and cord, but I am very pleased that you and your family got some good out of that parachute."

Lee concluded that he had underestimated the radius of the turn *Bottoms Up* was in during its final death plunge. He had been searching the map for the specific intersection of stone walls along a much smaller circle and farther away from any buildings, since he had not seen any buildings in the area in 1944. Zlatko Cetina's home and several others were not there in 1944.

So the search for Lee's past was nearing an end. All that remained was to locate the exact site where he touched down under the canopy of his parachute that bright November day in 1944. Lee nodded up the hill. "Would have been up there, the highest part of that field. Landed right on a big, flat rock poking up through the soil."

I headed up the hill to look, meandering toward the top around the overgrowth and stunted trees. The slope was not steep, but noticeable, and the incline at last gave way to a slight flattening of the field. Through the trees, I could see the tops of houses in Krvavici. I worked my way through a small copse of oaks, and there at my feet was a large, flat stone, worn smooth by exposure. An area about five feet in diameter seemed to mark the highest point in the field. Nearly breathless, I stood on it, looking around, and I could imagine—no, could feel—what it must have been like sixty-three years earlier, to be twenty-three years old, hitting the ground in a parachute while you saw your airplane crash and burn less than a mile away.

I went back for Lee and the rest of the crew, and soon we were standing in a circle on the stone itself. It was, Lee declared, the very spot. Luka pointed out the direction of the aircraft crash site, while Kirt pressed some buttons on the GPS unit he had brought along.

"Lee, how far away did you guess you were from the plane?" he asked.

"A half to three-quarters of a mile."

Kirt grinned. "Sixty-one hundredths of a mile."

Recognizing the enormity of the moment, Lee's grandson Kraig, who was studying to become a minister, asked to pray on the site of Lee's return to earth and deliverance from death in his bomber. We stood on the perimeter of the flat, exposed rock, with our arms around each other, while Kraig offered up a prayer for all the young men on every side who had been called up to fight in that global war.

"Thank you for saving my Grandfather. We know Your hand was in this."

And so we had completed Lee's final mission. We had returned to the place where he had been shot down nearly sixty-three years earlier, and found the exact spot on which he had landed under the canopy of his silk 'chute. We had discovered the hiding place where he had hurriedly buried that parachute, and talked to the man who had discovered it a week later. We had visited the site of the final resting place of *Bottoms Up*, and proved beyond any doubt that the pieces of wreckage discovered by Luka Bekic and his team of archaeologists were indeed the remains of Lee's B-24J. Lee said he was not interested in the least in finding the site of his capture by German soldiers, so we did not pursue that thread.

We spent the next day visiting archaeological sites that Luka had been instrumental in excavating, including the bronze-age fortress of Monkodonja. Here, on a hilltop that commanded a view of the Adriatic as well as the countryside for miles around, he led us through the ancient ruins, and we gained a new appreciation for his professional experience. He pointed out a depression outside the walls of the old fort. It was here that his team had discovered the remains of about twenty people—men, women, and children—who had been discarded there in what was essentially the garbage pit for the garrison. The right hands of each of the men had been lopped off, leading Luka to believe that they might have been newcomers who had rebelled against the Romans and their power over the region.

War, it seemed, had been interwoven through the history of this region for thousands of years.

There were a few more things to come, events that continued to display the courtesy and respect that Croatians had for Lee and all the young airmen of that long ago war.

We rented an aircraft to duplicate the final flight over Pula of *Bottoms Up*, from the Brijuni Islands, in a great left-turning arc over the city and finally to the village of Krvavici. Lee, Luka, and Mike Horine with his camera rode in the Cessna, looking down on the splendor of the Adriatic sparkling in the bright August sun, seeing the iconic Roman amphitheater in Pula itself, and experiencing the final descent of the bomber as the pilot followed the flight path down to a few hundred feet. The pilot turned over the controls of the Cessna 172 to Lee; it was identical to an aircraft he had owned after the war for many years, and he delighted in simulating the evasive turns he and Darden had made so many years before. At the end of the flight, which lasted more than an hour, the Croatian aircraft owner refused any money, saying no one could accept payment for contributing in any way to Lee's final mission. It was very touching to witness the awe in which he held Lee.

Near the end of our adventure in Croatia, Luka told us of something he had witnessed as a direct result of Lee's trip: the old Partisans, who had vanished into the population at war's end despite facing horrendous dangers and doing heroic deeds, were at last being given the attention and honor of veterans.

"It has been wonderful to see," Luka said. "In the past, these men have simply been viewed by the children of the village as old people with no histories, and they have been largely ignored. Now, with all of the news stories about Lee and the Partisans on television and the newspapers, young children are going up to them and asking, 'Grandfather, tell us about the war.' It has truly brought generations together."

Luka also made crystal clear what we were beginning to understand on our own: the story of Lee and *Bottoms Up* was as much a Croatian story as it was an American one. It was Croatian Partisans and ordinary citizens who had risked their lives to rescue many of the crew, valorous deeds that were duplicated hundreds of times during the war. It was a Croatian team of archaeologists who had so carefully and relentlessly pursued the story behind the wreckage they had recovered at the Roman villa, with the help of aviation enthusiasts and history professionals in and around Pula. And it was Croatian news media which was keeping the story alive for the week we were there, and prompting many veterans and older citizens to tell their stories for the first time since the war.

There always had been a special place in the hearts of Croatians for the American and British flyboys who thundered overhead in long streams of hundreds of bombers, escorted by nimble fighters, people told us.

"We would look up and see all those planes, and no Luftwaffe, and we knew the war would soon be over and the Germans would lose," one man told us. "It gave us hope, after so many years of darkness. That is why so many were willing to risk their lives to save those young men who had to bail out."

We met in Marcana for a reception honoring Lee, and he displayed a Croatian flag he had carried on his journey and presented an Old Glory to the mayor, Marijan Kostesic. The mayor and other dignitaries handed out gifts to those in our party. Luka once more interpreted the proceedings, and translated for Lee when he spoke to the assembled group. Those attending included Herman Bursic, the history professor and former Partisan from Pula who had been instrumental in helping Luka determine the origins of the crashed bomber.

We had a final lunch with Luka and several of the old Partisans, including Bursic, a nostalgic repast which lasted for several hours. No one wanted this to end. But at last, we began to board the bus for the last ride into Pula, shook hands with the Partisans and hugged Luka, and then quietly rode back to our hotel. There was little conversation, each of us lost in our thoughts.

After an all-night bus ride from Pula to Venice, we were at last ready to board our airliner for the flight back to the U.S.

"Lee, was this everything you hoped for?" I asked as we headed for the gate.

He paused, giving the question serious thought.

At last he grinned. "I'd have to say, Mission Accomplished."

Notes

CHAPTER 1

1. *B-24: Pilot's Training Manual for the Liberator,* AAF Manual No. 50–12, revised 1 May 1945 (reprint). The cockpit of a Liberator could be intimidating. The pilot's training manual lists eighty-three gauges, switches, controls, levers, knobs, buttons, indicators, and meters. In fact, there were many more, since instruments such as fuel pressure gauges, cylinder temperature gauges, oil pressure, and other monitors were replicated for each of the four engines. Additionally, a complicated device such as the C-1 autopilot—which had many buttons, lights, and switches—was counted as a single instrument in the cockpit layout detailed in the pilot's manual. There was a kind of order to what first appears technological bedlam, however. Basic flight instruments, such as altimeter, air speed indicator, gyro horizon, rate-of-climb, and turn-and-bank indicator, were displayed directly in front of the left seat, that of the pilot. Engine instruments, including fuel pressure, cylinder temperature, oil pressure, oil temperature, as well as starter switches, oil dilution switches, and primer switches, were on the right side in full view of the co-pilot. Each pilot had a complete set of controls for the ailerons, rudder, and elevators. Throttles, propeller pitch controls, and fuel mixture, were on a console between the pilots. Sitting atop the panel were the remote indicating compass beside the magnetic compass, and above those was the clock. Overhead directly above it was a small panel with a protective cover; four buttons there were the propeller feathering controls. In addition to these and others in the flight deck, many more instruments were at stations throughout the bomber, particularly at the flight engineer's position, as well as the bombardier and navigator's stations. And of course oxygen, heating, and communications systems were at every combat airman's station in the Liberator.

2. Chris Chant, *Aircraft of World War II* (London: Barnes and Noble/Brown's, 1999), 91.

3. Duane L. Bohnstedt and Betty J. Bohnstedt, *460th Bomb Group History* (Charlotte, N.C: Fine Books Publishing, 2001), 110–11.

4. For an account of the wartime flying career of George McGovern, see Stephen E. Ambrose, *The Wild Blue: The Men and Boys Who Flew the B-24s Over Germany, 1944–45.*

5. Bohnstedt and Bohnstedt, *460th Bomb Group History,* 31–111.

6. Aircrew Flak Map-Italy, Reproduced by 941st Engineering Battalion, 27 March 1945. This map, issued to B-25 pilot Lt. John Morris, shows a cluster of red dots around the islands, each dot representing an enemy anti-aircraft battery. The map displayed known flak batteries in the area but was not considered definitive since the Germans frequently moved batteries by rail. It is marked in red, "May be taken into air," but Lamar said his crew rarely had one with them since flak positions could be assumed to be concentrated around sizeable cities in northern Italy. Map made available to me through the courtesy of Lt. Morris's son, Dr. Terry V. Morris.

7. Jon A. Maguire, *Gear Up! Flight Clothing & Equipment of USAAF Airmen in World War II,* 130. Here is shown a reprint of Technical Order 13-5-39. According to the TO, the two types (rings and snaps) of harness and parachute were to be clearly identified by color: red for group 1, yellow for group 2. It was the pilot's responsibility before each flight to ensure that harnesses and 'chutes matched for each crewman.

8. *B-24 Pilot's Manual,* 211–12. Procedures for bailing out were specified, including the recommended departure points for each crewman. It is important to remember that no actual practice of bailing out was incorporated into the training of aircrew.

9. Edgar Lee Lamar, personal interviews with me on many occasions from 2007 to 2010. Lamar's memory is sharp and clear, and he has retained an impressive collection of books, documents, and memorabilia from his service days.

CHAPTER 2

1. Luka Bekic, "Krvavici–Boskina: Aircraft Crash Site," 197–212.

2. Bekic, multiple interviews with me, August 2007.

3. Despite the severe flak damage to the aircraft, all of the crewmen managed to escape from the bomber. The "glove with a hand in it" was never explained, but probably can be attributed to more than sixty years distance between the event and the recalling.

CHAPTER 3

1. Lamar, "Seven Seconds Aircraft to Ground: Reflections of a World War II Bomber Pilot," unpublished memoir, 1–31. Additionally, much of the information in this chapter came from personal conversations with me from 2007 to 2010.

2. Antoine de Saint-Exupery, *Wind, Sand and Stars* (New York: Reynal and Hitchcock, 1939), 105–6.

3. Civilian Pilot Training Program, National Museum of the Air Force, online at http://www.nationalmuseum.af.mil. Accessed 28 August 2010.

4. A good account of the Piper J-3, drafted into the Army during World War II and designated the L-4, is given by Ken Wakefield in *Lightplanes at War: US Liaison Aircraft in Europe, 1942–1947.* In addition to duties as trainers during the war, similar light aircraft, essentially civilian models painted in olive drab, were used as liaison and courier vehicles, artillery spotters, and occasionally as ambulances. They were produced by Aeronca (L-3), Taylorcraft (L-2), and Piper (L-4) as simple-to-fly, easy-to-maintain "flying jeeps" in every theater. The Taylorcraft was also produced in Great Britain under license by Auster; the British army used it as an Air Observation Post (AOP). I own and fly a restored U.S. Army 1942 L-2B.

CHAPTER 4

1. Lamar, *Seven Seconds,* 48–49.

2. Kevin Murphy, "Fairchild PT-19 / PT-23 / PT-26 Cornell," www.warbirdalley. com. The PT-19, built by Fairchild, was a 2-place, tandem-seat low-wing trainer powered by a 200-hp Ranger engine. More than 7,700 were built. PT was Primary Trainer, and the most commonly used were the Fairchild and the Stearman PT-13 and PT-17, open-cockpit bi-planes differing only in the size of the engines. Most World War II pilots with whom I have spoken agree that the Fairchild was easier to fly than the Stearman, which had a reputation for ground-looping because of the narrow main landing gear. The wider track of the Fairchild made controlling it after landing a bit easier.

3. Lamar collection.

4. Ibid.

5. Lamar, *Seven Seconds,* 57.

6. At each phase of flight training—Primary, Basic, and Advanced—the aircraft were more sophisticated, with greater horsepower and more equipment. The plan, obviously, was to take aviation cadets incrementally through a training program that would qualify them to fly combat aircraft.

7. Donald L. Miller, *Masters of the Air: America's Bomber Boys Who Fought the Air War against Nazi Germany* (New York: Simon and Schuster, 2006), 143.

8. Ellington Field also was home to a flight navigator training school. My uncle, Tage Okerstrom, received his navigator wings there in 1944. He was 19.

9. Lamar, *Seven Seconds,* 70.

10. Ibid., 73.

11. Ibid., 79.

12. Maguire, *Gear Up!,* 11–13.

13. Lamar, *Seven Seconds,* 79.

14. Ibid., 88.

CHAPTER 5

1. *The Luftwaffe,* Epic of Flight Series (Alexandria, Va.: Time-Life, 1982), 15.

2. For a detailed, day-by-day account of the Battle of Britain, see Richard Collier, *Eagle Day: The Battle of Britain* (London: Cassell, 1966).

3. For further reading about the Tokyo Raid, the reader should see Doolittle's autobiography (with Carroll V. Glines), *I Could Never Be So Lucky Again* (New York: Bantam, 1991), and Ted Lawson and Robert Considine, *Thirty Seconds Over Tokyo* (New York: Random House, 1943).

4. Walter J. Boyne, *The Influence of Air Power upon History* (Gretna, La.: Pelican, 2003), 228–30. Boyne concludes that the defeat was decisive and the turning point of the war against Japan.

5. Edward T. Russell, "Leaping the Atlantic Wall: Army Air Forces Campaigns in Western Europe, 1942–1945," The U.S. Army Air Forces in World War II, Air Force History and Museums Programs, 1999 (www.usaaf.net) Accessed 29 August 2010. According to the American Battlefield Monuments Commission, 405,399 Americans died in World War II; the figures for the 8th and 9th AAF indicate a disproportionate number of casualties for aircrews.

6. Miller, *Masters of the Air,* 33–36.

7. *Jane's Encyclopedia of Aviation* (New York: Portland House, 1989), 258.

8. Austin Weber, "A Historical Perspective," *Assembly Magazine*, 1 August 2001. On-line at www.assemblymag.com. Para. 8. Accessed 12 September 2010.

9. Lamar, personal conversation with me, November 2009.

10. *B-24: Pilot's Training Manual for the Liberator*, 9.

11. Philip Kaplan, *Bombers: The Aircrew Experience* (London: Aurum Press, 2000), 94. Kaplan and others have suggested that the Norden bombsight was the most effective weapon used by the U.S. flying forces. In terms of technology, the top-secret device was certainly highly regarded, particularly those commanding the bombing campaign. But I would argue that the young men who willingly climbed into those cramped and primitive airplanes were in fact the most effective weapons of the war.

12. Lamar, *Seven Seconds*, 97. Details added through conversations with me during 2008.

13. Lamar, interview with me, March 2008.

14. Lamar, *Seven Seconds*, 101.

CHAPTER 6

1. Rick Atkinson, *An Army at Dawn* (New York: Henry Holt, 2003), 359–92.

2. Lamar, personal interview with me. "I am not sure whether I considered it a minor breach of security, or if I just didn't want to be delayed," Lamar told me. "But I never said anything to anyone about it. Not to the enlisted crew, not to the officers."

3. Lamar, personal interview with me.

4. *B-24 Pilot's Manual*, 7. The manual reminds the aircraft commander that the performance and morale of his crew are his business:

> It is no business of yours whether a crew member spends his free hours in prayer, gambling, or hunting turtle's eggs unless these habits interfere with the performance of his duty. Then his business is your business. You can't afford to see a mission jeopardized because a crew member doesn't get enough sleep, comes to duty with a hangover, starts on a high-altitude mission with gas-producing food in his stomach, or is so distracted by worry that he cannot concentrate on the task at hand.

CHAPTER 7

1. Lamar, *Seven Seconds*, 112.

2. The 12th and 15th Air Forces were combined into a fictitious 27th Air Force in Joseph Heller's iconic novel *Catch-22*. Heller was a bombardier on B-25s flying out of Corsica against targets in northern Italy.

3. Lamar, *Seven Seconds*, 112.

4. Bohnstedt and Bohnstedt, *460th Bomb Group History*, 8–9.

5. Ibid., 9.

6. Ibid., 10.

7. Ibid., 12–13.

8. Keith W. Mason, "nothing to fear . . . ": Recollections of a World War II Bomber Pilot (Privately printed, 2009), 205–27. Mason was the operations officer of the 760th; he and Lamar got to know each other better long after the war. Mason told Lamar at a 460th Bomb Group reunion that during the war he had lost so many friends that he

stopped trying to know new crews as they reported. It was simply too hard on him as they went missing. Mason lives in Waukon, Iowa.

9. Bohnstedt and Bohnstedt, *460th Bomb Group History*, 22.

10. Lamar, *Seven Seconds*, 122.

11. Ibid., 122.

CHAPTER 8

1. The number of missions constituting a full-tour and a ticket home varied during the war. Joseph Heller's *Catch-22* details this in frenetic, dark humor, as his characters all go bonkers or die as the number of missions they must fly is increased. In practice, the first "magic number" for bomber crews flying out of England was twenty-five. Mark K. Wells, in his *Courage and Air Warfare*, says that the first commander of the bomber component of the 8th AAF, Brig. Gen. Ira Eaker, had to balance operational needs with the obvious physical and mental toll that sustained combat flying would take on the crews. He and his staff accepted an estimated attrition rate of 2-to-2.5 per cent per mission, and settled on twenty-five missions for a tour. However, in the first year of the war, that seemed impossible to attain as loss rates sometimes approached 10 percent per mission. The B-17 *Memphis Belle* flown by Capt. Robert Morgan and crew was celebrated in a widely distributed documentary film as the first crew to complete twenty-five missions, although Donald Miller (*Masters of the Air*) notes that the crew of *Hell's Angels* actually completed their twenty-five on 14 May 1943, three days before Morgan's crew (145). Later, the number of required missions was raised to thirty, then thirty-five, after it was apparent that the Allies were gaining air superiority and the odds for survival of crews increased. In Italy, later in the war, the number of missions was set at fifty for heavy bombers. My friend Robert P. Zulauf (1922–2010) was a B-25 pilot flying off Corsica in 1944–45; when he started his tour, the required number of missions was sixty, and it was increased to seventy while he was in theater. He finished his seventy missions 15 April 1945 with a Distinguished Flying Cross and nine Air Medals and returned to the states in June. The procedure in Italy for counting missions—no credit, credit, double credit—is explained more thoroughly in Chapter 9.

2. Gideon Jones was the veteran pilot who replaced Lamar on this first mission for the Darden crew. Experience was no guarantee of completing a tour, however, as Jones himself was shot down a few missions later. Jones at the time of this writing was still active in 460th BG reunions. He lives in LaPorte, Texas.

3. History of the 460th Bombardment Group (H), 1 September 1944 to 30 September 1944. Included in the monthly reports were individual narratives for each mission. Narrative report, Mission 100, 18 September 1944. In this mission, the group's 100th, thirty bombers from the 460th BG were launched; three returned with mechanical malfunctions. These monthly reports constitute the official history of the group, and they were sent to the Commanding General, Fifteenth Air Force. They are available through the Air Force Historical Research Agency (AFHRA), Maxwell Air Force Base.

4. Bohnstedt and Bohnstedt, *460th Bomb Group History*, 33–34.

5. History of the 460th, monthly report, 3. 1 September 1944 to 30 September 1944. The report shows that Lt. Col. Babb led three missions (4 September, 12 September, and 23 September) and was awarded an Oak Leaf Cluster to his Distinguished Flying Cross on 26 September. He was named Group Commander by GO No. 45. Additionally,

the monthly report makes clear the cost in personnel during September 1944: seven officers and seven enlisted men were killed in action; thirty officers and forty-seven enlisted men are listed as missing in action. Twenty-four replacement crews arrived at Spinazzola during the month, including the Darden crew.

6. James Dugan and Carroll Stewart, *Ploesti: The Great Ground-Air Battle of 1 August 1943* (New York: Bantam Books, 1963).

7. Michael S. Breuninger, *U.S. Military Combat Aircrew Individual Survival Equipment: WWII to Present* (Fairview Village, Penn.: Breuninger, 1994), 76. Survival kits and equipment evolved throughout the war, and they were theater specific. Flying over Europe generally did not call for a great deal of survival gear, but escape and evasion were emphasized. In the Pacific and Far East, more elaborate survival equipment was provided to bomber crews, and it would often include machetes, signaling mirrors, first-aid supplies, fishing gear, water purification tablets, malaria pills, mosquito netting, waterproof matches, and additional .45-caliber ammunition, both ball and shot, and field rations, all contained in the B-2 Jungle Emergency Back Pad Kit. Additionally, my father-in-law, Lynn Johnston, a B-29 crewman, carried numerous silk maps and a "blood chit," also of silk, displaying the U.S. flag and the following message in English, French, Tamil, Sumatran, Thai, Burmese, Malay, Chinese and several dialects:

> Dear Friend.
>
> I am an Allied fighter. I did not come here to do any harm to you who are my friends. I only want to do harm to the Japanese and chase them away from this country as quickly as possible. If you will assist me, my Government will sufficiently reward you when the Japanese are driven away.

8. *B-24 Pilot's Manual.* The procedures for any specific or individual aircraft might vary slightly if modifications had been made or additional equipment installed. The pre-flight inspection and checklist is a time-honored tradition that most pilots (and all commercial and military pilots) adhere to religiously. I have been a flight instructor for more than twenty-five years, and I have often told my students to honor the checklist, since each item probably represents a pilot killed because an item had not been listed.

9. Lee Lamar and I experienced a very minor taste of this when the Collings Foundation, which owns and flies the last remaining B-24J, very generously offered to fly us from Fort Collins, Colo., to Kansas City. Sitting on the spartan floor of the Liberator in the waist compartment, leaning back against the bulkhead and with a restraining strap across my waist, I could feel to the core of my body the tremendous power of the bomber's engines as the vibrations from 4,800 horsepower shook the entire aircraft. Of course, this was peacetime, and the bomber was lightly loaded, with no bombs or live ammunition. Still, the physical memory of that takeoff remains with me.

10. Lamar, *Seven Seconds,* 147.

CHAPTER 9

1. C. G. Sweeting, *Combat Flying Clothing: Army Air Forces Clothing during World War II* (Washington, D.C.: Smithsonian, 1984), 24–34.

2. History of the 460th Bombardment Group (H). Narrative report, Mission 101. 21 September 1944. AFHRA.

3. Lamar, personal interview with me, August 2007.

4. History of the 460th. Narrative report, Mission 102. 23 September 1944. AFHRA.

5. Peter Darman, *World War II: Stats and Facts* (New York: Fall River Press, 2009), 235.

6. History of the 460th. Narrative report, Mission 102, 23 September 1944. AFHRA.

7. Bohnstedt and Bohnstedt, *460th Bomb Group History*, 87.

8. Ibid., 87.

9. Ibid., 86. Mayo is buried in the Sicily-Rome American Cemetery, grave 10–25. More than sixty years later, Lamar still vividly recalls the tenderness of those who removed Mayo's body from the tail turret of the Liberator, and the profound, respectful silence accorded him as crewmen from other bombers surrounded the damaged bomber.

10. Lamar, personal interview. I have heard Lamar relate this experience several times in talks to university classes and other groups. His voice always catches and his eyes water as he momentarily relives one of the most horrific experiences of his wartime career. His own experiences seem to pale before the realization that the ten young men in that Liberator simply vanished in a split second.

CHAPTER 10

1. Lamar has visited several times with Mason at 460th Bomb Group reunions, and he has confirmed that the former Operations Officer was unfazed by the close formations the group flew. In a conversation with me in October 2010, Mason said he did not recall the specific incident related by Lamar, but doesn't doubt that it occurred: "I was an instructor at Randolph Field following my graduation from flight school in October 1941. I spent three years in Training Command doing all I could to get into combat. You just never think about the danger."

2. The Capri bells, as they were known by the flight crews, were as much the mark of a veteran combat flier as the colorful combat ribbons below their wing badges. Only combat crews with a significant number of missions were granted leave to Capri, and they were much envied by those who had yet to earn the privilege of wearing them.

3. Lamar, *Seven Seconds*, 129–31, 149–50. Lamar expressed much disgust with the British controller over this incident. In several conversations with me, Lamar was still in disbelief that a wind sock was not in use at the field, and that the controller directed them to land without giving wind direction and velocity.

4. Bohnstedt and Bohnstedt, *460th Bomb Group History*, 90.

5. Lamar, *Seven Seconds*, 117–22.

6. Lamar collection.

7. Lamar collection.

CHAPTER 11

1. History of the 460th. Narrative report, Mission 113. 21 October 1944. AFHRA. This incident is also detailed in Bohnstedt and Bohnstedt, *460th Bomb Group History*, 94. The accident happened at 1110 on 20 October 1944 over the Gulf of Venice. All ten

men aboard the aircraft piloted by Lt. Seldon Campbell, and three crew members—the three who bailed out—in the crew of Lt. Francis Galarneau were killed. Their names appear on the Wall of the Missing, Florence American Cemetery.

2. History of the 460th. Narrative report, Mission 109. 13 October 1944. AFHRA. This incident is also detailed in Lamar, *Seven Seconds,* 150, and Bohnstedt and Bohnstedt, *460th Bomb Group History,* 92–93.

3. Edward J. Devney, 460th Bomb Group (privately printed, 1946), unnumbered pages.

4. Gregory A. Freeman, *The Forgotten 500: The Untold Story of the Men Who Risked All for the Greatest Rescue Mission of World War II* (New York: Penguin, 2007). We would learn more about the divisions among the people of the region during the war when we visited Croatia in 2007.

5. Christine Peterson, "They Served with Honor: Staff Sgt. Kazmer Rachak, Casper," (Casper, Wyo.) *Journal,* August 18–24, A7. As I was completing this manuscript, my good friend Joel G. Heiney, of Casper, Wyoming, sent me a clipping from his local newspaper. Ninety-year-old Kazmer Rachak, a gunner aboard a B-17, was on a mission over Breman, Germany, 4 August 1944. Visibility was poor, and another bomber collided with his; Rachak and the navigator, 2nd Lt. Quentin Ingerson, bailed out and were captured by German troops. However, the pilot, 2nd Lt. Harvey Walthall, managed to crash land the ship on the small island of Borkum in the North Sea. The crewmen survived the landing but were all shot by townspeople. Six Germans were convicted of war crimes; three were executed.

6. History of the 460th. Narrative report, Mission 120. 7 November 1944. AFHRA.

7. General Orders, No. 3604, Headquarters, Fifteenth Air Force, 24 September 1944. Although the Unit Citation was approved in September for a mission that occurred in July, the official ceremony presenting the award and streamer was in November. GO No. 3604 notes that the target was a fighter assembly plant at Zwolfaxing, and the defense was spirited and intense. Three Liberators were shot down in flames, two were badly damaged and forced to drop out of the formation, and fourteen sustained severe damage. The GO states, "Unwavering, despite the intense enemy opposition, these gallant crews continued through the enemy defenses for a highly successful bombing run, inflicting grave damage to a vital enemy installation." All members of the 460th Bomb Group were entitled to wear the blue ribbon, whether they had participated in the raid or not.

8. Lamar, interview with me, March 2009.

9. Jadyn Stevens, *The Final Mission of Lt. Wade Moore Craig, Jr.,* as told to Jadyn Stevens (Nashville: Eveready Press, 2000), 4. The navigator's nephew wrote this short memoir, based on interviews with his uncle and a written account by Craig from March 1945.

10. Bohnstedt and Bohnstedt, *460th Bomb Group History,* 83. A small photograph of Col. Babb in front of the nose art of *Bottoms Up* shows that the painter was someone with talent. The decorative—and often risqué, if not obscene—paintings were normally done by someone in the squadron, with varying degrees of ability. For more on World War II aircraft nose art, see J. P. Wood, *Aircraft Nose Art: 80 Years of Aviation Artwork* (London: Salamander Books, 1996), or Gary M. Valant, *Vintage Aircraft Nose Art* (Osceola, Wis.: Motorbooks International, 1987). Not all nose art featured undraped or scantily clad young women, but a large percentage did. Readers should

remember that combat crewmen were generally single and in their late teens or early twenties. Mark K. Wells, in *Courage and Air Warfare: The Allied Aircrew Experience in the Second World War* (London: Cass, 1995) wryly observes: "Nose-art frequently displayed a healthy regard for the opposite sex" (cutlines, illustration no. 19).

11. Illustrations of the tail markings for the various bomb groups can be viewed at www.15thaf.org/55th_BW/460th_BG.

12. Lamar, *Seven Seconds,* 152.

13. Ibid., 153.

CHAPTER 12

1. Howard Nemerov, "The War in the Air," in *War Stories: Poems about Long Ago and Now* (Chicago: University of Chicago Press, 1987), 31. While I was in graduate school at the University of Missouri-Kansas City, Nemerov spent a week in residence delivering three public lectures and conducting graduate seminars. During that week, I had the opportunity to go for dinner and a beer with the national poet laureate, thanks to the kind invitation of Dr. James McKinley. Nemerov had been a pilot in the Royal Air Force, flying a hundred missions in a twin-engine Beaufighter for Coastal Command. He and his navigator were the only crew to survive the war, from an initial class of twelve crews at his OTU (Operational Training Unit). I asked him why he had waited more than forty years to write of his war experiences. He looked across the table, his neon-blue eyes unblinking. "Because it took me that long to stop shaking." Nemerov died of cancer three months later.

2. It is impossible to estimate with any accuracy how many cigarettes were distributed free to servicemen during the war, but undoubtedly it ran into the millions. Whether this was because of patriotism and largess on the part of tobacco companies or because they saw an opportunity to hook an entire generation, I will leave to others to decide. However, the ubiquity of smokes during the war is reflected in the camps around LeHavre for returning servicemen: nine camps, all named after cigarette brands, including Lucky Strike, Chesterfield, Pall Mall, Philip Morris, and Old Gold.

3. James R. Mund, "A One Way Ticket to Udine: A True Story," unpublished memoir. Mund was a gunner in the 763rd Squadron of the 460th, and his aircraft was one of two lost on the Udine mission. The other, of course, was *Bottoms Up.*

4. Lamar obtained a copy of a flimsy for a mission on 8 July 1944 from another 460th BG pilot who somehow had managed to retain it. It is a blizzard of numbers and directives; its content is proof of the need for its existence.

5. I interviewed a B-17 pilot many years ago, Roy Pendergist of Raytown, Missouri, who had to bail out of his bomber directly over Berlin. Coming down under canopy, with bombers still roaring overhead and explosions from their bombs shaking the city below him, Pendergist removed his .45 from its holster and field-stripped it, throwing the parts in all directions. "I didn't want to arm any civilians with it, and maybe get shot with my own gun." He landed, hid in a drainage culvert until he spotted German soldiers, and then surrendered. It was the first mission of his second tour of duty.

6. William Butler Yeats, "An Irish Airman Foresees His Death," *Selected Poems* (Franklin Center, Penn.: Franklin, 1979), 89.

7. History of the 460th. Narrative Report, Mission 126. 19 November 1944. AFHRA. The very real human drama of the mission has been eviscerated from the official

narrative report, which in ten numbered paragraphs details the logistics and results of the raid. Paragraph 8 comes closest to hinting at the human cost:

> 24 a/c returned to base with a mean landing time of 1325 hours. Two a/c with wounded aboard landed at friendly fields, Foggia and Bari. One of these a/c, Foggia, has since returned. The a/c at Bari blew up upon landing. Seven crewmembers are in hospital. One member was killed. Three escaped unharmed. Two a/c are missing: a/c # 512 was last seen at 45618N-1310E) headed toward Yugo, at 1122 hours. A/c # 926 was last seen at (4350N-1400E), headed towards Ancona at 1152 hours.

926 was the Darden crew.

CHAPTER 13

1. Associated Press, "Telegram Passes Into History," 2 February 2006. Western Union sent the last telegram early in 2006, as the company evolved from a communications company to a financial services firm. Email, text messages, cheap long-distance telephone calls, and other communications options had rendered the venerable telegram obsolete.

2. Lamar collection. Lamar's family saved every letter from him, and after he was shot down, saved all of the official correspondence related to his Missing in Action and later his Prisoner of War status. Today, he has all of the letters in addition to virtually every document related to his war service. All of the letters and documents cited in this chapter are from this collection.

3. I will admit to being unable to read this aloud without feeling deep emotion.

CHAPTER 14

1. B-24 Pilot's Manual, 210–12. Specific instructions for determining when to bail out, what to do before doing so, signals to the crew, and procedures for bailing (including which crew members should use which escape route) are detailed in a section titled "Bailout, Ditching and Fires." Lamar, in the interest of saving valuable seconds, disregarded this warning:

> It is extremely important in all cases to face the front of a B-24 and roll out headfirst. The airplane is traveling fast, and if you jump toward the rear there is danger of being slapped up against the airplane. If you jump feet first, the wind can catch your legs and bang your head on the edge of the hatch (212).

2. Lamar, *Seven Seconds*, 167. Six decades later, Lamar is still able to recall with precision exactly what occurred on 18 November 1944. Some experiences sear themselves into a person's memory.

3. After Lamar was captured, he received from the International Red Cross a package that contained, besides food, a couple of items of clothing and a notebook. The booklet, about six by eight inches, bound in gray cardboard, bore a label with a "Y.M.C.A." stamp and the legend "War Prisoners Aid." He used this as a journal, in which he recorded dates, names, events, hopes for the future, and daily life at the POW camp.

4. For longer missions, most crewmen carried a couple of candy bars in a pocket, but the flight to Udine was expected to be quite short. Lamar had packed extra socks and a bit of food in a separate bag but left it behind in the bomber.

5. Letter from Lamar to Swante Norlund, radio operator on *Bottoms Up*, 1988. Lamar kept a copy of the typed, eleven-page letter explaining what had happened to him after the bomber was hit over Pola. The crew never saw each other again as a complete crew after 18 November 1944.

6. Lamar, *Seven Seconds*, 169–70.

7. Ibid., 170.

8. Lamar wrote this phrase—"Vor You, Der War iss Ofer"—as the title of his POW journal.

9. Lamar learned this from Reynolds when they had an impromptu reunion at Truax Air Field near Madison, Wisc., shortly after the end of the war.

CHAPTER 15

1. Martin W. Bowman, *USAAF Handbook 1939–45* (Thrupp, Gloucestershire, UK: Sutton, 1997), 232–33. Germany had signed the 1929 agreement that came to be called the Geneva Convention, and aircrews were generally accorded good treatment if military personnel captured them. Prisoner of War camps for fliers were run by the Luftwaffe, and provided that the SS did not get their hands on captured crew, they could expect to be sent to the Dulag Luft for interrogation and then on to one of several large camps across Germany or Poland. Of ninety thousand U.S. airmen captured by Germany, about 1.2 per cent died in captivity. Japan also had signed the Geneva Convention, but the government never ratified it. Treatment of U.S. troops there was especially horrific: 40.4 per cent died in captivity.

2. Stevens, *The Final Mission of Lt. Wade Moore Craig, Jr.*, 7–8.

3. Lamar, *Seven Seconds*, 173–75.

4. The Dulag Luft, used by American troops after the war during the occupation of Germany, was renamed Camp King.

5. Dulag-Luft. Kriegsgefangenenkartei. Prisoner of war card, Prisoner number 6424. Dated 30–11–44. After German troops left Stalag Luft I at Barth, Lamar was able to locate his German POW record sheet with the photos at the bottom. He still has the pink record, a sobering reminder of that chapter of his past.

6. Lamar personal interview with me, 2008.

7. Lamar, *Seven Seconds*, 185.

8. Lamar, personal interview with me, 2008. When telling of this experience, Lamar's voice broke, and he pounded his fist in unconscious imitation of his movements under the pile of men in his train car. It was a moving experience for me to see such visible reminders of the psychic scars on a warrior more than sixty years after the events.

CHAPTER 16

1. A good account of life for a U.S. flier in a Stalag Luft can be found in Thomas Childers, *In the Shadows of War: An American Pilot's Odyssey Through Occupied France and the Camps of Nazi Germany* (New York: Henry Holt, 2002). The camp

described is Stalag Luft III, which was the location of the Great Escape, the breakout by allied fliers in March 1944. A firsthand examination of that escape can be found in Paul Brickhill's *The Great Escape* (Oxford, Eng.: Isis Publishing, 2009). Brickhill was a POW at the camp, but was not among the seventy-six who broke out. All but three were recaptured, and fifty were subsequently executed by the Germans.

2. C. Ross Greening, *Not as Briefed: From the Doolittle Raid to a German Stalag* (Pullman, Wash.: Washington State University Press, 2001). This is an excellent resource for both a firsthand account of life in Stalag Luft I and for the numerous watercolor paintings done by the author while a prisoner there. Greening had been the pilot of one of the sixteen B-25s that launched from the U.S.S. *Hornet* in April 1942 to bomb Tokyo. Later, he flew B-26s in North Africa, and was shot down 17 July 1943 in Italy.

3. Roger A. Freeman, *Zemke's Wolf Pack: The Story of Hub Zemke and the 56th Fighter Group in the Skies Over Europe* (New York: Orion Books, 1988).

4. Roy J. Morris, *Behind Barbed Wire* (New York: Richard R. Smith, 1946). This is a very rare book, written by one of Lamar's fellow Kriegies. Lamar wrote a check for the planned book while still at the Stalag; having no checkbook, he wrote it on a piece of scrap paper, and his bank honored it.

5. Lamar collection.

6. Ibid.

CHAPTER 17

1. The issues of combat stress, its manifestations, and treatment in the Army Air Forces are covered in some detail by Wells in *Courage and Air Warfare*, 60–88, and Miller in *Masters of the Air*, 128–36. For Lamar, this was the first outward sign of his inner stress. Years after the war, he was adjudged by the Veteran's Administration to be suffering from Post-Traumatic Stress Disorder and was entitled to a monthly stipend.

2. Lamar, *Seven Seconds*, 225–26. Lamar later heard that the young man became a priest a few years after the war.

3. Even today, sixty-five years later, his voice breaks as he describes that once-in-a-lifetime flight.

4. Seine Section, U.S. Army, "United States Army Paris Guide: For Leave Troops." N.d.

5. *Seven Seconds*, fn. 235.

CHAPTER 18

1. Col. A. C. Ramsey, Quartermaster Corps, "Effects Depot," *The Quartermaster Review*, September October 1945. (On-line at www.qmmuseum.lee.army.mil/WWII/effects_depot.htm) Accessed 11 September 2010. The logistics involved in retrieving, tagging, storing, and transporting the personal effects of the hundreds of thousands of U.S. military personnel in Europe who were killed, missing in action, captured, or otherwise missing was daunting. For all servicemen in Europe, the first repository was Q-290, in Folembray, France. After a few months, if the serviceman were still missing, the package would be shipped to the National Personal Effects Bureau in Kansas City, Missouri. Ramsey, writing shortly after the war, noted the seriousness with which the delicate matter was taken:

The detail involved in receiving, storing, safeguarding, and shipping personal property is prodigious. Each package must be handled separately in order that the name, status, and other pertinent data may be correctly recorded; and too, the consignor must have a receipt. There is no "O.S.&D." report in the handling of personal property. In order that each package may be immediately available upon request, numbered bin storage is necessary; recording the wrong storage space is tantamount to losing the property. A master file must be maintained indicating the status of all property on hand and the disposition of that which has been shipped. Transcribing a name incorrectly from a package, or misfiling a card, may make the property unavailable. Checking the files for receipt or disposition of property in order to reply to thousands of letter inquiries daily is a major clerical undertaking. Mistakes must not be made because they affect the morale of soldiers who have been casualties, or their next of kin. (para. 7)

Lamar confirms the efficiency of the unit. When he signed the forms on the seventh floor of the large building in Kansas City, the young woman helping him told him to drive his car to the dock in the rear of the building. He took the elevator to the ground floor, and the box containing his personal effects was waiting for him when he backed the car up to the dock. It had been no more than five minutes.

In 2009, our mutual good friend Ronald Wright, an Overland Park dentist and a retired Army Reserve colonel, volunteered for a tour in Iraq. Six months after his return, he was flown to a reunion of his unit. Wright and Lamar concluded that the Army must have learned something about the value of closure for military personnel who have served in a combat zone.

CHAPTER 20

1. Stevens, *The Final Mission of Lt. Wade Moore Craig, Jr.,* 7–8.

2. Missing Air Crew Report, # 9888. The MACR was maintained until the status of the entire crew was determined, a process that often took many months; in some cases, it took years. Included in 9888 is a three-page report, labeled "Secret," that contains the escape statements of four of the crew: S/Sgt. Henry L. Alder, S/Sgt. John F. Nordback, S/Sgt. Bernard Sturtz, and S/Sgt. Mario A. Briganti. They were returned to their squadron 1 January 1945; the report notes, "Never in enemy hands." They linked up with Partisans who assisted them in their evasion and return. The report is spare in its details and descriptions, but one can get some idea of their ordeal from this: "Moving via the safe area escape route from day to day many hardships were endured. Sleeping in the open and going without food for as many as six days at a time."

3. Reynolds to Lamar in numerous conversations after the war. The two kept in close contact until Reynolds's death in the 1970s.

4. Lamar, personal interview with me, 2008.

5. Lamar, conversation with me, 2009.

CHAPTER 21

1. The eight students selected for the trip were Adrienne Barr, Janice Gerke, Jackie Sloderbeck, Darrin Manna, Rachel Tharp, Tessa Elwood, Selvir Abidovic, and Stacy Weidmaier. All were helpful in researching a variety of topics prior to leaving, and

they assisted the film crew throughout the sometimes grueling days in Croatia. I thank them for their keen interest and professional attitude during the entire experience.

2. For many years, O'Neal sang the national anthems of the U.S. and Ireland at the start of the Kansas City St. Patrick's Day parade; he was an avid collector of flight jackets, and a good friend of mine. He died of cancer in July 2010 while I was presenting a paper at a conference in Lausanne, Switzerland.

CHAPTER 22

1. HMSO Manual, "Signal Training: Procedure for Radio Telephony," (Pamplet No. 5, Signal Procedure Part 1, War Office, 5 June 1943). The phonetic alphabet, intended to maximize clarity and intent by eliminating possible mistakes over similar-sounding letters, has changed over the years. Over a radio, possibly with a weak signal and perhaps with static or interrupted reception, it might be difficult to distinguish between the letters *B, C, D, E, G, P, T,* or *V.* Today, the phonetic alphabet begins with Alpha, Bravo, Charlie, and Delta. The letter *J* is designated Juliet. In World War II, the American phonetic alphabet was virtually identical to that used by the British, and began: Able, Baker, Charlie, Dog. J was for Jig.

Bibliography

AAF: The Official Guide to the Army Air Forces. New York: Pocket Books, 1944.

Ambrose, Stephen E. *The Wild Blue: The Men and Boys Who Flew the B-24s Over Germany*. New York: Simon and Schuster, 2001.

Ardery, Philip. *Bomber Pilot: A Memoir of World War II*. Lexington: University Press of Kentucky, 1978.

B-24: Pilot Training Manual for the Liberator. AAF Manual No. 50–12. Revised 1 May, 1945. Office of Flying Safety, AAF. (Reprint)

Baudot, Marcel, et al., eds. *The Historical Encyclopedia of World War II*. New York: MJF Books, 1989.

Bekic, Luka. "Krvavici-Boskina: Aircraft Crash Site." In *Rescue Archaeology on Magistral Gas Pipeline, Pula–Karlovac*. Zagreb: Hrvatski Restauratorski Zavod, 2007.

Bohnstedt, Duane L., and Betty Bohnstedt. *460th Bomb Group History*. Charlotte, N.C: Fine Books Publishing, 2001.

Bota, Jadranka. *The Magic of Istria*. Kastav, Croatia: Extrade, 2007.

Bowman, Martin W. *B-24 Combat Missions*. New York: Fall River Press, 2009.

——. *USAAF Handbook, 1939–45*. Thrupp, Gloucestershire, UK: Sutton Publishing, 1997.

Boyne, Walter J. *Clash of Wings: World War II in the Air*. New York: Touchstone, 1997.

——. *The Influence of Air Power upon History*. Gretna, La.: Pelican, 2003.

Breuninger, Michael S. *U.S. Military Combat Aircrew Individual Survival Equipment: World War II to Present*. Privately printed, 2009.

Childers, Thomas. *In the Shadows of War: An American Pilot's Odyssey through Occupied France and the Camps of Nazi Germany*. New York: Henry Holt, 2002.

——. *Wings of Morning: The Story of the Last American Bomber Shot Down over Germany in World War II*. Reading, Mass: Perseus, 1995.

Darman, Peter. *World War II: Stats and Facts*. New York: Fall River Press, 2009.

Davis, Harold E. *The Heart and Soul of America: Experiences and Antics of World War II Flyers*. 2005: Privately published.

Devney, Edward J. *460th Bomb Group*. Privately printed, 1946.

Dugan, James, and Carroll Stewart. *Ploesti: The Great Ground-Air Battle of 1 August 1943*. New York: Bantam Books, 1963.

Fifteenth Air Force Association. *The Fifteenth Air Force Story*. Dallas: Taylor Publishing, 1986.

Freeman, Gregory A. *The Forgotten 500: The Untold Story of the Men Who Risked All for the Greatest Rescue Mission of World War II*. New York: NAL Caliber, 2007.

Freeman, Roger A. *Zemke's Wolf Pack: The Story of Hub Zemke and the 56th Fighter Group in the Skies Over Europe*. New York: Orion Books, 1988.

Greening, C. Ross. *Not As Briefed: From the Doolittle Raid to a German Stalag*. Pullman, Wash.: Washington State University Press, 2001.

Hammerton, Sir John, ed. *The Second World War: An Illustrated History of WWII*. Vol. 8. Trident Press International, 2000.

HMSO Manual. "Signal Training: Procedure for Radio Telephony." Pamphlet No. 5. Signal Procedure Part 1. War Office. 5 June 1943.

Jablonsky, Edward. *Airwar: An Illustrated History of Air Power in the Second World War*. Garden City, N.Y.: Doubleday, 1971.

Jane's Encyclopedia of Aviation. New York: Portland House, 1989.

Lamar, Edgar Lee. "Seven Seconds Aircraft to Ground: Reflections of a World War II Bomber Pilot." Unpublished memoir.

——. "Vor You Der Var Iss Ofer." Unpublished journal of Lt. Lamar while a prisoner of war at Stalag Luft I. 1944–45: Barth, Germany.

Maguire, Jon A. *Gear Up! Flight Clothing & Equipment of USAAF Airmen in World War II*. Atglen, Penn.: Schiffer, 1995.

Mason, Keith W. *Wings of the Morning*. Unpublished manuscript of the operations officer of the 460th BG in Italy.

——. *"nothing to fear . . . ": Recollections of a World War II Bomber Pilot*. Privately printed, 2009.

Miller, Donald L. *Masters of the Air: America's Bomber Boys Who Fought the Air War against Nazi Germany*. New York: Simon & Schuster, 2006.

National Archives. Missing Air Crew Report, No. 9888. 18 November 1944.

Nemerov, Howard. *War Stories: Poems about Long Ago and Now*. Chicago: University of Chicago Press, 1987.

Ong, William A. *Target Luftwaffe: The Tragedy and the Triumph of the World War II Air Victory*. Kansas City: Lowell Press, n.d.

Peterson, Christine. "They Served with Honor: Staff Sgt. Kazmer Rachak, Casper." In *Casper, Wyo., Journal*. August 18–24, 2010. A7.

Ramsey, A. C. "Effects Depot." *The Quartermaster Review.* September October 1945. Online at www.qmmuseum.lee.army.mil/WWII/effects_depot.htm (accessed May 2011).

Roy, Morris J. *Behind Barbed Wire.* New York: Richard R. Smith, 1946.

Saint-Exupery, Antoine de. *Wind, Sand and Stars.* New York: Reynal and Hitchcock, 1939.

Stevens, Jadyn. *The Final Mission of Lt. Wade Moore Craig, Jr.* Nashville: Eveready Press, 2000.

Stokesbury, James L. *A Short History of World War II.* New York: William Morrow, 1980.

Sweeting, C. G. *Combat Flying Clothing: Army Air Forces Clothing during World War II.* Washington, D.C.: Smithsonian Institution, 1984.

Tolliver, Raymond F. *The Interrogator: The Story of Hanns Scharff, Luftwaffe's Master Interrogator.* Fallbrook, Calif.: Aero, 1978.

United States Army, Seine Section. "United States Army Paris Guide: For Leave Troops." N.d.

United States Army Air Forces. Headquarters, 460th Bombardment Group. Mission Report, Mission # 126. 19 November 1944.

Valant, Gary M. *Vintage Aircraft Nose Art.* Osceola, Wis.: Motorbooks International, 1987.

Wakefield, Ken. *Light Planes at War: U.S. Liaison Aircraft in Europe, 1942–1947.* Charleston, S.C.: Tempus, 1999.

Wells, Mark K. *Courage and Air Warfare: The Allied Aircrew Experience in the Second World War.* London: Cass, 1995.

Wood, J. P. *Aircraft Nose Art: 80 Years of Aviation Artwork.* London: Salamander Books, 1996.

In addition to the above texts, the author found these websites to be useful:

www.nationalmuseum.af.mil is a good source of official Air Force information regarding all phases of the air war.

www.b24.net is full of information related to the Liberator.

www.15thaf.org contains helpful information on the command and organization structure of the USAAF in Italy.

Paul.rutgers.edu/~mcgrew/wwii/usaf/html. Good day-by-day chronology of the air war in each theater.

www.376hbgva.com has a good archive of stories and photos of the air war in Italy.

www.b24bestweb.com is another useful site with a trove of archived material.

http.historyofwaronline.com contains very technical information on a variety of subjects, including German antiaircraft weapons.